PORTFOLIO / PENGUIN

DEBT-FREE U

Zac Bissonnette is a writer and editor with *AOL Money & Finance*. He writes daily for DailyFinance.com, AOL's financial news and analysis destination, and has appeared on CNN, written for the *Boston Globe* and the *Daily Beast*, and been quoted in media outlets such as WSJ.com, the *Salt Lake Tribune*, Bloomberg, and Reuters .com. He is an art history major at the University of Massachusetts, Amherst.

DEBT-FREE U

How I Paid for an Outstanding College
Education Without Loans, Scholarships,
or Mooching Off My Parents

Zac Bissonnette

PORTFOLIO / PENGUIN

PORTFOLIO / PENGUIN
Published by the Penguin Group
Penguin Group (USA) Inc., 375 Hudson Street,
New York, New York 10014, U.S.A.
Penguin Group (Canada), 90 Eglinton Avenue East, Suite 700,
Toronto, Ontario, Canada M4P 2Y3
(a division of Pearson Penguin Canada Inc.)
Penguin Books Ltd, 80 Strand, London WC2R 0RL, England
Penguin Ireland, 25 St. Stephen's Green, Dublin 2, Ireland
(a division of Penguin Books Ltd)
Penguin Books Australia Ltd, 250 Camberwell Road, Camberwell,
Victoria 3124, Australia
(a division of Pearson Australia Group Pty Ltd)
Penguin Books India Pvt Ltd, 11 Community Centre, Panchsheel Park,
New Delhi – 110 017, India
Penguin Group (NZ), 67 Apollo Drive, Rosedale, North Shore 0632,
New Zealand (a division of Pearson New Zealand Ltd)
Penguin Books (South Africa) (Pty) Ltd, 24 Sturdee Avenue,
Rosebank, Johannesburg 2196, South Africa

Penguin Books Ltd, Registered Offices:
80 Strand, London WC2R 0RL, England

First published in 2010 by Portfolio Penguin,
a member of Penguin Group (USA) Inc.

10 9 8 7 6

Publisher's Note
This publication is designed to provide accurate and authoritative information in regard to the subject matter covered. It is sold with the understanding that the publisher is not engaged in rendering legal, accounting or other professional services. If you require legal advice or other expert assistance, you should seek the services of a competent professional.

Library of Congress Cataloging-in-Publication Data

Bissonnette, Zac.
    Debt-free U : how I paid for an outstanding college education without loans, scholarships, or mooching off my parents / Zac Bissonnette.
        p. cm.
    Includes bibliographical references and index.
    ISBN 978-1-59184-298-9
    1. College costs—United States.   2. Finance, Personal—United States.   3. Education, Higher—United States—Finance.   4. Investments—United States.   I. Title.
    LB2342.B52 2010
    378.3'8—dc22

                                                                                          2010018510

Printed in the United States of America
Set in Granjon
Designed by Alissa Amell

In memory of Margaret

CONTENTS

CONTENTS

FOREWORD BY ANDREW TOBIAS

A hundred years ago I bought a brand new Acapulco blue Ford Mustang with money I had earned in college. It had sport stripes, yellow turn blinkers embedded in the hood so I could see them flashing, and a horn that went "toodela-toodela-toodela." It cost $2,511—as you can see, it really *was* one hundred years ago (well, 1967)—and I had earned every penny selling class rings and helping to publish a student travel guide. I loved that car. I loved earning the money even more.

Technically, I majored in Slavic languages and literatures—which for me meant reading *War and Peace* in English. In the crib notes edition. (Do they still have those? Now it would be Wikipedia.) What I really majored in was the student business enterprise, which was a great deal more fun, not to mention useful. That's the reason I jumped at the chance to write this foreword.

Zac Bissonette is one of the sharpest financial writers around. The fact that he is only twenty—Doogie Howser meets the boys from Facebook—*freaks me out.* (His first worldly wise e-mail to me, years ago, involved some kind of sophisticated stock market situation he had found suspect, and I assumed he was a middle-aged hedge fund manager. Turned out, he was in *high school.*) But listen, Mozart was five when he wrote his first stuff,* so by that standard Zac is lagging far behind.

The point is, you should listen to this guy—and you will have fun doing it. You may still decide to bury your family in debt to

---

* Though Tolstoy was fifty—so don't let any of this intimidate you. Even if your eighteen-year-old hasn't yet appeared on CNN, there's still hope.

enroll your offspring in an expensive private school; but you will have had the benefit of full and thoughtful consideration of the choice.

And your kids should listen to him, too, because college is the start of a lifetime of being out on their own. (Or at least you'd better hope so—I know it tears at your heartstrings to think of their leaving the nest, but you do *not* want them back at thirty.) Getting a handle on money, and on the real world, now, at the outset, can help them steer a course toward prosperity, security, and happiness.

It's all too easy, through lack of attention to these things ("I'm a kid! I'll worry about that later!"), to fall into an "I'm terrible with money" mentality. That may seem to brush the issue aside—"oh, I'm terrible with money"—or may even seem cool in some way. ("I'm into more important things!") But it is a terrible early misstep that becomes a significant life handicap. If your kid is bright enough to go to college, she or he is bright enough to be *sensible*, not terrible, with money. (Which, by the way, couldn't hurt *you* in your dotage either. Look how nicely Oprah provides for her mother.)

Whatever school your son or daughter decides on, Zac's advice will help get him or her through in the best financial shape possible. And when it comes to building a life, there's nothing like getting off to a good start.

ACKNOWLEDGMENTS

It takes a lot of people to help someone as stubborn as I am put together a book that's anything close to publishable. For everything that is good about this book, the credit goes to:

Andrew Tobias, the bestselling financial writer turned savior of the planet who helped me formulate the idea for this book and introduced me to . . .

David Kuhn, the best literary agent on the planet—who went so far beyond the norm of literary agents to make this book happen. Also: his lovely assistants Jessi Cimafonte and Billy Kingsland.

My aunt Jodi Tussing, who, in addition to being the most ethical person in the history of the real estate business, is one of the best people in the world.

All the "big shot" financial journalists and personalities who have been so generous with their time and expertise, especially Gary Weiss, Farnoosh Torabi, Herb Greenberg, Suze Orman, David Bach, Stuart Elliott, Jean Chatzky, and Ali Rogers.

Everyone at Penguin/Portfolio: Adrian Zackheim, Adrienne Schultz, Brooke Carey, Maureen Cole, and Will Weisser.

My publicist, Barb Burg, who took me on as a client even after I totally slept through our first breakfast meeting and left her alone at a diner waiting for me. It was an alarm clock malfunction, I swear!

The entire team at *AOL Money & Finance, WalletPop, Daily-Finance, BloggingStocks*, and whatever other brands we've launched by the time you read this. Especially the following people, who have been wonderful friends, colleagues, mentors, and tough editors: Amey Stone, Beth Pinsker, Sarah Gilbert, Julie Tilsner, Andrea Chalupa, Todd Pruzan, Tobias Buckell, Sheldon Liber, Michael Rainey, Melly Alazraki, Aaron Crowe, Jon Berr, Tom Barlow, David Schepp, Geoff Williams, Jason Cochran, and Josh Smith.

The lovely Tracy Coenen, who, in addition to being supersmart, can always make me laugh when she isn't making me cry. And of course Kevin Kelly, who encouraged me to get started in writing and made all this happen. He will be very famous in a few years.

My two ex-con sources, who helped me learn everything I needed to know about how people get financially screwed: Barry Minkow and Sam E. Antar, who is almost as awesome as he is crazy.

All my friends at UMass, who are living proof that smart people can get a fantastic education at public universities, but especially the original members of the Badd Boys Club: Ryan, Tommy, and Onri.

A good teacher is one of the most powerful things that can make someone's life better. I've been fortunate to have a bunch of good teachers (in chronological order): Becky Lash, Mrs. James, Mr. Brown, Mr. VanSant, Mr. Metzger, Mr. Pontes, and Mr. Hillebrand.

My family: Grandma, Dad, Nate, Ramsey, and my Jewish mother, Beth Wechsler. My life's ambition is to one day be as successful as she already thinks I am.

DEBT-FREE U

INTRODUCTION

The Four People You Meet When You Apply to College, and the Lies They Tell

I wrote this book because I've met, spoken with, and read e-mails from hundreds of families who are struggling with the burden of college costs—worrying about how they'll pay for college without bankrupting their retirement accounts or burdening their kids with massive debt loads.

If your child is preparing to apply to college (or is in college right now), are you worried about the financial impact of higher education both in terms of your own ability to finance it today and the effect student loans will have on your child's future? A recent poll conducted by the *New York Times* and CBS News found that 70 percent of parents were "very concerned" about how they would pay for college. Only 6 percent said they weren't worried. The 2003/2004 National Postsecondary Student Aid Study revealed that two thirds of Americans were graduating with an average of $19,202 in student loan debt[1]—and it's getting worse. For the 2006/07 graduating class, the figure was $22,700[2]—an increase of 18 percent over a three-year period when job and wage growth remained largely stagnant.

Student loans now constitute about 25 percent of all non–real estate consumer debt[3]—alarming when you consider that thirty years ago, student loans were practically nonexistent. While part of that gain can be attributed to the increasing percentage of Americans attending college, most it comes from changes in the way college is financed, driven by cost increases that have far outpaced the rate of inflation. In 1993 just 32 percent of students took out a college loan (which was a record high at the time).[4] Today, about two thirds of students borrow money to pay for college. Nationally, close to $600 billion in student loan debt is outstanding, compared with $850 billion in credit card debt.[5] Analysis of government statistics suggests that a full third of student borrowers today will end up in default—and student loans lack most standard consumer protections and cannot be discharged in bankruptcy. Missed student loan payments can lead to massive fees and penalties that trap a borrower in a cycle of debt. Social Security benefits can, believe it or not, be garnished for student loan payments.

Worse, studies have shown that people who graduate from college with significant debt loads are more likely to suffer from anxiety and depression and are less likely to pursue the careers they want—the ones that excite and inspire them—in favor of those that offer higher starting salaries.

It doesn't have to be that way.

In this book I'm going to show you and your college-bound child how to use the college years to develop the skills and a financial platform that can make her a millionaire by the time she's forty, doing the work that she loves. If that doesn't sound at all appealing, stop reading now. Are you still there? Good.

Before we go any further, I should say that there are two groups of people who may not need to hear most of what I have to say in this book. If you have the resources to easily pay for your child to go to his first-choice college without any impact on your lifestyle, put this book down right now, and go for it! Or if your child is an exceptionally gifted student with a high school GPA of, say, 11.6, and who was also president of her class, and only missed church when she was helping old ladies cross the road, you'll probably find that most schools she wants to go to will be happy to foot the bill—at least if your income is low enough to demonstrate financial need. So this book isn't for you, either.

But for the other 90-plus percent of families—those in which parents earn a living but for whom the average cost of four years at a private university (in 2009 that was more than $100,000,[6] not including room and board) is prohibitive, and whose kids will have to take out an average of $22,000 in loans over those four years—I have a lot to offer.

In this book I will

- Show you just how dangerous student loans can be to both the student and the parents
- Show you how your child can get as good an education as, or even better than, his peers without going into debt, and still have fun in the process (without the benefit of scholarships and financial aid, or having to resort to ramen noodles and panhandling)
- Help you resist the societal pressures to send your kids to expensive private colleges and universities when state schools can be just as good at one fourth the cost
- Prove to you that forgoing the diplomas from those "elite" schools will not hurt your child's career or future income one bit
- Show you how your child can make any college into an Ivy League college by looking at the characteristics that make elite schools elite and exploring how they can be duplicated anywhere! I'll also provide some not-so-obvious tips on how the choice of a major will (but mostly won't) affect your child's career options and earnings potential
- Tell you about the unique opportunities the current generation has for networking, and show how today's college students can, with a little bit of extra effort, prepare themselves for career success

- Give you tips about how students can earn money during college, and show how even just a little bit of saving now can set up your child for a lifetime of prosperity—just as surely as bad choices about college and the financing of college can set your child up for a life of poverty. I'll tell you everything your kid needs to know about financial management, credit, and banking before he heads to college, so that he can avoid being one of the more than 10 percent of college students who owe an average of more than $7,000 in credit card debt[7]

I say all this with such confidence because I know it can be done. I know because I'm doing it. When people find out that I'm a twenty-one-year-old college student with no student loans, a stock portfolio, rental property, and a job as a financial writer for AOL, they often assume that I come from a wealthy family.

The reality is that nothing could be further from the truth. As I write this, my dad's home—the home that I grew up in—is in the midst of foreclosure proceedings, and my dad has been stuck at a friend's house for the past few days because he doesn't have money for gas. My mom is a social worker who's devoted her life to helping those less fortunate than she is. Unfortunately, such work doesn't pay as well as it ought to, except in a karmic sense. She lives in a condo with my grandmother.

Throughout this book, I'm going to be letting you in on the strategies—some secret, others blindingly obvious but rarely discussed or put into practice—that will allow your student to get a great college education, a great degree, lifelong friends, and (this is the part that makes this so unique) *a strong, debt-free financial foundation that will prepare your child for tremendous success in life*. A quick detour on this topic, because I know what you're thinking: "tremendous success in life" is about a lot more than money. I agree. It is. But the reality is that in most cases, the foundation for happiness and a fulfilling life is at least partly financial—and while having enough money won't make you happy, not having enough can definitely make you miserable.

Back to my dad: a few weeks ago we were sitting on his couch watching the Red Sox game and, as is often the case, discussing his financial woes. My dad is, in his heart, a hippie. He's one of the most brilliant, generous, loving people I've ever met, and for the entire sixty years of his life he's thought about money as little as possible. But it dawned on him during our conversation that now money is all he thinks about—because he doesn't have any. And it's making him miserable. "I wonder who thinks about money more: you or Bill Gates," I asked him.

He laughed. "Without a doubt, me. Bill Gates has devoted his energy to pursuing a dream that brought him tremendous wealth, and he's able to focus on that, not money per se. It's like money is exacting its cruel revenge on me for ignoring it." That's why, even if you know money isn't everything, you and your college-bound child should read this book. Preparing a solid financial foundation for your future as well as hers will make your lives richer, and afford you the time and freedom to focus on what is truly important in life.

A bitterly cynical Lexus ad from a few years back proclaimed, "Whoever said money can't buy happiness isn't spending it right." I don't know about that, but the latest research is unambiguous on this point: people who are reasonably financially secure are happier than people who aren't. A recent Gallup poll found that 90 percent of people in households earning more than $250,000 per year consider themselves to be "very happy." In households with incomes below $30,000, only 42 percent consider themselves to be "very happy."[8]

Who has time to be happy when juggling credit card and rent bills, fielding calls from Sallie Mae, and staying just one car breakdown or illness away from bankruptcy? But the outcome of another study is interesting: this one, conducted by Dr. Daniel Kahneman of Princeton, found that earning about $60,000 per year—enough for a prudent person to live reasonably comfortably in many parts of this country without worrying about money too much—was enough to make most people as happy as they could get: people earning $200,000 per year are not likely to be much happier than those earning $60,000, but people earning $61,000 are much happier than those earning $40,000.[9]

I mention these statistics because I have a lot of college-age friends whose eyes glaze over when the topic of money comes up. They want to help people, to do interesting things, and to have wonderful friends, and money just isn't that important to them. I think that's a terrific outlook on life, and, believe it or not, it's actually closer to my own philosophy than most of my friends think it is. But to help people and do interesting things, it helps to have enough money.

Watching my parents struggle with money when I was young has been the key factor in making me as financially responsible and ambitious as I am today. I wasn't interested in wealth (and I'm still not interested in luxury travel or exotic cars) until I witnessed the stress that money was causing in my parents' lives, eventually ruining their marriage. I remember lying in bed with White Bear, when I was four, listening to my parents argue about finances in the dining room, wishing that we could just have enough money so they didn't have to worry.

In some ways, because of those experiences—and also perhaps because I'm genetically hardwired with entrepreneurial instincts—I spent a good chunk of my youth figuring out various ways to make money. When I was in second grade, I stumbled on a copy of the catalog for the Oriental Trading Company, which was filled with all kinds of tacky imported toys, games, and crafts, with prices like "$8.60/gross" for bouncy balls. I biked over to the local video rental store owned by a friend of my parents and told him that I had an idea for a business: I'd sell small trinkets for kids—nothing more than two dollars—in his store, and he'd collect the money for me. There was just one problem: What was in it for him? I hadn't thought of that, but Jamie had a plan: if I'd come in and vacuum once per week,

I could sell my wares on his counter. I'd place them in a little box with a slot for people to put their change in. It would be "the honor system," but he'd keep an eye out for aspiring Bonnies and Clydes wanting to abscond with my paper doll sets.

My dad built a wooden display box that would fit on the counter but still provided plenty of space for a variety of kids' items. Then I got out the Oriental Trading catalog and, with my savings and a loan of fifty dollars from my mom, bought stuff that I thought kids would want to buy (at the suggestion of some friends, I ordered a big box of Bomb Bags, those little fifty-cent exploding bags, which turned out to be my bestseller).

I ran that "business" for a couple years in the mid-nineties—before I decided to move on to other things—but during that time it made me about eight dollars a week, which was a lot more than most kids got as a weekly allowance. And it wasn't a handout from my parents. I was proud.

Since then I've pretty much always been embarking on some business venture or other, some successful, some not. When I was in middle school, I made a good deal of money on eBay selling old video games and rare books that I found at yard sales with my mother. One of my proudest moments—I now find it vaguely shameful—was the time I bought a first-edition book for fifty cents and sold it on eBay for $130 (and I'd haggled the seller down from one dollar). After seventh grade I got my first real "job," working at a grocery store. I scrimped and saved every single penny that I earned that summer, opened a brokerage account, and bought my first stock. I soon got bored with the grocery store, though, and got a job at a small candy store within walking distance from my home. I continued with my obsessive saving regimen, investing every dime I earned. By my first year of high school, I had a five-figure brokerage account, and I was happy. In the middle of all this working (and high school), I was reading business, investing, and personal finance books obsessively—five or more each week. I had a great idea: a column called TeenMoney, which would offer financial advice to young people and run in dozens (hundreds?) of small newspapers all across the country.

The plan was this: I'd write to a thousand or more newspapers and offer them my "syndicated" weekly column at the low, low introductory price of four dollars per week. I wrote a bunch of sample columns—my teachers said they were really good!—spent a thousand dollars on expensive stationery, fancy envelopes, and postage, and sent out my proposal, with order forms, to around a thousand newspapers. All that was left to do now was wait for the orders to pour in. And wait. And wait. That was four years ago and I still haven't received a single order. It was a massive failure—think New Coke, HD DVD, the Ford Edsel, and *Gigli* poured into a blender and served on the rocks.

I was devastated. I'd screwed up before, but had never poured my heart, soul, and money into something and achieved exactly nothing. But there was a silver lining: as part of my effort to promote the project, I'd started my own blog writing about stocks, business news, and investing. Online I met a really brilliant, cool kid from New York who referred me to someone he knew, and, before I'd even fully recovered from the TeenMoney flop, I had a gig as a blogger for AOL's BloggingStocks.com, a financial news and opinion site. Then we launched our new personal finance site, WalletPop.com, and I was hired to be the co-leader: planning features, finding story ideas, hiring writers, and, my favorite activity, writing. Somewhere in the middle of all that I started my college career at the University of Massachusetts, Amherst, where I was accepted into the honors college.

It was during the process of applying to college and figuring out how to pay for it, which involved months of research and study, that I realized a lot of the conventional wisdom about college is just plain wrong. My high school guidance counselor had urged me to apply to more "elite" (read: expensive) schools because of my GPA and SAT scores, but I realized that the benefits of attending a $40,000-per-year private college are greatly overstated, especially in comparison to the costs. Using the knowledge and wisdom I've gained from my own experience, extensive research, and witnessing the experiences of my friends and peers, I've come up with the philosophy, strategies, tips, and ways of thinking that inform the following chapters. I think my advice will make the college selection experience more fun and more fulfilling, and, most important, leave the graduate better positioned for a wonderful life. I also think I can make the college application and admissions process infinitely less stressful by exposing the fallacies that underlie so much of the "college fever" that sweeps high school juniors (and increasingly sophomores and freshmen) every year. This book offers a foolproof system for graduating from college with a financial head start rather than an anchor around the neck.

The Four People You Meet When You Apply for College, and the Lies They Tell

When I'm looking for help in understanding the psychological side of financial decisions, I call on a source who happens to have served seven and a half years in jail for securities fraud, a term that started before he was old enough to drink. Barry Minkow was the boy-wonder mastermind of ZZZZ Best Carpet Cleaning, a California-based start-up that he took public before his eighteenth birthday. The stock market valued the company at several hundred million dollars, but it all came crashing down when a reporter exposed the company as a massive Ponzi scheme. Today Barry is out of jail, and he's helped the FBI and the SEC uncover billions of dollars in investment fraud. So it's fair to say that very few people understand the psychological forces that separate people from their cash better than Barry does— even though I'm still not sure whether I trust him!

One day I asked Barry for the best piece of advice he had about how to avoid getting pressured into making financial decisions that aren't in our own best interests. Here's what he said: "It may seem obvious, but you'd be surprised at how many people don't understand this: Never take anyone who has a vested interest in lying to you at their word. Even if he's an ethical person, his incentives and motivations are different from yours and his advice will be geared toward his interests, not yours."

What does this have to do with college? Plenty. When I started looking into how Americans think about and pay for college, I was reminded of Barry's words. Keep them in the back of your mind as you consider the four sources of wisdom that most families rely on when making decisions about sending kids to college:

- high school guidance counselors
- admissions officers
- financial aid officers
- family and friends

If you're like 100 percent of parents, at least one of these four groups has influenced, is influencing, or will influence your thoughts and actions regarding your child's college education. Here's the bad news: none of these fine people can be trusted. Let's break it down.

High School Guidance Counselors

Guidance counselors are usually intelligent, well-intentioned people, but let's face it: they make their schools look good (and their bosses happy) by sending graduates on to four-year colleges with strong name recognition. This is especially true at private schools and charter schools that are competing aggressively to attract top students. If you're the parent of an eighth grader, which prep school will look more appealing: the one sporting banners from Harvard, Yale, and Princeton or the one with banners from a handful of community colleges and a couple of state universities? Guidance counselors are considered most successful when they get students into name-brand schools. The problem is that, in all probability, your guidance counselor has literally no training as a financial planner and is ill equipped to advise your kids on the long-term ramifications of large debt loads, much less to counsel you on depleted retirement savings accounts and home equity.

The MoneyWatch.com columnist Lynn O'Shaughnessy noted, "Many high school counselors know precious little about financing a college degree. The counselors I have met through UCLA and elsewhere often seem to be intimidated by financial aid issues. . . . From what I've seen, the financial advice that many high school counselors dispense focuses a great deal on meeting deadlines." This certainly meshes with my experience and the experiences of most students I've spoken with, but the problem actually goes beyond that: not only are most guidance counselors completely incompetent when it comes to providing students with ideas on how to get financing for college, but they also lack the financial background to analyze college expenditures in the broader context of long-term financial health.

One high school guidance counselor took exception to O'Shaughnessy's remarks and commented, "We counselors are not financial advisors." This is *terrifying*. Imagine a weight-loss counselor who suggested cocaine as an effective way to lose weight and, when confronted with the ill effects of the drug, replied, "We weight loss counselors are not doctors." The impact of a college decision is inextricably linked with the cost and means of payment.

The good news? Researchers are catching on to just how poor the performance of so many guidance counselors is. According to a report prepared by Public Agenda for the William and Melinda Gates Foundation, 62 percent of high school students felt that their college counselors did a "fair" or "poor" job of educating them about different career possibilities. And 67 percent felt that their guidance counselors did only a "fair" or "poor" job helping them select a school.

Admissions Officers

Admissions officers are salespeople. That's not a dig; it's a job descrip-
tion. Colleges and universities task them with attracting as many
applicants as possible so that the school can build a student body
that is as elite as possible—and obtain a low acceptance rate that
will boost its ranking in the all-important *US News & World Report*
rankings of the top colleges (more on this in Chapter 3). They work
for the school, not for you, and they are deserving of a tremendous
amount of skepticism.

A help-wanted ad for an admissions offer published in the
Chronicle of Higher Education read: "Must be articulate, engaging,
savvy and have the ability to close."

The reality is that admissions officers have far more in common
with car salesmen than with the world of academia they are ostensi-
bly part of. In recent years marketing-driven universities have sought
to suck high school guidance counselors into their plot: in 2004, the
New York Times reported that Regis College, a Denver-based school
rated "more selective" by *US News*, had embarked on an ambitious
campaign of influence involving all-expense-paid trips to Colorado
that included skiing, facials, and a stay at a luxury hotel.

Centre College, based in Danville, Kentucky, actually gives
guidance counselors money so that they can go to the track and bet
on horse racing. Goucher College in Maryland offers theater tickets.
John Carroll University has rented out the Rock and Roll Hall of
Fame and Museum for a night to have a party for guidance counselors who referred students to the college. The University of Southern
California took guidance counselors to the Orange Bowl.

Here's what is so appalling about all this: college is among the
largest investments most people will ever make, and there are no laws
regulating these perks or requiring that they be disclosed to students.
If your stock broker sold you shares of a stock after the company gave
him something of value, and didn't disclose the conflict, he could

lose his license, face severe civil penalties, and possibly end up in jail. That's right: Wall Street is held to higher standards of ethics than the college industry.

Treat them like you would treat a salesman at a car dealership: ask questions and always do your own research. As Barry Minkow likes to say, don't trust. Just verify, verify, verify.

Financial Aid Officers

These guys are like salespeople too, but in this case I do mean it as a dig. The role of the financial aid office is to make sure that the students the school has admitted are financially able to attend—through whatever means necessary. Here's one conversation you will probably never have.

FINANCIAL AID OFFICER: Well, here's your financial aid. I've been able to work it out so you'll have access to all the funds you need.

PARENT: That's great!

FINANCIAL AID OFFICER: No, trust me, it's really not. You'll have to take out a lot of loans and so will your child. He'll have to move back home when he graduates to service his debt—that is, if you still have a home. You could go here, but I really don't recommend it. There are a lot of more affordable options that can be just as good. We'd love to have your child, but it's just really not a good deal for him.

Interestingly, though, there is one school that has recently begun doing, to its credit, something quite similar. New York University graduates boast the highest average debt load by far—$33,600 and rising—and MoneyWatch.com's Lynn O'Shaughnessy recently reported that NYU "called the families of 1,822 admitted students in April and suggested that they might want to do some soul searching about whether the price, even after any financial aid, was beyond their means." That's a rare, rare phone call, and NYU deserves a gold star for it. But remember, with an average debt load of $33,600 at NYU, many students graduate with hugely excessive quantities of student loans and receive no such phone call.

Bottom line: looking to the financial aid office for advice on financing is, to use a metaphor coined by Warren Buffett, like asking a barber if you need a haircut. They will tell you how much they can offer you in grants and may direct you toward other sources of financing (sometimes with nefarious motives, as we'll cover in Chapter 1), but you should never look to them for advice about how much you can afford to spend on college and never let a financial aid officer tell you that you can afford to take out a Parent PLUS loan (also in Chapter 1) or a home equity loan.

Family and Friends

These trusted individuals, at the very least, affect many of your buying decisions and, at worst, inspire some pretty unwise purchases. Have you ever succumbed to the peer pressure to buy a bigger TV, a bigger house, or a bigger car so that you can keep up with the Joneses? If so, please remember one thing: the Joneses don't have any money! They are upside-down on their mortgage and one car breakdown away from bankruptcy! Many families feel pressure to send their kids to more expensive private schools so that they won't look bad at backyard barbecues. Who wants to say their kid is going to Bonzo University when the neighbor's kid is going to Upper Crust College? No one. But, as I will show in later chapters, in many cases both families would be better off sending their kids to Bonzo. Peer pressure has led to an arms race that can send both parent and child to the poorhouse, and your neighbors and, yes, your relatives in all probability aren't informed enough to be worthy of influence in your child's college selection process.

When it comes to taking college advice from family and friends, people would do well to remember that great LendingTree commercial with the happy family man who proclaims that he has a beautiful house, new cars, and a great new grill. "How do I do it? I'm in debt up to my eyeballs."

So whom can you trust? The sad truth is that there are very few people who can provide you with objective, knowledgeable advice on college. Nearly everyone who is providing information is either ignorant, too invested in the outcome to be unbiased, or both. Luckily, there's an alternative. Evaluating college decisions objectively is something that every parent is smart enough to do. My goal here is to give you the tools to educate yourself about the selection and financing process in a way that pretty much no one ever really has: with logic, rationality, data, and one of the coolest tools in the economist's toolbox: cost-benefit analysis.

When I mention in my columns and blog posts my ideas about why people are wrong in the way they think about college, I get more than a few skeptical responses. The reason for this is that the conventional wisdom about college is so deeply ingrained in readers' beliefs that they erupt in anger at the suggestion that it might be wrong. They, and probably you, are suffering under the influence of at least some—and more likely, most—of the nine myths of college:

1. It's important for parents to do what they can to help pay for their kid's educational expenses, even if that means taking out a loan.

2. Scholarships and financial aid will alleviate the burden of spiraling college costs.

3. It's unreasonable to expect students to be major sources of financing for their educational expenses while they're in college.

4. Student loans are a *good* form of debt: leverage. My child will be able to pay them off out of his future earnings. Student loans are unfortunate, but they won't have a serious negative impact on his life.

5. The name of the school on my child's diploma will have a strong impact on her career and life prospects. The better the college she goes to, the more doors she'll have open to her.

6. "Thrifty" approaches to education like community college will have an adverse effect on my child's life. You get what you pay for.

7. The most important thing when it comes to selecting a college is finding a good fit.

8. Guidance counselors, admissions officers, campus tours, and anecdotes from former students are great sources of advice and wisdom on the college application and financing process.

9. The quality of the education my child receives will be largely a factor of the college he attends. Guides like *US News & World Report*'s "America's Best Colleges" are valuable resources in evaluating possibilities.

By the time you finish this book, you will be absolutely convinced that every one of these statements is not only false, but hazardous to you and your child's current and future wealth and well-being. Here's the best part: you don't even have to trust me. I'm a twenty-one-year-old student at a large public university. What do I know? You'd have to be out of your mind to take my word for anything! But what you should do is look at the data and draw your own conclusions. In the next few chapters I will show you the results of some little-known studies that are likely to change the way you think about paying for college. Throughout, I'll offer guidance and practical tips to help your child secure a more enjoyable and less stressful financial life before, during, and after college.

Unlike the vast majority of sources providing advice on college, I'm giving you my thoughts on a topic that I'm actually living. A large portion of the advice in this book is hugely counterintuitive, but guess what? I'm living it. I've worked very hard to keep this book short in the hope that you—and maybe even your kid!—will actually read it. If you do, and act on half of my advice, I have no doubt that you, and your child—and maybe even your grandchildren!—will be looking for me in a few years to thank me.

So grab a pad, a pen, and a highlighter, and have a seat. The first topic is one that you've probably been pondering for a long time: How the heck are you going to pay for college?

CHAPTER 1

How Much Can You Afford, and Where Will You Get the Money?

If you're like most parents, you want to help pay for your kid's education. The question is, How much can you afford to contribute? Chances are you think you can afford to spend a lot more than you actually can.

According to a 2007 study conducted by Country Insurance and Financials, Americans are evenly split on whether it is more important to save for their children's college education or for their own retirement. Forty-three percent believe that college should be the priority, while another 43 percent believe retirement is more important. Contrast that with the fact that in 2006,[1] the Center for Retirement Research (CRR) at Boston College found that 43 percent of American families are at risk for being inadequately prepared for retirement.[2] This was *prior* to the collapse in the housing and stock markets, so it seems fair to assume that that number is substantially higher now.

To those parents who think saving for their kids' educational expenses is more important than saving for retirement: I admire your devotion to your children. Your spirit of self-sacrifice is heartwarming. Now let me explain to you why you're insane. Your kids have a lifetime of work ahead of them to earn money for retirement. You, on the other hand, only have a few years. One of the best gifts you can give your children is your own financial independence in your golden years. Your kids love you, but that doesn't mean that they—or their future spouses—will want you crashing in that extra bedroom when they're in their forties or fifties. Unfortunately, that's a trend that is already developing. The number of parents, siblings, and other adult relatives who live with adult heads of households grew 42 percent from 2000 to 2007, according to U.S. Census data.[3]

Parents Borrowing: Don't Do It!

If you fall into the majority of the population that is at risk for being inadequately prepared for retirement, you really cannot afford to contribute much to your child's education. No financial aid officer or guidance counselor will tell you that, but it is the absolute truth. However, that doesn't mean there isn't plenty of pressure on parents to go ahead and do just that. While I was doing research on parents borrowing money for college, an ad popped up courtesy of JPMorgan Chase, pitching the Chase Home Equity loan as a "simple, flexible solution to the challenge of financing a higher education. . . you'll receive a response to your college financing request in minutes."

That's right! It only take a few minutes to find out whether you'll be able to put a lien on your house—the largest asset most families have—to pay for your kid's education.

The question is not how much of your home equity you *can* contribute. The question is how much of your home equity you *should* contribute. If you're like the vast, vast majority of parents, the answer is zero. You need that home equity for your retirement because you most likely don't have enough in IRAs, 401(k)s, pension entitlements, or Social Security benefits to guarantee a comfortable retirement. And making payments on a home equity loan may be difficult if you get laid off or sick, and you may need to preserve that equity for any number of curveballs that may come your way in your golden years.

In addition, taking out a mortgage will lead to monthly payment obligations that could well extend into your retirement years. The easiest way to make your retirement years less stressful is to have a house that you own free and clear.

The federal government goes a step further and actually thinks it's prudent to encourage parents to borrow money with no collateral—that is, nothing to sell to repay the debt in the event that they are injured, laid off, or otherwise financially compromised—to help their kids pay for college. On its Web site, Sallie Mae describes the federally sponsored Parent PLUS loan as a "student loan for parents of undergraduate, dependent students. With a Parent PLUS loan, families can fund the entire cost of a child's education."

When I was about four years old, I was eating at the counter in a diner with my mother, and she got up to go to the bathroom. I sat there slurping at an already empty milkshake making a fair amount of noise, and an older man sitting next to me said, "Ya know, in French that means it's empty." It's the same with parents borrowing for college: if you don't have enough money to pay for your child's education, you have no business slurping at the straw of the Parent PLUS loan.

But colleges love the federal PLUS loan program because it's so easy: they send the family a letter with the financial aid package, and whatever expenses aren't covered by that can be covered by a PLUS loan provided that the parents are (a) creditworthy and (b) stupid. In a letter to a student detailing its financial aid award, Allegheny College suggests that the parents cover the additional $24,000 of annual expenses not met by financial aid with a PLUS loan: "We recommend an excellent financing option for families, the PLUS loan for parents. . . . Maximum Plus eligibility: $24,000."

Ah yes, a great option indeed—for the college! What strikes me as so manipulative about this letter is that the federal PLUS loan is mentioned alongside the financial aid award in a letter addressed to the *student*.

So imagine this scenario: A high school senior races home from band practice every afternoon to check the mailbox to see how much financial aid he's been awarded by his first-choice college. He sees the name of the college in the left-hand corner, rips open the envelope, and reads that the financial aid office thinks it would be "excellent" for his parents to borrow $24,000 per year to pay for his education. Now Mom and Dad have to be the bad guys to say, "We love you, but we'd also like to avoid spending our golden years eating ramen noodles every night. No deal, Howie!"

Who wants to be that guy? No one, and the financial aid office knows that. So they send a letter to the *student* suggesting that his *parents* borrow $24,000 with no collateral. In 2004 the parents of 15.3 percent of graduating college seniors took out federal PLUS loans, carrying an average debt load of $17,709.

Of all the dirty tricks that financial aid offices play, this one irks me more than just about any other. If you are going to suggest that someone borrow $24,000 per year for four years, you should send a letter to that person. It is sneaky and unethical to send someone a letter suggesting that she try to convince another person to borrow up to $24,000 per year for four years.

But home equity loans and federal PLUS loans are only a couple of bad ways to borrow money to pay for college. There are more!

Some experts recommend borrowing against your retirement assets to pay for college. Superficially, borrowing from your 401(k)—you can't borrow from an IRA—seems to make sense. You can borrow up to half of the vested value of the account or $50,000, whichever is less. There is no penalty for the withdrawal and because you're borrowing from yourself, the interest on the loan is paid back to yourself. There's no 10 percent penalty for taking a loan and you won't have to pay taxes on it.

Doing this is still a mistake. Here's why:

• The loan must be repaid in five years and, if you lose your job or quit, the loan can come due immediately—at exactly the time when you're most likely to have a problem paying it back. In that case, you might have to convert the loan to a withdrawal and pay ordinary income tax on the money plus the 10 percent penalty. This can easily work out to more than 40 percent of the total loan amount in additional taxes and penalties. Then, just to add insult to injury, you have to deal with the consequences of reduced financial aid because that withdrawal from your 401(k)—which is really just a loan to yourself that you forgave yourself for—is now part of your income. Got that? This is insanely bureaucratic and nonsensical, but I don't make the rules. I just make fun of them.

• The interest on the loan is not tax deductible, and by borrowing the money from your account, you are losing any interest that you would have been earning. So the argument that "the interest you pay goes back to you!" that you'll hear from financial aid officers is really pretty lame. In addition, the interest you pay comes from after-tax income and is not tax deductible, so you're losing the tax shelter benefit that is the whole point of retirement accounts in the first place.

Two More Payment Methods to Avoid: Looting Your Savings and Withdrawing from a Retirement Account

Many parents recognize that when they're in their forties and fifties, borrowing money isn't a good idea, and so they look at other options: withdrawals from 401(k)s and IRAs. In some cases, you can get a hardship withdrawal from your 401(k). But beware: you will need to demonstrate that you need the money and have no other way of accessing it. That means you must have no home equity to tap, no money in savings, and no gold stashed in a lockbox buried in your backyard. This is a catch-22. If you have no assets other than your 401(k) plan and can qualify for the hardship withdrawal, you have absolutely no business taking it.

Withdrawing money from an IRA or a Roth IRA is easier and potentially less costly than taking the retirement account loan approach. If you're using the money for qualified educational expenses for a child, you won't have to pay a withdrawal penalty. If you withdraw principal (money you put in) from a Roth IRA, you won't even owe taxes because your contributions come from after-tax money. If you withdraw from a traditional IRA, you will owe incomes taxes on that money. But the worst thing of all about withdrawing money from a traditional IRA is that it can affect your eligibility for financial aid next year. That's right. The FAFSA formula calculates a $10,000 withdrawal from a retirement account the same as it does a $10,000 raise at work. Bottom line: don't do it.

In addition, the current market environment, in which many investors are sitting on some substantial losses in their stock portfolios, means that you may have to sell stock in a bear market without receiving the tax benefit that comes with taking a loss in a non-retirement portfolio. If you have non-retirement assets that are trading at a price lower than you paid (stocks, mutual funds, etc.), this is a much better option than a withdrawal from a retirement account because it can have the effect of lowering your taxes—and your reported income for financial aid purposes—but only by a maximum of about $4,000 per year.

All these explanations of why it's a bad idea to withdraw or borrow from retirement assets are technical and procedural—reflections of current IRS rules that could change if someone with an IQ larger than the average shoe size ever was in charge there (so they won't be changing anytime soon). But the larger reason that it's a bad idea to use retirement money to pay for college is that it's your retirement money. You need it for your retirement.

If there is only one thing that you get out of this book, let it be this: *do not risk your own financial well-being to help your kids go to college.* Helping your kids pay for college is great if you can afford it. But if you can't, relax: they'll be able to go anyway. Read on, and I'll show you how.

Save Money Instead of Borrowing It: Downsize Your Way to College Savings

If you're a typical middle-class family whose retirement prospects are up in the air, I have a rule about the one way that you can contribute to your kid's educational expenses: *every dollar that you contribute must come as a result of cost cutting in some other aspect of your life, not from a reduction in savings.* In his book *The Automatic Millionaire*, the financial planner David Bach used the "Latte Factor" to explain how much of an impact seemingly minor cost cuts can have on a family's financial future.

The key to this strategy is that parents contribute to college by downsizing their lifestyles, not their emergency funds, home equity, or retirement accounts. It's a pay-as-you-go system: slum it up a little bit while your student is going through college, and then emerge with your net worth intact—and no debt!

Here are a few examples of ways that you could cut costs to raise cash for your kid's education:

Quit smoking: If you smoke a pack a day, seven days a week, at five dollars per pack, that's $1,825 yearly that could be redirected toward college—if you quit smoking. That's enough to cover more than half of a semester's tuition bill at the average public college or university.

Vacations: Do you like to travel? Skiing? Cruises? If you want to make sacrifices to help your kids pay for college, this is one way to save thousands of dollar per year. According to the Travel Industry Association, the average family spends $2,200 per year on leisure travel, not including any lost wages.[4] If you can chop that in half—or perhaps go the staycation route—you'll have a four-figure sum that can go straight into the coffers of a college of your choice.

Drive your car for an extra year: When I was in eighth grade (and my brother was in tenth), my mom bought an old Volvo and proclaimed it her "college car"—an unattractive but reliable hunk of steel that she would putter around in for years at great personal embarrassment, all for the sake of helping to pay for our college tuition. If you have a car that's been paid off and you're contemplating trading it in . . . keep driving it! The average car payment is around $384 per month. That means that if you go without a car payment for the entire four years of your child's education, you will have saved $18,432. And you can buy a couple of textbooks with the savings from taxes and registration. My mom got a new-to-her Honda when I was able to pay for college without her assistance, and now I drive the old Volvo.

Lattes, energy drinks, and the like: This one's similar to cigarettes without the whole dying-a-slow-and-painful-death part. If you spend six dollars per day on miscellaneous junk (candy bars, energy drinks, Starbucks, lottery tickets, etc.), that's $2,190 per year that you could have for your child's college education.

Assuming that you smoke, travel, drink lattes, and have car payments, I have just shown you how you can save an extra $9,000-plus per year for your child's education.

If your kids are still in high school (or, better yet, younger), I urge you to look at your own personal spending habits and find ways that you can cut out the pork. One way to keep track of the savings and keep yourself motivated is to keep a separate account where you put all your savings associated with an end to bad habits. If you give up a pack-a-day smoking habit, you could deposit forty-two dollars per week and brag to your family by showing them the bank statements full of found money.

The best part of cost cutting your way to a debt-free college education during the college years? It's completely tax free and won't cut your financial aid eligibility. *There is no tax or financial aid consequence resulting from that latte you didn't buy.* There are also no interest charges to be paid and no origination fees.

It's also a good idea to involve your kids in this process of cost cutting for college, because young people should develop a respect for thrift as early in life as possible. Plus they might help keep you on track when you're having a weak moment at the corner store. Does your college-bound high school student have younger siblings? Get them in on the college saving bandwagon! If you have the means, consider matching any money that your child puts aside for college by depositing the same amount into the account. But be careful: when your child reports his assets on the financial aid form, a large chunk of whatever he has saved will be deducted from his financial aid. Savings accounts should be in your name, not in his.

Get a Second Job

In the first part of this chapter, I expressed skepticism about the amount of money that so many parents are contributing toward their children's educations. The average parent who borrows through a Parent PLUS loan takes on $23,300 in debt[5]—which is actually more than the average student's indebtedness. Worse, this figure does not even include home equity loans or other forms of debt. That's just Parent PLUS loans.

I passionately believe that parents should borrow a maximum of zero dollars to help their kids pay for college, and the reasoning is simple: if you don't have enough cash to pay for college, it means that you are probably underprepared for retirement, have an inadequate rainy day fund, and need to focus on those areas—you cannot afford to divert future earnings toward payments on college loans!

But I'm not suggesting that parents not make sacrifices to help their kids pay for college. As I showed in the last section, you can probably find a number of opportunities to cut costs in your personal life. But as a very smart person once said, the best place to go when you need money is work.

Would you be willing to put in more hours at work if it would help your child graduate from school debt free? I hope so. And if you can't get more hours at work, you could easily earn a couple hundred bucks a month throwing pizzas, delivering newspapers, or working the register at Wal-Mart. That might seem degrading if you have more degrees than a thermometer, but it's a great alternative to being stupid and taking out loans. Less melodramatically, it is worth looking into freelance, overtime, and per diem opportunities within your field. Be creative! If you increase your take-home earnings by $200 per month every year your kid is in high school, you'll have $9,600 by freshman year: enough to cover nearly three semesters' worth of tuition and fees at the average public college or university.

Another option is to sell your stuff. Most families have plenty of stuff lying around that they could part with. Have a yard sale. Post stuff on Craigslist. Sell on eBay. You'd be surprised how much money you can earn from what's lingering in your basement and at the back of the closet. What you can't sell, you can donate to a local thrift shop in exchange for a tax write-off that can free up cash for college (although you only benefit from the write-off if you itemize your deductions).

A Walk Through the FAFSA Form

Unless you are very, very early in the college financing exploration process, you have probably heard of the FAFSA form. FAFSA stands for Free Application for Federal Student Aid—but for our purposes let's think of it as the Federal Assault on Families' Savings Accounts. It's a form provided by the federal government that asks for all kinds of information about your finances and those of your child; how much you, your spouse, and your child earn, and what kind of assets you have. Then it puts all that information into a formula and spits out your expected family contribution (EFC) or the amount of money the government believes you should—or can afford to—contribute to your kid's college education. If you really care about the details, you can log on to the federal government's federal student aid Web site and read a thirty-five-page PDF that purports to explain it, although scientific studies have shown that anyone who can get through the whole thing without falling asleep is high on cocaine. United States Secretary of Education Arne Duncan has said, "You basically have to have a Ph.D. to figure that thing out." I would take it a step further and say that if a student can figure out how to fill out the FAFSA form on her own, she should automatically be awarded a bachelor's in finance, accounting, and Greek mythology.

If you haven't yet filled out the FAFSA form and are curious about what your EFC will be, log on to FinAid.org and use that site's EFC estimator.

There are a few things to keep in mind about the FAFSA form, the first of which is that it's arbitrary and out of touch with how much families can actually afford to contribute to college. Think about it: this formula that purports to show you how much you can responsibly spend is produced by the federal government, which has the largest debt in the history of the world. It's like asking Cher how much plastic surgery you can have before it looks tacky.

The FAFSA formula basically takes into account the parents' income(s), savings and other assets (not including retirement assets or the primary residence), and age, along with the student's income and assets, which are, in most cases, not particularly material. This seems like a perfectly rational way to assess financial need, but there are tons of problems with the simplicity of the formula. For most families, the expected family contribution has nothing to do with what that family can prudently afford to contribute toward college expenses. Here are some specific things to watch out for:

1. The FAFSA form determines your EFC based on a formula that has nothing to do with how much families will actually

contribute. What if FAFSA says your expected family contribution is $15,000 per year, but you decide that you only can contribute $8,000? Your child is on the hook for the rest. What if you have special circumstances? Do you spend a significant portion of your income caring for aging parents? Was your income higher last year than you expect it to be in the near future (like if you're a real estate agent, for example)? Good for you: FAFSA doesn't care.

2. The FAFSA form does not take into account retirement savings when determining the expected family contribution. To understand how nuts this is, take a look at this example: The parents in family A have a combined income of $90,000 per year, with $12,000 in retirement assets. The parents in family B have a combined income of $90,000 per year, but also $4.2 million in retirement savings (Mom was a secretary at Apple back when it was located in Steve Jobs's garage). All the parents involved are fifty-eight years old. Under the FAFSA formula, both families are expected to contribute the same amount of money toward college expenses. But doesn't it seem obvious that, at fifty-eight years old with just $12,000 in retirement funds, family A needs to get crackin' if it has any chance at an even reasonably comfortable retirement? And in that case, wouldn't they be ill-advised to contribute even a small portion of their income to college? I've never heard a single person intelligently explain how a family with a net worth of $4.2 million has the same ability to fund educational expenses as a family with a net worth of $12,000. This reinforces my point that the EFC is produced by an arbitrary formula that has absolutely nothing to do with the long-term financial outlook for the parents. Without looking at home equity and retirement savings, the EFC calculated by the FAFSA is the equivalent of calling up a nutritionist and asking, "I'm five-nine. Am I overweight?" The FAFSA form has insufficient information to determine how much a family can afford to contribute.

3. I mentioned this earlier, but it's worth saying again: be extremely careful about methods of paying for college that will

artificially inflate your income for the purpose of the FAFSA form. For instance, let's say that you own a few hundred shares of stock that are worth $10,000 more than you paid for them. This seems like a great way to pay for college, but it's actually a *horrible* way to pay for college. Why? Selling the stock will cause you to realize a $10,000 gain, which in addition to subjecting you to any capital gains taxes will also raise your income by $10,000 and harm your ability to qualify for financial aid. One alternative, if you dare, is to borrow against that stock holding on margin. You'll pay interest on it but, because you didn't sell the stock, it won't increase your income for tax and FAFSA purposes. If your family doesn't qualify for financial aid, then by all means sell stock for big gains, but remember to factor in the taxes.

4. If your child works hard and saves a lot of money, he will be penalized by the FAFSA form. One of the worst things about the formula used for calculating a family's expected contribution is that, each year, 35 percent of a student's savings is deducted from the financial aid eligibility on top of half of his after-tax income over $3,000 per year. Then there's the double whammy: if an ambitious and frugal student devotes half her income to college expenses and then saves the other half, FAFSA comes back and grabs 35 percent the next year, because now it's savings! I find it appalling that we have a financial aid system in this country that offers more financial aid to students who don't work or save than to students who work and save. Why should a student who sits at home in his underwear and plays Halo all summer (if you don't know what that is, consider yourself lucky) get more government assistance than one who works full-time and barely has time for a social life?

5. The FAFSA formula does not take credit card debt into account when calculating the EFC. What this means is that two families with identical finances—except that one has $100,000 in credit card debt and the other has no credit card debt—will have the same expected family contributions, even though their capacity for paying tuition bills is extremely different. One tip here is that if

you do have credit card debt, you should pay it off before submitting your information on the FAFSA form, if you have the cash available and can dip into it without jeopardizing your emergency fund. This will reduce your expected family contribution somewhat by reducing your savings, possibly qualifying you for more financial aid.

The current system for student earnings and assets is so messed up that college financial aid officers can't even talk about it without lying. On the PBS special *Paying for College with the Greenes*—an epic that makes *Gigli* look like *Casablanca*—one financial aid director explained that the notion that families who prioritize hard work and saving are penalized in the financial aid process is a myth. He explained that, on average, parents are only expected to contribute 5 percent of their savings to college but did allow that it's "a little bit more" for the students' assets.

I was stunned. A financial aid director at a prestigious college was staring viewers in the face and simply lying about how financial aid works. I've been told that I shouldn't accuse people of lying, but there really isn't any other way to describe it. Let's break down the two lies he told:

1. "Only about 5 percent of parental savings are expected to be contributed to college." That one is technically true, except that college is four years. So it's really 20 percent, because I'm told five times four is twenty. (Yes, I know: it might be a little bit less, because if your savings are depleted 5 percent every year, 5 percent will be a little less the next year. But if you rebuild your savings each year, it could be more than 20 percent.) The other problem is that parent assets are not counted nearly as heavily as parental income when it comes to the FAFSA form. So if you have very few assets but a high income, know that your low assets won't protect you from a large expected family contribution.

2. Students are expected to contribute "a little bit more" of their assets than parents. Parents are expected to contribute about

5 percent of their assets (with the caveat that that's an average: the actual percentage varies considerably based on income) and students are expected to contribute 35 percent of their savings each year. Thirty-five percent is not a little bit more than 5 percent, any more than weighing 350 pounds is a little bit more than weighing 50 pounds. This is yet another example of college salespeople (admissions and financial aid staff) spinning and not telling the truth: if they're so brazen as to lie on national television, how can you possibly trust anything they say in unrecorded phone conversations?

Here's what you need to know about the "financial aid office." These people work for the college, not for you. Don't be confused by their innocent-sounding titles: their job is to help students come up with the money to attend their institutions through whatever means necessary. It may be helpful to think of financial aid people as mortgage salesmen who are happy if and only if you find a way to send your kid to their school.

Ultimately the problem with the FAFSA form goes back to the retirement equation: more than half of parents of college-age kids face serious questions about their financial readiness for retirement, but most of those people will still be expected to contribute cash toward college. In fact, studies have shown that the percentage of financial aid given to low-income students is disproportionately low. According to a 2008 study conducted by the National Center for Public Policy and Higher Education, low-income families contribute, on average, 55 percent of their earnings toward their children's public, four-year institutions, which is an increase from 39 percent in 2000.[6] And you can be sure that most low-income families aren't pulling that money out of college savings accounts. They're most likely borrowing it or diverting funds from their already too lean retirement savings. For more information on the FAFSA form and how you can get the most out of it, check out FinAid.org. It's an excellent resource for navigating the bureaucratic minefield of FAFSA.

Look at the expected family contribution that you'll arrive at from the FAFSA form the same way that an intelligent person looks a preapproval on a car loan: it's an amount of money that someone with a vested interest in overextending you says is appropriate. Don't be fooled. I'm asking you to take an honest look at your finances and decide how much you can afford to contribute to your kid's educational expenses without jeopardizing your own retirement or rainy-day fund. The EFC calculated by the FAFSA form has absolutely nothing to do with the amount that you can actually afford to contribute to your child's education. That is the largest problem with financial aid, so it's worth repeating and putting in italics, bold, and underlining: ***The EFC calculated by the FAFSA form has absolutely nothing to do with the amount you can actually afford to contribute to your child's education.*** It couldn't possibly, because it doesn't take into account retirement assets or your career outlook or any major expenses you may have in the future. What you need to do is take an honest look at your financial situation and calculate your IFC: intelligent family contribution—that is, the amount that a reasonably sane person could comfortably contribute. If that number is zero or something close to zero, relax! You're in the majority, and I'm going to show you ways that your child can still get a great education without raiding your savings or putting you in debt. And I can say this from my own personal experience: those of us who are putting ourselves through college without significant parental assistance will leave with a sense of accomplishment and a work ethic that is probably more valuable than the diploma itself.

Two Types of Financial Aid Methodology

For most parents this won't be an issue, but I should say here that when I discuss FAFSA, I'm talking about the federal methodology for calculating financial aid. But just to make this a little bit more fun, there is another method called the College Scholarship Service's Financial Aid Profile Institutional Methodology, which is employed mainly by very expensive private colleges. This method for calculating expected family contributions is then sometimes rejiggered in different ways by different schools, but the key difference to worry about between this method and the federal one is this: the CSS's Financial Aid Profile counts home equity against you when calculating expected family contribution. The more home equity you have, the more you'll have to pay.

Most colleges don't count home equity when calculating expected family contributions, which doesn't make any sense at all. Even if we agree that people shouldn't use home equity loans to pay for college, doesn't a parent's net worth have something to do with their college financing ability? And since the primary residence is the largest asset that most people have, how can you determine their financial need without taking it into account? I don't think that families should use home equity loans to pay for college, but it's ridiculous to argue that a family that owns a $3.5-million estate has the same means as a family that rents. The *New York Times* reports that "of the roughly 2,000 four-year colleges nationwide, only about 250 require applicants for financial aid to disclose a home's value and outstanding mortgage debt.

The CSS's Financial Aid Profile is generally only used by the most selective, most expensive schools in the country, and it's definitely worth looking at whether schools your child is considering use this measure, as it can add quite a chunk to your EFC. At Sarah Lawrence College, for instance, parents with an adjusted gross income of $100,000 and $150,000 in available home equity were expected to contribute 5.65 percent of their home equity each year as part of their educational contribution.

In other words, if you are "house poor"—that is, your home makes up the largest portion of your net worth and you have little in the way of other assets to tap for college—the financial aid packages offered by private colleges that use the CSS's Financial Aid Profile are likely to be poor because they will take into account home equity that other colleges don't even ask for.

Why this difference? It's simple: because expensive schools require larger family contributions, they have to come up with a methodology to rationalize it. Sure, they could send people letters that say, "Your EFC is $10,000, but we need you to come up with $25,000. K thx ttyl!" but that would be distasteful. So instead they invent a parallel system of financial aid that leads, in most cases, to higher expected family contributions.

It's also worth noting here that the institutional methodology that leads to higher EFCs also exposes a key fraud in the advertising by so many private colleges that they "meet 100 percent of financial need!" The problem? Their calculation of financial need is completely different from that of other colleges, rendering their promise to meet financial need completely—or at least mostly—meaningless.

A FAFSA Loophole: Stuff Your Money in Your House

To maximize your financial aid eligibility, you can take advantage of the FAFSA rules that disregard home equity when determining EFC. This is a somewhat risky strategy because you might end up house poor—too much equity in your house and not enough cash in the event of an illness or layoff. But as a strategy for maximizing financial aid eligibility, it's hard to beat. Here's how it works: take any money that you have in savings accounts or the stock market (outside of retirement accounts, which don't count against you in the financial aid race) and use it to pay down your mortgage.

This will prevent FAFSA from looting your savings account to the tune of 5 percent per year (or a total of 20 percent over four years) to pay for your child's education. If you have $100,000 in savings and use it to pay down your mortgage while your child attends a school that uses FAFSA to calculate EFC, this could qualify you for an extra $20,000 in financial aid. If you pursue this approach, please make sure that you still retain an adequate emergency fund in case you need cash quickly. Apply this method only to cash reserves in excess of your needs.

Scholarships Are Overrated

So now I've shown you two things: you shouldn't take out a loan to help your kid pay for college, and you should also completely ignore the expected family contribution spit out by the FAFSA form or, if your child is applying to more selective schools, the CSS.

Many families believe that scholarships and financial aid will help alleviate the burden of spiraling college costs. This one is especially tragic because, from my experience, many families put a lot of faith in it. And guidance counselors play into the fraud by constantly talking about the availability of college scholarships, encouraging students to fill out countless applications and write numerous essays.

The reality is that the role that scholarships and financial aid are likely to play in financing college is vastly overstated. Of course some kids will get full rides to their dream colleges, but most won't. When I was shopping the proposal for this book to publishers, one of the most common suggestions I got was "You should provide more advice on how to get scholarships." I don't do this for a few reasons. First, one of my goals is to have a positive long-term impact on the financial future of college students and their families. Offering tips on how to get scholarships is a zero-sum game. If one student learns tricks for how to win, he receives the cash at the expense of another student who might have otherwise been the winner. The net societal benefit of offering advice on scholarships is zero.

The other reason I don't talk about scholarships is that the role they play in financing education tends to be greatly exaggerated, giving families a sense of false hope. According to Scholarships.com, high school students hoping to receive merit-based scholarships generally "need to get exceedingly good grades and, most likely, graduate in the top five to ten percent" of their high school class. At Wake Forest University, for example, only 5 percent of the most recent freshman class received any merit-based scholarships at all—and don't forget that the vast majority of scholarships cover only a tiny fraction of the overall cost of attendance. What about those much-celebrated athletic scholarships? A recent *New York Times* study found that those cover, on average, only about a third of college expenses. And unless your child is a really elite athlete in a major sport, she's probably out of the running.

According to the College Board, about two thirds of all full-time undergraduate students receive grant aid. In 2008/09 estimated aid in the form of grants and tax benefits averaged about $2,300 per student per year at public two-year colleges, about $3,700 at public four-year colleges, and about $10,200 per student at private four-year colleges.[7] That's hardly chump change, but with the total cost of attendance at many private colleges coming in at well over $40,000 per year, it's nowhere close to enough to alleviate the burden of college costs. Even though private colleges offer more grant aid per student on average, they are so much more expensive than public colleges that, unless your child is able to secure an especially large scholarship, the cost of attending a private college will be far higher.

And what about private scholarships—those that gurus and guidance counselors are urging you to apply for because thousands go unused every year, leaving a couple thousand dollars just yours for the taking? Remember what your grandmother told you: if it sounds too good to be true, it probably is. According to the Institute for Higher Education Policy, only about 7 percent of all college students receive college scholarships from third parties—with an average award of $1,982. Private scholarships represent only about 2 to 3 percent of all college aid awarded each year.[8] Worse, those private scholarships are often only for one year, so your child will have to start the scholarship application race all over again each year. If you're counting on scholarships to cover the cost of college, this can be highly stressful and potentially disastrous if they don't come through as well sophomore year as they did freshman year, which they often don't because the sense of urgency is gone. The student's already there and he's unlikely to drop out, so why send him more money? Let him figure it out!

But by far the biggest problem with scholarships has to do with the way that the expected family contribution is calculated on the FAFSA form. If your family qualifies for a significant amount of need-based financial aid, there is a very good chance that obtaining additional outside merit-based scholarships will be completely useless in terms of helping you to pay for college.

Here's why. When the FAFSA form calculates the expected family contribution, that is the amount of cash that you (or your child, her grandparents, etc.) are expected come up with. Earning additional scholarship money does not reduce that number because it must be reported on the FAFSA form. Unless you earn enough outside scholarships to more than cover the amount of financial aid you were awarded, you're probably helping out the college more than yourself.

From the college's perspective, it makes perfect sense. They provide financial aid to help students afford an education, and make a calculation of how much a family can afford to contribute. If a student is able to find some cash on his own, that's great. But his family can still afford to contribute, so why not make that financial aid available to someone else? The effect of this well-meaning policy is that filling out countless third-party scholarship applications often does a lot more for the university than it does for the student.

None of this is to say that you shouldn't look into scholarships—and indeed some schools do find a way to reward students who secure substantial scholarships by reducing work-study or loan aid before reducing grant aid. And if your child doesn't qualify for much in the way of need-based financial aid, scholarships can be fantastic and he absolutely must look to apply to outside sources for financial assistance with college. If you'd like to learn more about scholarships, the best resource is Ben Kaplan's *How to Go to College Almost for Free*, in spite of its hyper-ambitious title. I wonder what percentage of people who bought that book were able to go to college for anything resembling free. Books like this and Web sites like Scholarships.com offer tons of advice and links to scholarships and applications. Advice and information on scholarships are also things your high school guidance counselor is good for. Encourage your child to apply for tons of scholarships, but don't count on them to make a meaningful dent in the college bill. Be pleasantly surprised if they do.

Another thing: the world of scholarships is full of gurus, hucksters, and downright charlatans. You should never, ever pay anyone a nickel to help you find scholarships, nor should you pay an "application fee" to apply for a scholarship. People in the nonbusiness of handing out thousands of dollars to young people out of generosity do not need to collect fees and anyone who says they do is likely to be a crook.

How to Get the Most Merit Aid

Everyone wants to go to the best school they can get into on a full ride, but here's how it really works. If you're hoping to score merit aid for college, the best bet is to look to schools where your student will be in the top 10 percent. If your child wants to apply to some private colleges—and he absolutely should, because he just might get a miraculous financial package—the best bet for cost-conscious families is to look to schools that qualify as safety schools.

Many schools, especially larger ones, offer scholarships automatically to accepted students with certain GPAs and certain SAT scores. Obviously, the cutoffs will be lower at less selective schools.

Colleges disperse their merit aid to their best students. So a student who just barely squeaks into a college gets nothing. Therefore, look at schools where your child's SAT scores and GPA will be at or above the high end of the college's range. "Reach" schools—those applications that guidance counselors encourage students to send in even though they probably won't be accepted—should generally be avoided because applying there can lead to heartache: "You got in! But you can't go!"

In the financial aid world, there is a practice known as gapping. That is, selective colleges generally offer weaker financial aid packages to more marginal students—with a large "gap" between the expected family contribution and financial aid offered to meet the total cost. For many families, this can lead to a need for the aggressive use of private student loans, retirement account looting, and general overextension.

For a handful of the most selective schools in the country—Harvard, Princeton, Yale, Amherst College, and a few others—this "gapping" policy doesn't happen. The endowments are large enough so that everyone who gets in gets a fantastic financial aid package. But for the best of the rest, it's a compelling reason to avoid reach schools. It flies in the face of the conventional wisdom that students should "go to the best college they can get into" but, financially, it's the smart approach.

There's another problem with applying to a lot of colleges that seldom gets addressed: those application fees add up quickly. According to the College Board, the average college application fee is thirty-five dollars—some charge sixty dollars and others charge no fee, but that's a rough average. So let's say your child spends $420 to apply to twelve schools—that's more than 6 percent of the tuition and fees at the average public university for the 2008/09 school year! And it's an out-of-pocket expense that isn't tax deductible, nor—in most cases—can you get financial aid to help you cover it.

Add to that the fact that, for most students, an in-state public college, university, or community college will offer the best deal, and it just doesn't make sense to follow the old "cast a wide net" wisdom and apply to tons of colleges to "see what kind of packages you get." As Dr. Martin Nemko wrote in his book *The All-in-One College Guide*, "The easiest, most powerful way to make college affordable is to choose a college with a low published (sticker) price."

Keep it simple. If your child has a fetish for a few schools, go ahead and apply, with the understanding that they're out of the picture unless they offer some kind of miraculous financial aid package *that isn't loaded with loans.*

Another reason not to spend a lot of time applying to a ton of different colleges is that it takes a lot of time—time that could be spent working a part-time job to help raise money to pay for college, reading, hanging out with friends, or engaging in tons of other activities that help young people develop the passions that can turn into livelihoods and lives.

Financial Aid

A lot of parents put all their faith in financial aid. Financial aid, they hear, will bridge the gap between what they can afford and what college costs. The average financial aid package in America today comprises 60 percent loans—which isn't really financial aid at all, because you can always get loans from other sources. According to the United States Department of Education's National Postsecondary Student Aid Study, nearly all federal financial aid given to families with incomes over $60,000 came in the form of loans. Of families with incomes between $40,000 and $59,999, only 31 percent received federal grant aid. Of families with incomes between $60,000 and $79,999, only 2.3 percent received any federal grant aid.[9]

The key thing to remember about financial aid is this: if it were that great, student loan debt wouldn't constitute 25 percent of all consumer debt in this country. It's that simple.

One of the reasons that so many people have inflated hopes for financial aid is that there's a huge amount of bad information out there coming from sources most people consider reliable. Understanding the financial aid packages offered by colleges and how much money you're really likely to receive is like looking at Enron's statement of cash flows and trying to figure out where the money comes from. *US News & World Report*'s annual guide "America's Best Colleges" (which will be the victim of a thorough debunking in Chapter 3) lists the average financial aid package per year for each college in the directory, but if you read the footnotes, there's a little catch:

> Financial Aid: Here you'd find the percentage of undergraduates determined by the school to have financial need and amount of the average aid package (including grants, loans, and jobs) in the 2007-2008 school year. We also list the phone number of the financial aid office.

Oops! Isn't a loan different from a grant? Because, you see, if my friend lends me his Ferrari to take a date to dinner, that's different from his giving it to me. At least, I think it is. But in the Alice in Wonderland world of financial aid, a loan is no different from a gift. That will help induce students into attending whatever college strikes their fancy, but there will be hell to pay once the loan comes due.

Similarly, an opportunity to work a low-paying job is also different from a grant. For instance, if you offer me eight dollars an hour to do your laundry, that is fundamentally different from your simply giving me eight dollars. This all seems obvious to me, and I don't mean to be patronizing or to insult your intelligence, but apparently *US News & World Report* is having some difficulty understanding the thin distinctions between grants, loans, and jobs. If you go to the college's Web site or check out any of the better college guides (especially the Department of Education's College Navigator site, which is

free and data-driven and not full of hype designed to lure advertisers
and sell magazines) with detailed directories of colleges, they'll have
a breakdown of how the financial aid is distributed.

But it isn't just *US News & World Report* that's confused. The
world of financial aid is byzantine and, I believe, obfuscatory: a
deliberately confusing world of smoke and mirrors designed to lead
students down a path of poverty. There is evidence that, in their
enthusiasm to help their children fund higher education, many families don't really think about student loans with any sort of objective
analysis and look at them as part of the package, a minor concern
to be thought about later. In "Financial Aid Packages and College Enrollment Decisions: An Econometric Case Study" (NBER
Working Paper No. 9228), the authors, David Linsenmeier, Harvey
Rosen, and Cecilia Rouse, looked at the change in enrollment decisions that occurred when one university tried to attract more low-
income students by entirely replacing offers of student loans with
grants for low-income applicants. This change in financial aid policy
increased the likelihood of a low-income student actually starting
college at the school by only three percentage points, a statistically
insignificant sum.[10]

In other words, students didn't really seem to draw a clear distinction between grants and student loans, even though it is clearly in
their best interests to do so.

One of the most heinous methods that colleges use in awarding
financial aid is what I like to call the crack-dealer method. They
give you a good deal on the first hit and then jack up the price. It
works like this: A student is accepted to his dream school and the
college offers a strong financial aid package for the first year. The
student enrolls and then—poof! The financial aid package for
sophomore year drops and the student is faced with a few uncomfortable options: his parents can loot their retirement funds or home
equity, he can bog himself down with student loans he never anticipated having to take, or he can transfer to a less expensive college.

Attending a dream college and then transferring is one of the biggest wastes of money in the history of the world, but if you're overly reliant on financial aid packages that are up for renewal every year, it's certainly a possibility.

The crack-dealer method is especially common when you look at the distribution of financial aid between grants and loans. Because federal Stafford loan limits increase from year to year ($5,500 for freshmen, $6,500 for sophomores, and $7,500 for juniors and seniors), it is easy for colleges to shift students away from grant aid and into loans.

I'm not making this up—it really does happen. In November 2008, I was talking to a producer for CNN's morning show, going over topics for an upcoming interview. I mentioned to her that I wanted to talk about the problem of students at private colleges being forced to transfer to less expensive alternatives mid-year because of their parents' sagging retirement portfolios. "Oh yeah—that happened to me," she said.

Here's what's so messed up about this: Let's say that a family loots its retirement and borrows heavily to pay for their kid to go to the private college of his dreams. After two years (or one or three), the family is out of money. What happens? Maybe Junior has to transfer and receive his diploma from a less prestigious public college, and whatever benefit you were hoping to get from the diploma you were buying for $50,000 per year has evaporated. Remember: the diploma comes from the college you graduate from, whether you went there for four years or one semester.

The scenario where families run out of money and students are forced to transfer to cheaper schools is expected to grow increasingly common. The poor returns of the stock market over the past decade have many college endowments feeling the pinch. Amherst College's endowment lost about 25 percent of its value in the span of four months, and financial need among its students is on the rise as their parents' net worths decline. Meanwhile, the alumni who are traditionally a reliable source of cash for many private colleges are less inclined to open their wallets because of their own financial woes. So far Amherst College has avoided cuts in financial aid partly because its endowment is still large for a school of its size—many other universities have not been able to do that.

The point is that there are always risks inherent in counting on other people to pay for expenses. Scholarships and financial aid are a wonderful thing, but you have to recognize that, for most forms of aid, it's back to the drawing board every year. You can, and should, ask the financial aid office for information about whether the aid will be renewed with the same package next year, but take everything they say with a grain of salt. It's their job but your and your child's lives. Remember Barry Minkow's advice: never take someone at her word when she has a vested interest in lying to you.

Students who are overly reliant on financial aid for college are depending on renewed generosity each year with no viable alternative if things change. The result is that students often end up graduating with far more debt than they anticipated having when they entered college.

Some Colleges Will Offer to Cover 100 Percent of Financial Need: True or False?

One of the latest marketing tricks used by colleges is the offer to meet 100 percent of a student's financial need. In 2005 CNN reported that nearly one hundred colleges and universities in the United States boast of being able to cover 100 percent of a student's demonstrated financial need.[11]

This sounds really good, but the truth is that it means nothing. For starters, that "100 percent of financial need met" thing can include student loans, which makes those schools just like every other school on the planet. Anyone who wants to go to a certain college badly enough will find someone willing to lend the money.

The other problem with this piece of marketing hype is that it's often based on the expected family contribution calculated by the FAFSA form, which, as I've already demonstrated, can be a completely unrealistic picture of the amount that it actually makes sense for you to contribute toward your child's education.

If it isn't based on the FAFSA form, it's based on the CSS—which is even worse, because it includes home equity.

In her otherwise excellent book *The College Solution*, Lynn O'Shaughnessy points to Case Western Reserve University as an example of a school that exhibits great financial generosity. Ninety-three percent of first-year students receive some financial aid, and the average financial aid package is $26,989, compared with a cost of attendance of around $44,000. The average merit award is $16,174, according to the College Board.

And yet according to the Common Data Set posted on the college's Web site, the average student borrower's indebtedness at graduation—not including parental debt—was a mind-numbingly high $37,892—and 65 percent of students took out loans. And this is an example of a college whose financial aid packages would seem to make it look affordable. But for the average student, Case Western Reserve University leads to an extremely serious debt problem that will interfere with her ability to pursue her dreams.

The next school O'Shaughnessy mentions is Juniata College, which, she says, provides most of its students with need-based financial aid and merit scholarships. And yet Juniata College still hands more than 80 percent of its graduates an average debt load of more than $23,000. Sure, that's better than Case Western, but it's only about average. If these are the best examples of private colleges that help out students with generous grant aid, I'm not impressed.

The point is that these cute ideas of "pursuing merit scholarships" and "finding generous colleges" simply don't seem to lead to debt-free graduates. The merit money that these schools award doesn't make them cheaper than public colleges. That's why the average public college graduate leaves with far less debt than the average private college graduate—even though the private college grads tend to have wealthier backgrounds.

Can You Negotiate for More Financial Aid? Maybe, Kinda, Sorta

One of the most common bits of advice that people are getting on financial aid is that you can negotiate for more. Occasionally that's true—if your circumstances are really unique. The financial aid expert Mark Kantrowitz of FinAid.org recently told *Fortune* (yes, even high-net-worth readers need help with paying for college),

> "Schools are not car dealerships where you can get a better deal through a combination of bluff and bluster. It's a much more formulaic process.
>
> "And you can't get colleges into a bidding war. If you come in and say, 'This other school gave us a better financial aid offer,' the school will ask for a copy of the other school's offer. Your financial aid package is based on the difference between the cost of education and your ability to pay for it, as determined by standard formulas. If two schools have come up with substantially different estimates of how much you can afford to pay, they will try to understand why there is such a difference."[12]

It's certainly worth trying to negotiate with colleges to get more financial aid, but Kantrowitz is right: the process is formulaic, and unless you have a fairly unique situation—you experienced a job loss, Bernie Madoff stole your savings, *and* you lost your house in a natural disaster—it's unlikely to yield much in the way of results, and it's definitely not going to alleviate the burden of paying for college. Universities dole out financial aid based on rigid formulas that, as I've shown, have basically nothing to do with the reality of what a family can actually afford to contribute toward educational expenses. That's just reality.

But Don't Private Colleges Offer More Financial Aid?

Many families have heard that private colleges offer more financial aid than public colleges. This is often true, but the post-financial-aid discount from private colleges is very, very rarely enough to make them an economically superior option to public colleges. This is because—unless your child is offered a huge pile of merit award—the school will only cover financial need as calculated by FAFSA or the CSS institutional methodology. So the financial aid will be larger because the tuition is higher, but at the vast majority of private schools, it will include more loans than would be required from a public college.

The Problem with Receiving Financial Aid

All of these problems with the byzantine world of financial aid have led me to this conclusion: all other things being equal, it's much better to pay for college without any financial aid. That sounds crazy and counterintuitive, but it's absolutely true. Take this example:

- Option A: Ritzy College has a sticker price of $45,000, but through its generous financial aid program, your child received a grant of $30,000, meaning that you have to come up with $15,000 each year to pay the bills.

- Option B: Rugged State College has a sticker price of $15,000 and your child received no financial aid, meaning that you have to come up with $15,000 each year to pay the bills.

Ten out of ten guidance counselors will tell you that these two offers are identical, and that you and your child should take whichever one strikes his fancy. But the problem with that is that under option A, your choices for coming up with that $15,000 are very limited. Under option B, they're unlimited, because you aren't beholden to the evil bureaucracy of FAFSA. Under option B, these are some of the ways you could raise the $15,000 in cash: (1) have your student take a part-time job to cover at least some of her living expenses, (2) sell stock you own that has appreciated, or (3) work more hours at your own job.

Under option A, none of these ways of making up the college funding gap will work. To the extent that they do, they also increase the cost of attendance. If your child earns $6,000 per year, having him earn an extra $2,000 to put toward college will increase the cost of college by $1,000 next year, meaning that he'll have to earn an extra thousand to cover that. But doing that will increase the cost of college by $500, meaning that he'll have to earn an extra $500, but doing that will increase his bill by $250, which . . . You get the picture. Having your kid work will have a tremendous adverse impact on his financial aid eligibility next year, and selling stock that has appreciated will create a bump in your adjusted gross income— which will also decrease your eligibility for financial aid. If you can find a college that is affordable without receiving need-based financial aid, it gives you far more flexibility.

That's why, all other things being equal, you want to be able to pay for college with as little aid as possible. This is especially true because receiving financial aid requires you to requalify each year— which means that you'll have to continue living your life in such a way as to maximize your financial aid. That can take a lot of time and energy that could be better devoted to other things, like learning how to crochet or play the violin.

The FAFSA Wedding: The Insidious, Truck-Sized Loophole to More Financial Aid

People get married for all kinds of really bad, cynical reasons. But marrying to pay for college? Huh? I want to tell you about a strange loophole in this whole mess that, if you, your child, and a friend are willing to do something really bizarre, could save you thousands of dollars. When you fill out the FAFSA form and derive your expected family contribution, your income will be taken into account. The more you earn, the less financial aid your child is likely to receive. Even if you elect not to contribute anything toward your child's education, it is likely to be nearly impossible to make him an "emancipated minor" for financial aid purposes so that he can receive full financial aid—nearly all students would qualify for far more financial aid if they were able to file the FAFSA form as independents rather than as dependents of their parents.

The process for securing a "dependency override" is arduous, and only around 2 percent of students qualify. If you are a concerned enough parent to be reading this book, it's unlikely that your child meets that category. The following standards are NOT sufficient to qualify a student for a dependency override, according to the Department of Education. Note that this list includes the most common reasons that students might feel they should be able to apply for financial aid as independents:

1. Parents refusing to contribute to the student's education

2. Parents unwilling to provide information on the application or for verification

3. Parents not claiming the student as a dependent for income tax purposes

4. Student demonstrating total self-sufficiency

So how can a child get a dependency override? In general, the circumstances have to be incredibly dire:

1. A documented history of physical or sexual abuse (police reports, etc.)

2. Incarceration of *both* parents

3. Both parents completely missing (don't get any ideas)

4. Child removed from home and placed in foster care

In other words, it's extremely unlikely that you'll be able to qualify under any of those standards. Here's the loophole: students who are married file their FAFSAs with their spouses, not with their parents. So two college kids earning close to nothing who are married would likely have an expected family contribution close to zero.

So all you have to do is find a like-minded, trustworthy friend who's as worried about paying for his kid's education as you are about yours, and marry the two kids off. Make sure they sign a prenuptial agreement so they can divorce quickly and painlessly upon graduation (simple divorces can cost less than $500). Also, make sure that you do it before you file the FAFSA form for freshman year, because once it's filed, you can't change the student's marital status.

What are the downsides to this? It's immoral, dishonest, and expressly intended to dump the burden of your child's college costs onto the lap of the financial aid office and the taxpayers. I mention it partly to provide an example of just how stupid the financial aid formulas are—a sham marriage could save you tens of thousands of dollars! But if your child is already married, this is information you should have: marriage is easily the fastest way to increase eligibility for financial aid.

The purpose of this chapter has been to alert you to the land mines you'll face if you overextend yourself in the pursuit of a college degree for your child. There is a vast industry aimed at convincing you to loot your savings and take on loans to further your kid's education, and most of the people parents listen to are part of this industry: admissions officers, financial aid officers, lenders, and the rest all have a vested interest in leading you to the decision that results in sending your child to their school or borrowing their money and paying them interest and fees. Always remember: no one is looking out for your interests except you.

Here's what you need to remember: you should not loot your retirement savings or borrow money to help your kid pay for college. If you have been diligent in saving money for your child's education, wonderful. If not, relax. Your child will be able to get a world-class education without breaking your bank. Take a look at your monthly spending and see how much cost cutting you'll be able to find to help pay tuition bills. Once you find an affordable school for your child to attend—I'll explain why that won't harm your child's future in Chapter 3—making up the difference with weekend and summer jobs along with whatever financial aid you receive and perhaps a small amount of student debt will be far easier than you may have been fearing.

How an Ambitious Student and His Penny-Pinching Family Could Finance a Bachelor's Degree with No Savings, No Loans, and No Financial Aid

One of the most common arguments I hear is this: "We get that student loans are bad. We get that parents shouldn't loot their retirements. But college costs are rising so fast that there's really no alternative."

That is where they're wrong. College is outrageously inflated and we do need to look at long-term solutions for bringing the cost down—or at least slowing the rate of increase. But when I look at the average prices for community colleges and state universities, the conclusion I reach is this: for families who can find fifteen dollars per week in cost cuts (Vitaminwater, cigarettes, soda, sugar-free gum, magazines, restaurant lunches, bikini waxes, movie tickets, etc.) and students who are willing to work hard—thirty hours per week, on average, including vacations—college *is* affordable: without any savings, student loans, Parent PLUS loans, retirement looting, organ sales, or heroin dealing. That thirty hours per week sounds like a lot, and it is, but once you figure that there's no reason students can't work hard on weekends while they're in college or during the four months off we have each year, it's really not so unreasonable to come up with an *average* work week of thirty hours. In Chapter 7, I go into more detail on why working during college could actually be good for your student—and certainly won't be bad.

This flies in the face of what generally passes for "wisdom" about paying for college. Be forewarned. I'm about to ask you to radically rethink the way that most people look at college.

Before you look at the numbers I've put together, please note: these are pro forma numbers and your individual situation will vary. I used the average tuition and fees for community colleges—yours may be higher or lower depending on where you are. I then looked at data from a variety of sources to try to spitball some numbers on what room and board and transportation would cost while attending community college—because these are informal costs that consist of direct expenditures by the student, it's hard to find concrete data on them. If you'd like to quibble over a few dollars, that's fine, but I think the broader point will stand.

A note about terminology: At the end of each year I refer to the "Year X surplus" (or deficit) and then I refer to the "Year X accumulated surplus." The way that this model for college financing works is that you save substantially more than enough cash to pay for the first two years at the relatively inexpensive community college—that leads to the "accumulated surplus," or what might be called in the corporate world "retained earnings." In the final two years at the four-year college, your penny-pinching and your child's slave labor aren't earning enough to cover the cost of college, but you have enough in that "accumulated surplus" savings account (which for ease of calculation I didn't bother adding interest to) to make up the difference.

Year 1 at a Community College

Average tuition and fees: $2,360

Books and supplies: $500

Room and board (at home), transportation, etc.: $4,000

Year 1 total cost: $6,860

How you pay for it:

> Parents spend $15 per week less on bottled water, snacks, etc: $780
>
> Student works 30 hours per week on average (less during the school year, more during holidays/summer) and saves the equivalent of 20 hours per week at $9 per hour (after taxes): $9,360

Year 1 intake: $10,140

Year 1 surplus: $3,280

Year 2 at a Community College

Average tuition and fees: $2,360

Books and supplies: $500

Room and board (at home), transportation, etc.: $4,000

Year 2 total cost: $6,860

How you pay for it:

> Parents spend $15 per week less on bottled water, snacks, etc: $780
>
> Student works 30 hours per week on average (less during the school year, more during holidays/summer) and saves the equivalent of 20 hours per week at $9 per hour: $9,360

Year 2 intake: $10,140

Year 2 surplus: $3,280

Year 2 accumulated surplus: $6,560

Year 3 at a Public University

Average tuition and fees: $6,600
Books and supplies: $1,000
Average room and board: $8,000
Year 3 total cost: $15,600
How you pay for it:

> Parents spend $15 per week less on bottled water, snacks, etc: $780
>
> Student works 30 hours per week on average (less during the school year, more during holidays/summer) and saves the equivalent of 20 hours per week at $9 per hour: $9,360

Year 3 intake: $10,140
Year 3 deficit: -$5,460
Year 3 accumulated surplus: $1,160

Year 4 at a Public University

Average tuition and fees: $6,600
Books and supplies: $1,000
Average room and board: $8,000
Year 4 total cost: $15,600
How you pay for it:

> Parents spend $15 per week less on bottled water, snacks, etc: $780
>
> Student works 30 hours per week on average (less during the school year, more during holidays/summer) and saves all earnings at $9 per hour: $14,040

Year 4 intake: $14,820
Year 4 deficit: -$780
Year 4 accumulated surplus: $380

And you still have enough left over to print some really nice résumés and, if you're a good shopper, to take your recent college grad shopping for a great outfit for her first job interview.

Now I know the problem with all this, and, admittedly, a large number of people won't find the plan satisfying: it involves hard work and short-term sacrifice. But unlike virtually every other plan for financing college, it is a pay-as-you-go method that doesn't depend on the kindness of strangers. It doesn't require you to play games with the FAFSA form, nor does it rely on an "enroll and hope" strategy of sending your child to college with a good financial aid package and then chatting with God every night about how happy you'd be if it gets renewed in the fall—and how screwed you'll be if it doesn't. All the sacrifices for college education are made during the time your child is acquiring that education: they aren't made from future earnings that may or may not materialize for your child, and most important, they aren't borrowed against your own financial security.

And although I assumed savings of just fifteen dollars per week on the part of parents, I would venture a guess that the vast, vast majority of parents could contribute considerably more than that.

But Wait! There's More! Tax Credits Will Pay a Large Chunk of College Costs

In 2010, Congress and the president acted aggressively to provide tax relief to families struggling with the high cost of college. The American Opportunity Tax Credit allows for a tax credit of $2,500 for parents who spend at least $4,000 on qualified educational expenses in a year. The tax credit begins to phase out for families with earnings over $160,000, or $80,000 for singles.

And please note: this is a tax credit, not a deduction, making it the equivalent of receiving $2,500 in cash from the government. That's enough to cover *35 percent* of the $7,020 annual cost of the average four-year public college in America today, according to the

College Board. So maybe you can send your kid to college with cash and still smoke (just kidding!). Another important component of this tax credit is the fact that because there is no additional tax savings available from spending more than $4,000 per year on college, it puts an even bigger gap in the cost differential between public colleges and private colleges.

The point is this: student loans are not a necessary evil in the way that most college writers assume they are. FinAid.org reports, "Few students can afford to pay for college without some form of education financing." I don't buy that and I've just shown above, mathematically, that it's not the case. I'm not saying that the pay-as-you-go method for higher education is easy. I'm saying it's worth it.

"Aha!" you say. "That method works, but what if I don't have the cash lined up at the beginning of the semester?"

For reasons that I don't claim to understand, very few colleges mention another option for financing college without paying interest: do it monthly.

Pay for College Monthly

Most colleges—especially large public institutions—offer monthly payment options that allow families to spread the cost of college out over the course of the semester. There's often no interest charged, just a small setup fee (under $100). This is a fantastic option for families that are paying for college with the pay-as-you-go option that I recommend because it makes it so easy—and doesn't require much savings going in. All you have to do is set up the program and find out how much the monthly bill will be. Then mom, dad, and student can all dig into their budgets to find sources of cash. For instance, here's how it might work:

John is going into his freshman year at the University of Georgia, and the tuition, fees, and room and board expenses for the first semester come to $6,000 after some minor financial aid and scholarships. He enrolls in a payment plan that allows him to pay the bill over five months—from August through December. So each month, a combination of John and his parents must come up with $1,200. That's a substantial amount of money, but it's very doable. If John works twenty hours per week at eight dollars an hour after-tax, he'll have $640. If Mom and Dad each spend five dollars less per day on coffee, lottery tickets, Vitaminwater, and so on, that's another $300—so now we're down to $260, an amount more than compensated for by the tax credits for education spending I discussed earlier. Alternatively, John's parents could sell stuff, work one night a week at a convenience store, or ask John to work more hours. Or maybe John worked more during the summer and has some savings from that.

I get screamed at when I tell people that the notion that "student loans are a necessity for anyone who want to go to college and doesn't come from a rich family" is bunk. But, mathematically, it is. We just proved it.

Monthly payment plans are a fantastic option for families who have a commitment to sending their kids to college without student loans but didn't rack up the savings. Ideally, your student will have some savings from working odd jobs during high school and a nice little nest egg from the summer before college starts that will make a dent. But if not, have no fear! Public colleges are quite affordable when you break them down into monthly payments—*without* paying interest.

Ask your college's financial aid or bursar's office for information on installment plans. The best thing about these plans, psychologically, is that they force you to commit to a semester of debt-free education. You simply must find a way to scrape together $1,200 per month—it might not be easy, but you can do it. It's worth it.

Graduate from College in Three Years

Most students who graduate from college do so in four years, and an increasing number are taking five or six years to accomplish the task. But getting through school in three years is one of the easiest ways to lop a year of tuition and fees out of the equation—and get into the workforce and start earning a good income more quickly. Here are a few ways students can graduate in three years:

1. Take the maximum course load every single semester. There's really no reason not to do this. You're paying for it, so you might as well take as many credits as possible each semester.

2. Take community college classes during the summer. Most universities offer summer classes to their students and advertise them heavily. But beware! For the cost of one public university summer class, you can get three times as many credits at a local community college—and you can probably take the classes online with minimal in-class assessment, so travel won't be an issue.

3. Keep very careful track of major requirements, general education requirements, and the number of classes needed to graduate. If a college requires 120 credits for graduation, that works out to five three-credit courses per semester for a total of 40 classes. Taking six classes per semester and then a total of four at community colleges makes graduation in three years possible. It's not for everyone, but it's one way to shave a year off the cost of college and get into the workforce quickly.

CHAPTER 2

Student Loans and Stagnant Wages: A Dangerous Cocktail for Future Graduates

"Those who understand compound interest are destined to collect it. Those who don't are doomed to pay it."

—Unknown

In the last chapter, my goal was to rid you of any notions that you should spend your retirement savings, mortgage your home, or borrow money to pay for your kid's tuition bill. I also tried to put a damper on all the hype about financial aid and scholarships, and show that you can pay for college with cash, as you go. This chapter is devoted to showing you why it is absolutely crucial that you do that. I haven't even talked about the other common way that students pay for college: loans taken out in their own name. According to the Project on Student Debt, 67 percent of students graduating from four-year colleges and universities in 2008 had student loans, with an average debt load of $23,200.[1] This represented an increase of 24 percent in just four years. In addition, the number of students borrowing also soared 27 percent over those four years.

In my search for some real-life examples of students who took out student loans and then lived to regret it, I e-mailed Alan Collinge, who runs the Project on Student Debt, an organization devoted to lobbying for better treatment of student borrowers. I asked him if he could direct me to a few people who had gotten into trouble with student loans and might be willing to talk to me on the record about it. He responded a few minutes later by attaching a spreadsheet of first-person horror stories written by more than three thousand student debtors—along with e-mail addresses in case I wanted to contact them for more information.

So if your child—or a guidance counselor or admissions officer or financial aid officer—tells you that student loans aren't really so bad, tell him I have three thousand people who can attest otherwise.

AOL Money & Finance recently featured a first-person story of student loan drama written by Fruzsina Eordogh, who borrowed $43,000 to pay for a private college at an average interest rate of 9.5 percent. In order to be debt-free, she will have to make monthly payments of $690 for fourteen years and eleven months, she says. She wrote, "That's more than I pay for rent, and in this economy, I do not have a full-time, or even a good, part-time job. I live with roommates, I rarely go out, and I agonize over every single financial decision (should I fork up $4.50 for the train today, or should I ride my bike in 20-degree weather?). . . . I can kiss my dreams of saving money for a car, a house, or even having children by the time I am 40 years old goodbye. And I didn't even go to graduate school!"

Her piece attracted 1,364 comments from readers, many of whom were college students going through the exact same thing. Because of space constraints, I don't want to go into student loan horror stories here—but before you or your student sign any loan papers, please log on to StudentLoanJustice.org and read through some of the stories of lives ruined by student loan debt.

Conventional wisdom says—and remember that conventional wisdom is the way that people knew the sun revolved around the earth—that student loan debt just isn't that big a deal. In fact, it's viewed by most as an inevitable part of the college experience. You almost never hear it talked about in the media as a crisis because most

Americans have convinced themselves, with the help of financial aid offices, that their diploma will increase their earnings by more than enough to service the debt. That is, student loans are leverage: a low-interest way to earn a high return. Ben Stein has likened it to a company borrowing money to build a factory—the earnings from the factory will cover the cost of the interest and principal payments. I can't even tell you how many times I've heard well-intentioned parents say that "student loans are a *good* form of debt—leverage. My child will be able to pay them off out of his future earnings. Student loans are unfortunate, but they won't have a serious negative impact on his life."

The student loan apologists are wrong when they say that increasing debt loads don't matter, and you only need to keep in mind two statistics to know that.

1. College costs have been rising at more than two times the rate of inflation, and that cost increase is being financed by student loans.

2. Wages are essentially flat after inflation, and experts, including the billionaire investor Warren Buffett, believe that the robust economic growth that the United States achieved over the past century is a thing of that past.

In other words, the monthly payments required of graduates to service their students loans are increasing extremely rapidly, while their monthly earnings aren't increasing at all. Over the last ten years, the average student debt load among graduating seniors has risen 108 percent (about 58 percent after inflation) in the face of essentially stagnant wages. In fact, from 2000 to 2007, college grads between the ages of twenty-five and thirty-four experienced an inflation-adjusted earnings decline of 8.5 percent, according to a *BusinessWeek* analysis of United States census data. How can the quality of life of college graduates not deteriorate rapidly if their student loan payments are doubling while their earnings aren't rising? It's a serious, serious problem, and that's the deadly cocktail that I'm referring to.

When you combine stagnant inflows with rapidly increasing outflows, something has to give. The other reason we know that everyone who says student loans aren't that big a deal is talking crap is that we really have never witnessed the havoc that enormous student debt loads can wreak on working Americans—the proliferation of college debt is a fairly new phenomenon. Remember all those people working in "safe" chemical plants who then got sick years later, because there was simply no track record and no one knew how the chemicals would affect workers? That's precisely the situation we're in right now. Few people over the age of sixty-five have or had student loans, so we don't yet know the long-term effect it has on graduates' ability to build wealth. Anyone (e.g., an admissions officer, financial aid officer, or banker) who says the current levels of student loan debt won't have a material impact on people's ability to build wealth is full of it because there is no one with this amount of debt old enough for us to know how it works out.

But we can run the numbers and try to figure it out. How would student loan debt have impacted your financial life? The average graduate will spend about $200 per month on student loan debt for twenty years before she's finally free. Were you rolling in dough to the extent that you could have done that when you were in your twenties and thirties? Given that more than half of Americans don't have enough in savings for retirement, the answer is most likely no. Let's add some numbers to the mix to make this more (or less) fun. Student 1 graduates with the national average in student loan debt. He spends the next twenty years dutifully sending in $200 per month. He does no saving. Student 2 graduates with no student loan debt and spends the next twenty years dutifully saving $200 per month and investing it at 11 percent per year. He does no other saving.

After twenty years, Student 1 will have achieved a net worth of zero. Congratulations! After twenty years, Student 2 will have $173,127.61. At this point, let's say that both graduates are forty-one years old, and have another twenty-four years until they reach retirement. Student 2 lets his savings ride and contributes nothing more. By the time he reaches retirement, he will have $2,397,069.89. All because he didn't have to make a couple hundred bucks a month in student loan payments. That's the average. If your child's monthly payments are $400 a month, double all those numbers. And, of course, life can intervene with the ability to make payments. If your child misses a payment or two for whatever reason, fees and charges can turn it into a real mess.

A woman recently e-mailed me to say that she and her husband have a combined $60,000 in student loan debt and refer to it as the little ski lodge in Wisconsin that they'll never actually have. This is a wonderful metaphor to think about when you evaluate student loan options. That ten- or twenty-year commitment to making monthly student loan payments represents money that could be used to finance dreams. Talk to your child about aspirations he has for his life, and then look at the ways that student loan payments can interfere with those dreams.

The impact of student loan debt on the lives of debtors is often immediate and painful:

• A 2008 Yale study explored the correlation between student debt loads and the occupational choices of recent graduates. The title of the article in the *Yale Economic Review* describing the findings tells the story: "Constrained After College." The study found that for every $10,000 in student loans students graduate with, they accept jobs that pay $2,000 more in annual salary. Other results from the same study back up the trend: every $10,000 in student loan debt results in a 5 percent reduction in the chances that a student will become a teacher, work at a nonprofit, or take a similarly low-paying, high-karma job. If a young person's goal is to get a good education and make the world a better place—at the possible expense of a lower starting salary—she should know that student loan debt will limit her ability to do so.[2]

- A 2008 Experience, Inc., survey found that 40 percent of recent graduates took a job that offered higher pay, but less career satisfaction, in order to help pay off their student loans. Forty-seven percent of the respondents said that their student loans had an impact on their decision to pursue a particular career; 88 percent said they had to make sacrifices in their budget because of their student loan payments; 23 percent sacrificed continuing education or graduate school to take a job in order to pay back loans.[3]

- According to a 2002 Nellie Mae study, 44 percent of recent graduates put off buying a home because of student loan obligations—up from 25 percent in 1991. Fourteen percent said that they put off marriage because of student loans, double the 1991 rate. Perhaps most troubling, 55 percent said that college debt had delayed their ability to start saving for retirement. Because of the way compound interest works—with the greatest gains coming in the later years of savings—starting retirement savings even just a few years later dramatically increases the amount of saving required. The study also found that 21 percent of student loan borrowers had delayed having children because of their debt—up from 12 percent in 1987.[4]

- A 2006 *USA Today* and National Endowment for Financial Education (NEFE) poll found that 60 percent of twentysomethings feel they're facing tougher financial pressures than their parents did at their age. Thirty percent said they worry frequently about debt.[5]

- A 2002 Myvesta.org survey found that 49.3 percent of people who struggle with debt can be classified as depressed, with 39.7 percent qualifying as "severely depressed." That means that having a substantial debt load increases your chances of depression by about

400 percent. Seventy percent of respondents said that they think about their debt "very often" or "constantly."[6]

You might look at these numbers and feel a lump in your throat at the prospect of your child contributing to these statistics. A common rebuttal to the data suggesting that student loan debt will push them into choosing a higher-paying job is "I want to make a lot of money anyway!" For students who are interested in pursuing careers based on financial gain, there is some truth to this, and I have no problem with it. The problem is that there is a difference between short-term greed and long-term greed. When you're coming out of college, it may well be that the job that puts a graduate on the best long-term career path financially is not the one that offers the best starting salary—short-term greed motivated by student loans may lead to depressed earnings over the long run. I'm not making this up. The University of Texas professor Alexandra Minicozzi found that "higher educational debt is associated with higher initial wage rate the year after finishing school and lower wage growth over the next 4 years."[7]

There is not yet data on the longer-term trend, but it seems likely that out of the necessity to start making interest payments a few months after they graduate, many students are forgoing huge amounts of money in long-term compensation. The need or perceived need to be short-term greedy is hurting long-term earnings.

There are other signs that the student loan problem may be having an adverse impact on students' career options. In 2004, only about 6 percent of new graduates left their jobs voluntarily within one year of starting—the lowest "quit rate" in twelve years. And 2004 was a time of economic prosperity in a way that 1992 was not, so the low quit rate would not seem to be a reflection of a tough job market. Large monthly debt burdens can chain students to their desks— unable to quit jobs that they hate and that aren't going anywhere because their fixed expenses are too high to deal with the uncertainty of reentering the job market.

The first years after college graduation should be a time of great mobility—where young people pursue their passions and change jobs and locations with whatever frequency is necessary to give them a shot at a career worth having and a life worth living. Monthly student loan obligations—especially large ones—are just not compatible with the lifestyle that may be necessary if young people are to achieve their dreams.

What Happens When You Can't Pay

The items I've mentioned above—quality of life issues, inability to build wealth, and so on—are all systemic problems associated with student loans. These are problems even for people who are able to pay their loans and manage them effectively. For some borrowers it gets much, much, much worse, and the number of people who default on student loans is on the rise.

Understanding just how many students default on student loans is hard because the data produced by the federal government is really strange. Instead of saying what percentage of loans overall end up in default at some point, they use a number called the cohort default rate. The Department of Education reported that this cohort default rate for fiscal year 2007 rose to 6.9 percent, a 32 percent increase over 2006.[8] But what exactly is the cohort default rate? The cohort default rate is the percentage of students who entered repayment between October 2006 and October 2007 and fell at least nine months behind by September 2008. Two problems: that data doesn't include private student loans, and, more important, someone has to miss nine payments within two years to count as defaulted.

A report produced by the Office of the Inspector General criticized the way the cohort default rate is calculated because, get this, it includes people whose loans are in deferment or forbearance—presumably because they can't make loan payments right now—in the denominator but not in the numerator. That is, in calculating the cohort default rate, the data actually includes people who literally haven't had a chance to default.[9] The student loan expert Alan Collinge estimates that, long-term, roughly a third of students end up in default. That is far, far higher than the default rate on subprime mortgages, car loans, and credit card bills. And it's important to note that this number would likely be far higher if it were not for the standard consumer protections that student loans lack. Given a choice between defaulting on a credit card or car loan and defaulting on a student loan, most rational people will let the car or card go because it's easier to discharge. How many people default on other loans because of the need to meet student loan obligations? We don't know, but it seems fair to assume that it's a lot of people.

What's the overall, long-term default rate on student loans? We don't know because they don't say. But if 6.9 percent fall *nine payments behind within less than two years, not including students who put their loans in deferment,* it's got to be pretty high. According to StudentLoanJustice.org's analysis of a 2003 Office of the Inspector General report, between 19 percent and 31 percent of first- and second-year students with loans will be put into default on those loans at some point during their lives—numbers that are doubtless getting worse as college costs and the resulting student loan obligations soar. StudentLoanJustice.org pegs the long-term default rate at somewhere around 33 percent, and BridgeSpan Financial has said that one in three people borrowing for college right now will eventually fall behind on their payments. Though it's hard to know exact numbers because of the lack of available data, it's safe to say that the default rate on student loans is significantly higher than the default rate on literally any other consumer loan.

This reminds me of another tip from Barry Minkow—that ex-con turned fraud fighter I mentioned in the introduction. If someone will give you one piece of data but not another piece of data that seems similar and reasonable, it's probably because that other piece of data would present a more troubling picture of the investment than the first. I—and many, many others—have asked these companies and agencies a simple question: What percentage of people who borrow to pay for college will end up in default? No one will answer it.

The National Center for Education Statistics found that students who take on a lot of debt are more likely to default. That seems obvious, but it explains why default rates published by the government are misleadingly low. A large number of students take on a few thousand dollars in debt and get included in that statistic, even though their debt burden is not high enough to present a serious threat to their financial security. But if you look at the number in more detail, it gets extremely troubling: one in five students with over $15,000 in loan debt—well below the 2009 average—defaulted on their loans within ten years of graduation.

I'm going to repeat that because it's so important: one in five students who graduated with more than $15,000 in debt defaulted within ten years.

And the numbers are getting worse. According to the United States Department of Education, fully 10.6 percent of all borrowers who left school in 2002 had already defaulted on their student loans within five years. That's worse than the ten-year default rate for borrowers who left school in 1993. Who knows how many students are struggling and missing payments? But the number can't be good when more than 10 percent have gone 270 days without making a payment just five years after graduation.

So let's say one in three students who take out loans will end up in default. Those students will have their credit scores destroyed and will enter a world of fees and penalties that will make achieving a positive net worth even harder. What happens when you go into default? Here are just a few of the ways it can ruin your child's life:

1. He'll be responsible for huge penalties and collection costs.

2. He could be sued for the entire value of the loan.

3. His wages could be garnished, and any federal and state tax refunds he was set to receive could be intercepted by the lender.

4. His Social Security benefits could be garnished—and there's no statute of limitations on this, so it doesn't matter if he's seventy and the loan is from fifty years ago.

5. His credit will be destroyed.

6. He may not be able to renew professional licenses. This is the most bizarre and hypocritical part of the default process, but it's true. An engineer or doctor who defaults on student loans can be stripped of his ability to practice and find himself without the means to make his payments.

7. He could be denied entrance into the armed forces.

But remember, to go into default on a federal student loan, you have to go 270 days without making a single payment or making alternative arrangements with the lender. So many, many students will find themselves burdened by life-altering, unmanageable student loans, even if they never show up in the default rate.

This drives a huge truck through one of the leading myths about student loans. You've probably heard a guidance counselor or financial aid officer say that a graduate's earnings will be increased by a large enough amount to make the debt load bearable. In a large percentage of cases, that's just not the case.

Students and parents need to know that student loans are pretty much never dischargeable in bankruptcy. You can file for bankruptcy five hundred times and your student loans will still be there, *accumulating interest and fees*. As for the collection measures that can be taken, the Harvard professor and noted consumer credit expert

Elizabeth Warren has said that loan guarantors and collection agencies have powers that would "make a mobster envious." Default on your student loans, and you can be subject to the following draconian measures: wage, Social Security, and disability garnishment; tax seizure; suspension of state-issued professional licenses; and even termination of public employment.

In 2005, the once quasi-governmental but now publicly traded student loan agency Sallie Mae was called the second most profitable company in the nation by *Fortune*. This money was made from student borrowers, and many lenders have what are euphemistically referred to as "preferred lender agreements" with certain colleges. Here on earth these are known as kickbacks. In his book *The Student Loan Scam*, the nationally recognized student loan expert—and victim—Alan Collinge writes, "It is far more profitable for the industry when students default on their debts than when they pay back the loans on time. This is because when a loan is defaulted, not only is the lender paid nearly the full balance of the loan (both principal and interest), but the guarantors of the loan the collection companies contract with—which are often owned by the original lenders—can still collect on the defaulted loan, the amount of which is now vastly inflated by fees and accrued interest." CBS News estimated that one fifth of Sallie Mae's income is attributable directly to fees and penalties thrust on borrowers who default.

The point is that when life presents you with challenges, student loans have a way of making those challenges more challenging. In some cases they have contributed to the ruin of student debtors.

What Makes Student Loan Debt So Bad

Guidance counselors, admissions officers, and financial aid people—to say nothing of loan salespeople—will tell you student loans are a good kind of debt. The About.com debt experts advise readers,

"Another example of a good debt is a student loan taken out to finance a college education. Earning a college degree usually means that you'll make more money over your lifetime." Rebuild.org reports, "Analysts now say that student loans are considered a good type of debt. That's because a college education is classified as a worthwhile investment over the long haul. As a result, student loan debt is significantly different from credit card debt, which is considered a bad kind of debt, since the interest on credit card balances is not deductible and the goods you buy with your credit cards will depreciate over time."[10]

Putting aside the potential tax "savings" associated with student loans—which is really not that great, as I'll explain below—they have a number of characteristics that make them arguably the most insidious form of debt this side of payday lending. Some of these may seem obvious, but my experience is that few people actually think them through when evaluating college financing options.

You can't cash in your education to pay off your loans: A college education is the most illiquid investment on the planet. Let's say that you buy a house or car. A few years into owning the item, you realize that you really can't afford it. In the case of a house, you can sell the item and recoup—in the vast majority of markets throughout history—a large portion of what you put into it. If you can't, you can do a short sale and the lender might forgive the balance on the mortgage. This can harm your credit score but all in all, you'll be okay.

Alternatively, you could rent out that spare bedroom to help make the mortgage payments and hang on until your financial situation improves. What if you borrow $50,000 to pursue a bachelor's degree in finance and then decide that you want to join a monastery or become an alpaca farmer? You have a serious problem. The college education has tremendous value in increasing your earnings power but can't be used to raise quick cash in case of an emergency, and there's no way to "get out" of the investment. You can't sell the "present value of the future cash flows" the way you can with a bond. You're stuck. Financial giants like Bear Stearns and Lehman Brothers—along with their shareholders—learned the dangers of borrowing large amounts of money to finance illiquid investments, no matter how valuable those investments might be in the long run. On a much smaller individual scale—but cumulatively, much larger—college graduates are learning and will continue to learn in ever-increasing numbers the danger of using large amounts of debt with monthly payment requirements to finance an illiquid investment.

Lack of residual value: A college education has no residual value. One of the most overlooked aspects of college as an investment is the fact that the annual earnings must not only provide a good return on investment, they must also be good enough to cover the entire cost of college. If you buy an income-producing real estate investment, you get cash flow and you get back the equity you put in when you sell. With a college degree, there is no equity, only cash flow. No one shows up and refunds you the cost of tuition when you retire. That's a definite disadvantage.

Full recourse, no collateral: Student loans are made with no collateral and are full recourse in nature. The term *full recourse* means that if you default, the lender can do pretty much anything to get its money back. If you go into default on a car or home, the lender will repossess the item, and depending on the state and the type of loan (recourse or nonrecourse), that may be all that there is to be done about it. With a student loan, the lender has nothing to repossess and the loan is always full recourse in nature. That is, the lender can—and will—attach every asset your child has, right on up to Social Security benefits, to collect principal, interest, and the enormous penalties that will ensue if the borrower goes into default. Savvy business moguls separate their liabilities into various structures so that a problem with one can't torpedo an entire empire. For instance, Trump Entertainment Resorts, the holding company for Donald Trump's Atlantic City casinos, recently filed for bankruptcy. But that bankruptcy had no impact on Trump's other investments or on his own lifestyle. With student loans, there are no limited partnerships to protect your life from the inevitable dominoes that fall with a default on a student loan.

Don't believe me on college being a terrible investment to finance with debt? Listen to Milton Friedman, the Nobel Prize–winner whom the *Economist* called "the most influential economist of the second half of the 20th century . . . possibly of all of it." Friedman is mainly known for his work on macroeconomics, but he tackled the issue of student loans in an article way back in 1955. Friedman wrote of the "inappropriateness of fixed money loans to finance investment in training. Such an investment necessarily involves much risk. The average expected return may be high, but there is wide variation about the average. Death or physical incapacity is one obvious source of variation but is probably much less important than differences in ability, energy, and good fortune."[11]

None of this is to say that college isn't a great investment. College is a fantastic investment, both financially and in terms of quality of life. On balance, a bachelor's degree is a far better investment than real estate in terms of how it can improve your quality of life. But the factors described above make it uniquely poorly suited to debt financing.

For all those reasons, I am of the opinion that students should simply not borrow any money at all to pay for college. As I showed in Chapter 1, it is absolutely possible to get a four-year degree without debt.

If You Do Use Student Loans: Things to Remember

First, the only possible situation where students should even be considering taking out loans is in the later years of college, after all other options have been exhausted—and when unpaid internship opportunities may cut into the student's time to work for pay. If your child finds herself signing contracts and agreeing to interest rates before she has set foot in a college classroom, you have to rethink what you're doing. If your finances are stretched thin in the first year, you are at risk for a serious problem if things deteriorate. What if you lose your job or get sick? What if your retirement portfolio declines? Student loans should be viewed as the last resort to college financing, a way of making up the slack after all possibilities for cutting expenses have been explored.

Second, students should only take out federally chartered student loans, such as those offered through the Robert T. Stafford Student Loan program. Here is a quick summary of the federally chartered student loan programs, followed by a discussion of the only major alternative: private student loans, which absolutely no one should ever use.

Subsidized Stafford loans: These are federally guaranteed fixed-rate loans made available to students based on financial need. Interest does not accrue on the loan while you are in school at least half time, or during any future deferment periods, like grad school. The federal government "subsidizes" (or pays) the interest during these times. For the 2011/12 school year, the interest rate on subsidized Stafford loans will be 3.4 percent. About two thirds of subsidized Stafford loans are awarded to students with family incomes of under $50,000, one quarter to students from families with incomes between $50,000 and $100,000, and a little less than one tenth to students with family incomes of over $100,000. As you can see, students from relatively well-off families may still qualify for a subsidized Stafford loan.

Unsubsidized Stafford loans: These are federally guaranteed loans that are made available to all students without regard to financial need. Interest does accrue on the loan while the student is in school, but payments are deferred until after graduation. The interest rate on this loan is 6.8 percent.

On Stafford loans—subsidized and unsubsidized—the annual loan limits for a dependent student break down like this:

First year: $5,500 ($3,500 subsidized/$2,000 unsubsidized)
Second year: $6,500 ($4,500 subsidized/$2,000 unsubsidized)
Third year and beyond: $7,500 ($5,500 subsidized/$2,000 unsubsidized)

It's a little bit confusing because students who don't qualify for subsidized loans are eligible for the additional $2,000 per year in unsubsidized loans. That is, a first-year student who qualifies for subsidized loans might get $3,500 subsidized and $2,000 unsubsidized. A student who doesn't qualify for subsidized loans might get the full $5,500 in unsubsidized loans. Either way, the maximum is the same.

That works out to a total of $27,000 over four years for a dependent undergraduate student from the Stafford program alone. If that isn't enough, you have other options: schools will recommend the Parent PLUS loan but, as I explained in Chapter 1, you should never, ever take them up on this bit of generosity. But wait, there's more! If you apply for a Parent PLUS loan and are rejected because you have poor credit, the federal government will allow your child to borrow more money. In order to be rejected for a PLUS loan, you would need to have "an adverse credit history." This means that you are "more than 90 days late on any debt or having any Title IV debt (including a debt due to grant overpayment) within the past five years subjected to default determination, bankruptcy discharge, foreclosure, repossession, tax lien, wage garnishment, or write-off." Students whose parents are rejected for Parent PLUS loans can borrow up to $45,000 over four years. The limits look like this:

First year: $9,500 ($3,500 subsidized/$6,000 unsubsidized)
Second year: $10,500 ($4,500 subsidized/$6,000 unsubsidized)
Third year and beyond: $12,500 ($5,500 subsidized/$7,000 subsidized)

To summarize: if a student's parents have a track record of being unable to manage debt effectively, the federal government will provide the student with an opportunity to take on additional debt. You couldn't make this stuff up.

Here's the bottom line about Stafford loans: because they are available to all students regardless of financial need, the combination of a Stafford loan, part-time employment, and minimal parental assistance is enough for anyone to attend a public college or university for four years—without even taking into account any need-based financial aid. Therefore, you should never, ever, ever take out any student loan other than a federal loan. The end. Period. Ever.

Federal Perkins loans: This is a low-interest (5 percent) subsidized loan, and interest doesn't start accruing until after graduation. Students can borrow up to $4,000 per year, but the total eligibility depends on the financial need demonstrated on the FAFSA form. This is the best student loan available, but most students won't qualify for it because of parental income.

Private Student Loans

If your child is unable to meet his borrowing needs through federal student loan programs and is forced to look to the private sector, take this as a huge red flag. He is trying to borrow far more money than is necessary or prudent. Private student loans nearly always have higher interest rates (interest rates of 18 percent are not uncommon) and, because they're not standardized products the way that Stafford loans are, can lead your child into a cesspool of extra fees and charges. Fees of 10 percent of the loan value are common, and if you miss a payment, future payments can get really ugly. Worse, private student loans are often variable-rate loans, meaning that monthly payments will fluctuate with interest rates. It is not a good idea to pay for college with a product that gives you absolutely no idea how much the monthly payment will be. Private student loans can't be consolidated with federal student loans and forebearance deferment, and other repayment plan adjustments are basically at the sole discretion of the lender.

As college costs have spiraled upward, so has the private student loan market. According to the College Board, private student loan volume has grown by 989 percent in the past decade, and is currently going strong at a rate of 25 percent per year. If that trend continues, private student loans will make up a larger chunk of student loan volume than federal loans within a decade. FiLife .com offers this advice for students struggling to come up with enough money for college: "Students increase their chances of being approved for a private loan and getting lower interest rates if they persuade a parent or another creditworthy adult to be a cosigner. If parents are unwilling to take out a federal Plus loan—which they are legally responsible for paying back—some observers suggest that students offer to split repayment costs and put the agreement in writing."[12]

Here's a tip: don't cosign your kids' loans. College guides, bank employees, and financial aid people may recommend cosigning loans as an easy way to qualify for more loan money at lower interest rates. Do not fall for this trap! Banks have spent billions and billions of dollars over the years developing complex models to assess borrowers' creditworthiness, and if they decide not to lend money to your kid without a cosigner, they have a good reason. So by all means: cosign other people's student loans, but do so planning to pay off the loans yourself. If they miss payments, your credit score will be dinged too—and, more important, you could be sued by the lender for payment. And keep in mind that cosigning student loans is far, far riskier than cosigning a mortgage or even a car loan, because there is no collateral that can be sold off in case of default. You have full exposure and no recourse if things go south. What happens if you have some sort of falling out with your child and he decides to stop making payments on the loan? Guess what: it's your problem. That is why you should never, ever, *ever* cosign on a student loan for anyone. If you are in a situation where student loans will be necessary for your child to attend the college you're discussing, financial aid officers will certainly suggest this option. But remember: they do not have your best interests at heart.

A very smart friend once told me that there are no absolute rules in the world of personal finance advice, but I'm going to give you one here that almost no one else will: *neither you nor your child should ever, under any circumstances, ever, take out any private student loans.* I thought long and hard about it before committing this idea to paper because it's so definitive, but there you go. The Project on Student Debt reported, "The percentage of undergraduates borrowing private loans increased dramatically, from 5% in 2003-04 to 14% in 2007-08."[13] In my opinion, 14 percent of undergraduates did something incredibly stupid that they will very likely regret. Please don't let your child join that group. If a combination of federal student loans, need-based financial aid grants, work-study, and savings that you can afford to contribute to college aren't enough to cover the cost of college, you need to step back and look at other college options.

Another note here: the sleaziest of the sleazy private lenders will market directly to families, often trying to persuade them to sign up for their loans rather than filling out the FAFSA form. I recommend forwarding any such letters you receive straight to your attorney general's office—and also send a copy to me so that I can write about them.

And, just in case you aren't already feeling paranoid, a number of major scandals in recent years have raised grave concerns about the integrity with which college financial aid offices process student loans. Recall that in the introduction I explained that you cannot trust financial aid people. In the worst case scenarios, they are out-right criminals. In 2006, New York's attorney general, Eliot Spitzer, launched an investigation into the relationships between student loan companies and the colleges they helped with financing student tuition costs. What he and his successor, Andrew Cuomo, found was appalling: some colleges were operating financial aid hotlines that were secretly staffed by employees of the student loan companies. Imagine calling up a stop-smoking hotline and getting connected to a Philip Morris salesman without knowing it. Moreover, many financial aid directors were receiving compensation from student loan companies that magically ended up appearing on the preferred-lender lists. Ellen Frishberg, director of financial aid at Johns Hopkins, received over $155,000 in compensation from companies like Student Loan Xpress, American Express, and Global Student Loan Corporation. Ms. Frishberg maintains that she did nothing wrong and that her decisions were not influenced by all the money and free gala tickets she received. Right.

Of course, there have been some efforts at regulation to clean this stuff up in the wake of embarrassing media coverage. But just as the Sarbanes-Oxley legislation passed in the wake of Enron and World-Com appears to have done little to prevent the near total collapse of the financial markets under the weight of dodgy debt securities, there is no reason to think that the conflicts of interest have disappeared.

One of the biggest problems with student loans is that very few schools and even fewer lenders make a proactive effort to ensure that student borrowers are aware of the amount of debt they're taking on—and the amount they'll be paying monthly. One study found that one in three student loan borrowers is surprised at how large the payment is the first time they receive a student loan bill—meaning that you and your student alone have the responsibility of educating your-selves about how it works—and whether the amount you're borrow-ing really is as manageable as the salesmen would like you to think.

How Much Student Loan Debt Is Too Much?

Even if you decide, after taking a realistic look at your financial situation, that your child must take out some student loans to fund his education (and, as I showed earlier, I can't imagine why loans would be necessary), it's vital that you keep the amount of debt as low as possible. In 2002 Nellie Mae studied the impact of student loan debt and found that "borrowers who require *less than* 7% of their gross monthly income to pay their education debt generally do not feel difficulty." The "perception of difficulty" is "somewhat amplified" among students with between 7 percent and 11 percent of gross monthly income. After that, it starts to become highly stressful and difficult. And keep in mind that Nellie Mae is part of Sallie Mae, a publicly traded for-profit student loan company that has made millions of dollars on student debt, with a significant portion of that chunk coming from fees charged to student who miss payments or end up in default. So assume that the real goal should be monthly loan payments that amount to an even smaller percentage of income.

Using numbers as a guide, how much is prudent to borrow? Average starting salaries vary considerably by major and career choice (more on this in Chapter 4). The average chemical engineering major begins with a starting salary of about $59,000, while psychology majors start at around $31,500. So let's say the average starting salary out of college is $45,000—which is extremely generous given how bad the job market is right now, and how few recent grads land full-time work in their fields. That's $3,750 per month. Seven percent of that would be $262.50 per month. So let's call that the most that you would want your child to graduate with in monthly payments.

However, there's an important caveat: most students drastically overestimate the amount they'll earn upon graduation. One study found that many students overestimate their postgraduation earnings by an astounding 45 percent, and in 2004, more than one million college graduates were unemployed. More than one in three recent graduates work in jobs that don't require a degree. In his book *No Sucker Left Behind*, Marc Scheer recommends that, to be conservative, students should assume a starting salary of $31,000 when making borrowing decisions to finance their educations. This is good advice.

Nellie Mae adds that "17% of borrowers said student loans had a significant impact on their career plans. Fifty-nine percent said student loans were worth incurring because of the career opportunities provided."[14] Seventeen percent of students choosing careers based on student loan debt seems troubling to me. And what of that 59 percent? It's important to keep in mind that people can delude themselves as a way of coping with bad decisions. If you're struggling under the weight of a heavy debt load, telling yourself that it was all unnecessary would make you feel bad: the human brain does not like to feel stupid, and will construct narratives to avoid that uncomfortable experience. Writing a monthly check for $300 or $400 or $500 would be extremely painful if people believed that they were wasting their money.

Unfortunately, many college financing experts and financial aid officers don't look at the topic of student debt based on any kind of data and resort to clichés about education being a great investment. Mark Kantrowitz, publisher of FastWeb.com and FinAid.org, told the *New York Times* that he recommends students follow a simple rule of thumb. "Do not borrow more than your expected starting salary for your entire undergraduate education. If your starting salary is going to be $40,000, then you should borrow no more than $10,000 a year for a four-year degree."

Actually, one in every five students who graduated with a debt load of more than $15,000 in 1995 defaulted within ten years. Since $15,000 is well below the average starting salary—and was ten years ago too—I think it's a safe bet that Mr. Kantrowitz's "rule of thumb" could well lead students to take on way, way too much debt. Please don't fall for silly "formulas" like this. They're just made up. It's like saying, "Never borrow money at an interest rate larger than your shoe size." The 1:1 ratio is cute and memorable, but it won't keep your child from getting into a student loan nightmare.

In an e-mail, Mr. Kantrowitz defended the rule, saying, "A debt-to-income ratio of 1:1 corresponds to 13.8% of gross monthly income for Federal Stafford loans, assuming a standard 10 year repayment term (9.2% on a 20-year term). For private student loans it can be as much as 21.6% on a 10 year term and 18.5% on a 20 year term, although 15.9% and 11.6% would be more typical . . . Based on the Baccalaureate and Beyond Longitudinal Study, 2.9% of borrowers default when less than 10% of their gross monthly income goes toward servicing student loan debt. This increases to 5.6% for 10% to 13% and 14.3% for 13% to 15%. Clearly there is a cusp in the data at 13% of gross income."

Recall this little gem from get-out-of-debt guru Dave Ramsey, author of the fantastic book *The Total Money Makeover*. In a 2006 speech Ramsey said, "The average car payment in America today is $378 over 84 months. If you were to invest $378 from age 25 to age 65, you'd have $4.4 million. I hope you like the car!" In other words, the argument that a student loan the size of a car payment isn't the difference between great wealth and poverty is crap. A student loan payment the size of a car payment could be the difference between a life of wealth and a life of poverty. But wait, there's more: a student who starts out with monthly student loan obligations the size of a car payment (or larger) will very likely have difficulty in saving up the money to pay for a car with cash. The result will very likely be car payments that could have been avoided if the graduate had avoided student loans.

The other problem with Kantrowitz's magic formula is that it assumes that you know what your "expected starting salary" will be. I know quite a few people who majored in finance, planning on lucrative job offers from institutions like Lehman Brothers and Bear Stearns. But those companies filed for bankruptcy and the industry stopped hiring. Large student debt loads can make a tough job market a lot tougher, and high school seniors have no business trying to predict where the job market will be in four years—and then betting tens of thousands of dollars that they'll be right. And, as I mentioned above, students who do predict how much they'll earn are likely to be too optimistic: which ends in disappointment at best but, if you borrow money based on the prediction, it can end in disaster.

When you're looking at student loans, it's important to be very, very wary of rules of thumb that aren't based on anything other than catchiness. They make good sound bites (Kantrowitz's advice not to borrow more than your expected starting salary got quoted in the *New York Times*) but they can lead you and your child down a path toward poverty.

The *other* other problem with this "rule of thumb" is that student loan default rates continue to get worse—and by the time you get around to reading this, they will likely be a lot worse than they are as I write. In April 2008 the United States Department of Education reported that the cohort default rate on federal student loans rose 50 percent between 2004 and 2007, from 4.6 percent to 6.9 percent. The cohort default rate is defined as the percentage of borrowers who entered repayment and then defaulted within the next two years. So the cohort default rate is actually far, far lower than the percentage of students who actually end up defaulting. However, the increase in the cohort default rate suggests that in the long term, recent graduates will default at far higher rates than their older siblings.

I would amend Mr. Kantrowitz's rule on student loans to say this: "Never borrow more than your starting salary, but make sure that you know exactly what your starting salary will be when you graduate when you pick your college. Also, don't have a change of heart and decide to pursue a career that offers a low starting salary, and make sure that you don't graduate during a recession or jobless economic recovery and aren't one of the more than half of college graduates under age 25 who are unable to find work that requires a college degree."[15]

But let's say that we do accept Mr. Kantrowitz's 1:1 metric. It provides all the more reason not to take on debt to attend an expensive college. Consider for example this statistic: Boston University students paid an average of $33,000 per year in tuition and fees and achieved an average starting salary of $51,000. The University of Florida (Warrington), Gainesville, charged $2,968 for an average starting salary of $42,000.

That difference of $9,000 in starting salary would—if you buy into Mr. Kantrowitz's formula, which I don't—make it prudent to take on an additional $2,250 in debt each year to attend BU. As you can see, that would not be close to enough debt to finance the cost differential. Across the board, private college degrees simply do not correspond to an increase in annual earnings by an amount anywhere close to enough to make it possible to finance the difference in costs and come out with a 1:1 increase in student loans and annual earnings. On the other hand, affordable college options always lead to lower debt-to-income ratios.

Finally, it should be pointed out that there are ways to reduce monthly payments. *Kiplinger*'s Janet Bodnar advises student debtors to consider lowering payments by extending the payment term from the standard ten years to the extended twenty years. Of course, this will mean paying more interest and making monthly payments well into your forties—money that could be used for retirement saving, mortgage payments, or saving for college for your grandchildren so that they won't need this book. This advice isn't so much bad as it is obvious: extending loan terms always lowers monthly payments. This is one of the ways that car dealerships lure people into buying cars they can't afford, generally prefaced with a P. T. Barnumesque "Tell ya what I'm gonna do" and a flick of an oversized fake Rolex and then a few pen strokes reducing a monthly payment by

30 percent. If you're out of college and are really struggling, extending the loan term is a valuable option to have. But it is certainly not something you should plan on when you're picking a college.

The False Dichotomy of Student Loans and Low-Wage Jobs

One of the most common arguments you'll hear from people who aren't as bearish on student loans as I am is that college is a good investment and that the increase in earnings over the course of your life will more than compensate for the interest charges.

This is true: given a choice between not going to college at all and graduating with $50,000 in debt, graduating with $50,000 in debt would be a better option for college-ready students. But the point is that it's possible to get a great education without going into anywhere near that much debt. Peddlers of student loans try to reel in naive families by portraying the decision as student loans or Frialator operator. But what really matters here is the marginal decision: that is, $50,000 in student loans to attend a dream college versus the next best option. As I'll prove to you in Chapter 3, attending the "next best option" will not harm career or life prospects at all. College is an extremely good investment on average, but once you have already found a way to go to college, additional expenditures tend to be a poor investment on the margin. Spending $50,000 per year to go the University of Miami is a good investment on average in that it will yield a good payoff for the money compared to not going to college at all. But compared to spending $15,000 per year to go to a state university, it is a poor investment on the margin.

Worse, many colleges are overestimating the value of a college degree. It is an oft-repeated statistic that people who hold bachelor's degrees earn about $1 million more over the course of their lives than people who don't. But the economics professor Sandy Baum, the author of the College Board's "Education Pays" study, says that the value is really only about half that: $500,000 over the course of a life-time. Back in February, it was reported that the $800,000 increase in lifetime earnings that The College Board website claimed was associated with a bachelor's degree had been quietly reduced to just $450,000 based on further research—a decrease in return of 44%.[16] No apology was offered—and don't even think about asking for a refund. But the million-dollar figure remains a popular urban legend, and Arizona State University recently justified a proposed tuition hike by arguing, "Average annual earnings of individuals with a bachelor's degree are more than 75 percent higher than the earnings of high school graduates. These additional earnings sum to more than $1 million over a lifetime. And that is just the average. Many college graduates will earn two, three, four or more times that amount."

Right: it is just the average, and for every college graduate that earns two, three, four, or more times that amount, there will also be one who earns far less. What about him? Arizona State doesn't say. The average is the average and in order for "many college graduates" to earn "two, three, four or more times that amount," a corresponding number have to earn substantially less. This press release is a typical example of the spin college salespeople subject us to.

If You're Planning to Start a Family, Don't Take Out Loans

According to the Organisation for Economic Co-operation and Development, the average American woman has her first child at 24.9 years of age. While more women work full-time while raising families than at any point in history, recent data suggests that many would prefer not to do this. The Pew Research Center reported, "Among working mothers with minor children (ages 17 and under), just one-in-five (21%) say full-time work is the ideal[17] situation for them, down from the 32% who said this back in 1997, according to a new Pew Research Center survey. Fully six-in-ten (up from 48%

in 1997) of today's working mothers say part-time work would be their ideal, and another one-in-five (19%) say she would prefer not working at all outside the home. . . . Among all working mothers, there's a strong disconnect between the kind of job they say would be ideal and the kind of job they actually have. Some 60% of working mothers say they'd prefer to work part-time, but—according to figures from the U.S. Bureau of Labor Statistics—only about a quarter (24%) of all working mothers have a part-time job."

In preparing for a recent Money 911 segment on *Today*, my friend David Bach, the author of *The Automatic Millionaire*, asked me for advice on how to handle a situation a viewer had presented him with: Nicole and Aaron, a young married couple from Maryland, were expecting their first child. Aaron had $85,000 in student loans and earns about $38,000 per year. Their monthly payments are about $1,000 a month, and they've had to move back in with his parents in order to cut expenses. Nicole wasn't working at the moment—she's pregnant—but will need to get a job of some kind in order to help with the student loan payments. Nicole obviously had some hesitation—who wants to start a job hunt while pregnant and then continue working with an infant at home?—but there just wasn't any good alternative. If you want to stay home with your kid(s), don't borrow money for college. It really is that simple.

Remember, if a student takes out a ton of loans to pay for college and then opts for domestic life—as a stay-at-home mom (or dad) or a part-time worker—she'll still be responsible for all those student loans. Sure, maybe the other partner will be working hard and earning money to cover her student loan payments, but this is far from an ideal situation and can lead to resentment and arguments about money—which is, by the way, the number-one cause of divorce.

This is yet another example of what makes student loans so troubling: they are long-term obligations (ten to twenty years, with a decisive trend toward longer durations as debt loads increase) that can severely restrict life and career choices. I believe passionately that people should graduate from college and enter a world of limitless opportunity, without the constraint of monthly payment obligations.

Student Loan Interest Is Tax-Deductible, Sort Of

One of the common rationalizations surrounding the "student loans aren't so bad after all" argument is the notion that the interest on the loans is tax deductible. GoCollege.com reassures readers, "You may be worried about the amount of debt you have accumulated in student loans. However, there are some tax benefits to having student loans. Some, if not all, of the interest you pay may be tax deductible."[18]

Here's the thing: to call the student loan interest deduction a "tax benefit" is pretty ambitious. If you have a federal student loan that you pay the federal government $1,000 per year in interest on and you're in the 15 percent tax bracket, you actually only end up paying them $850 in interest ($1,000 in interest minus [$1,000 x 0.15] = $850). In other words, the "tax savings" are really just built into the interest rate you pay. With federal student loans, all the money is going to the same place: dinner parties for AIG's top earners (so at least it's going to a good cause).

Some other important things to know about the tax deduction on student loans, courtesy of GoCollege.com:

- Income limitations apply. If you are filing as a single, your modified adjusted gross income (MAGI) may not exceed $55,000, and $110,000 for married couples that file jointly. You may qualify for a partial deduction if your MAGI is between $55,000 and $70,000 for singles, and $110,000 and $140,000 for joint.
- Your maximum deduction may be $2,500.
- You may not use the 1040EZ form to file the student loan interest deductions.

Those mean, in this order:

1. If you graduate and earn a pretty good income, the student loan interest deduction won't really help you. Granted, you won't need it as badly in that scenario, but this means the savings from the student loan interest deduction only apply to students who are in low tax brackets anyway. The irony here is that the more you earn, the more valuable a tax deduction is, but the less likely you are to receive that tax deduction.

2. If your kid is in the 15 percent tax bracket, the absolute most student loans can reduce his tax bill by is $375 per year. That isn't nothing, but it's also far from a good reason to feel better about leaving college with a five-figure debt load. It is, to borrow a line from Christopher Buckley, "chump change we can believe in."

3. If you want to deduct student loan interest, you'll have to forgo the tax return the IRS invented to make filing taxes easy to understand. For a student who is shy about math or finance, that may mean having to hire a professional to prepare his taxes for him.

Bottom line: students who use debt to finance educational expenses may be able to save some money on taxes after they graduate. But the paltry savings will easily be overwhelmed by the interest and principal payments, making tax advantages a really, really lame rationalization for borrowing money to finance college. Students and parents should also know that that the IRS treatment of student loan interest as a tax deduction could change at any moment, especially in a time of mounting deficits and a need to increase tax revenue.

Another way of thinking about it: all the tax savings associated with student loans can also be achieved by not taking out student loans and donating some money to charity each year (provided that you itemize your deductions).

If You Want to Be a Teacher, DEFINITELY Don't Borrow Any Money!

As I mentioned, students who take on substantial debt loads often find themselves forced to take higher-paying jobs to service their debt. But students who are planning to pursue lucrative careers in fields like engineering may feel like they can prudently take on more debt. There is some truth to this, but be careful: flexibility is one of the greatest treasures of youth, and it's one that can be squelched by excessive borrowing. Most students change their majors while they're in college, so if you select a college and take out loans planning to be an engineer but then decide you want to be a writer, you could have a problem. Choosing a life path is challenging enough without adding large monthly debt obligations to the picture. For students who enter college planning to pursue careers that often don't yield tremendous monetary rewards, at least in the beginning, the situation can be dire. In a 2009 piece on huge student debt loads, the ABC News *20/20* correspondent John Stossel spoke to some disgruntled grads. One of them, Kris Alfred, took out $125,000 to earn multiple degrees in theater, and is now working at a call center earning ten dollars per hour.[19]

So here's the deal: if your child wants to become a writer or a social worker, educate him about the dangers of student loans. If your son wants to be an investment banker, recognize that he may end up taking a "Poets and Poetry of New England" class sophomore year, fall in love with the work of Emily Dickinson, and devote his life to traveling the country in drag reading her poems to crowds of fifteen people who pay a dollar each. Hey, it could happen. Do not try to get into a game of predicting future earnings. Look at college as a way to increase earnings and happiness, and stay out of debt.

Student Loan Forgiveness and Other Fairy Tales

The normally solemn BankRate.com reports that "Permanent disability or death will allow for 100 percent forgiveness of your loan, but obviously have serious downsides that limit their popularity." And keep in mind that in order to have loans forgiven, the student must be permanently disabled: maimed to the point where no possibility of ever earning an income at any point in the future exists. Terry Schiavo might have met that standard, but maybe not because all of the media attention could have made for a compelling reality show.

The good news is there are other ways to get rid of student loans. Teach math in an inner-city school and you might qualify for loan forgiveness. However, this creates a similar problem to the one I just mentioned: students with large debt loads go after high-paying jobs. If you're going to devote your life to the demanding work of teaching underprivileged students, your motive should not be ditching your student loans.

In addition, BankRate.com reports that "some hospitals and private health care facilities recruit candidates by dangling loan forgiveness."[20] Employers in a wide range of fields have been known to offer prospective employees help with their student loans, but remember the first lesson of economics: *there is no free lunch*. An employer who helps you with a student loan will generally do so at the expense of a higher salary. Student loan help can be a good recruiting tool from a marketing perspective, but it's certainly not something you should sign up for loans looking forward to. And it's also important to note that if you miss payments and end up defaulting on a student loan, you no longer qualify for any of these.

The best reason not to count on loan forgiveness programs for paying off student loans is this: all those programs are subject to change and, if Congress gets in a budget-cutting mood, they very well could go the way of the hula hoop. How likely is that? I have no idea and neither do you. Do not finance college with a plan to depend on the kindness of strangers like the federal government for your ability to pay back the loans. This is the equivalent of what got people into trouble during the real estate bubble: "I'll buy now with a variable-rate mortgage and then I'll refinance into a fixed-rate before it adjusts." But then the properties declined in value (making refinancing impossible) and interest rates didn't stay low for very long. All these loan forgiveness options are great, but you have no idea whether they'll be there in four years or ten years. Therefore, you absolutely should not factor them into postgraduation plans.

In May 2009, the *New York Times* reported on the sad tale of Travis and Stephanie, a Kentucky couple working as special education teachers, inspired in part by a generous student loan forgiveness program offered by the state. The plan was that after five years, they would be free from the $100,000 debt load. Then, he said, "we get a letter in the mail saying that our forgiveness this year was next to nothing." "I remember sitting in the financial aid office and them saying, 'Pay for every penny of it, pay for your books through loans, because they're going to be forgiven,'" he added. Now Travis and Stephanie have a serious problem, and may have to sell their home and move back into a rental in order to generate the cash needed to service their debt "and eat," he told the *Times*.[21]

What's most troubling is that many financial aid officers will tell high school seniors about various student loan forgiveness programs, without any kind of warning that those programs could very easily be cut by the time the student has graduated and worked as a teacher at a low-income school for long enough to qualify. If you (or your child) ever find yourself being fed this line of crap by a financial aid or admissions officer, here's my patent-pending takedown method:

FINANCIAL AID OFFICER: The loan does seem like a lot of money, but your child told me that she wants to be a teacher, in which case she could work teaching math to low-income students for five years and have her entire balance forgiven through a number of government programs.

PARENT: That sounds awesome! But I've heard that some programs like that are being canceled, and people who graduated from college with plans to participate in these programs are now finding themselves without a clear path toward student loan freedom.

FINANCIAL AID OFFICER: It's a really sad situation for those students, but it's just bad timing: we're going through the worst economic downturn since the Great Depression, but things will improve and we have a president who suffered through student loans himself, understands the issue, and is committed to helping students who want to take on jobs that give back to the community.

PARENT: That's very reassuring, and I'm really happy that you have such a confident, rosy outlook. But since I'm not as confident as you, can we make a deal? If the programs you're talking about don't exist when Stephanie graduates from college, will you pay off her entire student loan balance over five years, just like the programs you're talking about do?

FINANCIAL AID OFFICER: Ha ha!

PARENT: I can have my lawyer draft up a contract and fax it to you tomorrow.

Busted!

It's a sad situation and my heart goes out to all the young people in the country who were counting on student loan forgiveness programs, only to find that they were cut out of the budget. But the fact is that relying on government programs for anything is a lousy idea because they can lose their funding at the drop of a hat. Bottom line: if your child graduates from school and finds a great job that has the added benefit of paying off student loans, that's fantastic! But if you take out loans planning to pay them back with these programs, you may be setting yourself up for a miserable, miserable time. Taking out loans in anticipation of a loan forgiveness program four years from now is like booking a vacation in a certain town four years in advance because the weather there is nice today—except with far, far more money at stake.

One increasingly popular option for graduates who can't deal with their student loans is to flee the country. Seriously. They're called student loan refugees. If you leave the country, Sallie Mae has no ability to harass you or garnish your wages. The downside is that the penalties and interest will keep accruing, so once you leave, you really can't come back. Taking out student loans with the intention of living out your days in exile like the deposed dictator of a third-world country is probably not the best plan.

There Is a Better Way

I hope that you are now convinced that student loan debt is far more toxic than guidance counselors, financial aid officers, and admissions people have led you to believe. In fact I would argue that it's among the worst kinds of debt on the planet for these reasons:

- It can't be discharged in bankruptcy.
- It isn't asset-backed—if you have trouble making student loan payments, there is no underlying asset that can be sold to raise quick cash.
- It's likely to have a negative impact on your child's ability to choose a career that interests him.
- It will make it harder to start a family, get married, start your own business, buy a home, buy a car, and save for retirement.

- It's a big, big loan. Sure, the terms on payday loans are much more anticonsumer, but the denominations are usually relatively trivial compared to those of student loans.

But knowing that student loans are dangerous isn't enough for many families, who are convinced that, without them, people are destined to attend lousy colleges that will hurt their marketability in the workplace. Many parents say that "the name of the school on my child's diploma will have a strong impact on his career and life prospects. The better the college he goes to, the more doors he'll have open to him. When it comes to college, you get what you pay for."

Fasten your seat belt, because Chapter 3 will rock the very foundation of how you think about sending your kids to college.

CHAPTER 3

Does It Really Matter Where You Go to College?
The Solution to the College Funding Nightmare

The words *college* and *investment* get tossed together a lot, usually by people who are trying to sell you on the idea of parting with money in exchange for education. But what does *investment* really mean here?

I recently saw a glossy poster advertising St. John's University's master's degree programs hanging in one of the buildings at the University of Massachusetts. In the current economy, where people are watching their investments fall through the floor, St. John's is using the investment theme to pitch its programs:

> Invest in a Stronger Future with a Graduate Degree from St. John's. Here's a hot tip that guarantees big returns. Invest in a world-class graduate degree from St. John's University.

To get you in the mood for analyzing college as an investment, let's break down this advertisement. First this little bit of language: "Here's a hot tip that guarantees big returns." If a stock broker called up a client and offered him a "hot tip that guarantees big returns," he would lose his license, get sued by the SEC, and, very possibly, end up in Club Fed, sharing bologna sandwiches with Bernie Madoff. The fact is that no college can guarantee anything, much less returns, much less "big returns."

And what exactly are "big returns"? Someone who operates a Frialator might earn $23,000 per year while someone with a graduate degree might earn $70,000 per year. Does that make a graduate degree a good investment? Not necessarily. The are tons of other reasons why the Frialator operator tends to earn less than the person with a graduate degree, most of which have to do with something other than the graduate degree. What matters is the marginal return. That is, what would your child do without a degree from a certain college? Most likely get a degree from a different college. Beware of apples-to-oranges comparisons that make something sound like a more compelling investment than it really is. When you're looking at a college's return on investment, you need to compare it to other colleges that your child could also attend.

Colleges make extraordinarily vague claims about the "investment" value of their programs, but these are almost never substantiated (in Chapter 5, you'll learn about a few schools that have very substantiated data on the investment value of their programs). To try out this theory for yourself, perform this test next time you get a brochure from a college trumpeting its "investment" value. Call up the admissions office and ask these kinds of questions:

- When you say it's a "hot tip that guarantees big returns," what returns are you comparing it to?
- I'm looking at this college and another one. Admissions people at both say it's a "great investment." Show me the evidence that your college offers a better return on investment (ROI) than other colleges I'm looking at.
- What discount rate did you use when calculating the "big returns"?
- Investment advisers who guarantee big returns and then don't deliver can be sued and sometimes thrown in jail. If I enroll in your program and don't earn those "big returns," will you give me back my money with penalties and interest?

You won't be able to get intelligent answers to these questions from any admissions officer or high school guidance counselor. When college people talk about the "investment" you are making in your child's education, there is an overwhelming probability that they are spewing crap.

The notion of college as a "great investment" has become an outright cliché, parroted by so many people that it just becomes accepted as true. To a large extent, it still is true. But as wages stagnate and college costs rise, it becomes less true. Any reasonably intelligent investor will tell you that the worthiness of an investment depends on two factors: the cost of the investment and the return. For instance, let's say I offer to sell you a bond that will pay you interest of $100,000 annually. Is that a good deal? Would you buy that bond? Of course the answer is that I haven't given you enough information. If the bond costs $200,000, then it's a heck of a deal—you earn your money back in 2 years and then have a 50 percent yield on your investment every year! But if I'm charging $10,000,000 for the bond, it's less good of a deal. It will take you a century to get your money back with a yield of just 1 percent annually.

So if we look at college in these terms, where does it stack up? In 2009, the College Board released a study on how long it would take the average college graduate to earn a benefit from their four-year public university degree financed entirely with debt. In calculating the data, the College Board looked at average salaries for college grads versus non–college grads and then factored in the time spent in school that could have been spent working and the interest payments on the student loans, and found that it takes thirty-three years to recoup the cost of a college degree. That works out to an annualized yield of 3.33 percent, which is, let's be very clear, absolutely pitiful. If it takes thirty-three years to reach the break-even point and you retire at sixty-five, that means that someone who graduates from college at twenty-two has a whole ten years—age fifty-five to sixty-five—to realize the value of their college degree.

Now, there are a number of problems with this study. For starters, people without college degrees are at substantially greater risk
for unemployment than their educated counterparts in the workforce. People with bachelor's degrees had an unemployment rate of
2.8 percent in 2008, compared with 5.7 percent for high school graduates.[1] Failing to factor in the more than 100 percent greater chance
of unemployment associated with not earning a college degree leads
to numbers that are totally inaccurate.

The less granular problem with the numbers in that study is
that they fail to take into account the vastly limited career prospects
that those without college degrees face. As the percentage of young
people graduating with bachelor's degrees continues to grow, more
and more employers are demanding college degrees. Jobs that didn't
always require college degrees now do, and the flood of unemployed
graduates is putting those with a mere high school diploma or GED
at a substantial disadvantage. In 2008, CareerBuilder.com listed the
top five highest-paying careers available without college degrees,
each with an average salary of at least $70,000 per year, and they
were, in order (1) margin department supervisor, (2) air traffic con-
troller, (3) automobile service station manager, (4) real estate broker,
and (5) Web surfer.[2] If those sound intriguing, then go for it. But
for most people, a fulfilling and lucrative career will require higher
education.

But What College Will Offer the Best Return?

In his book *Harvard Schmarvard*, the Harvard graduate, *Newsweek*
business editor, and *Washington Post* reporter Jay Matthews puts it
like this: "What you will be measured by in life is your talent and
energy, not your college's name."

Superficial evidence seems to rebuke this claim. According to

a 2008 Payscale, Inc., survey, Ivy League graduates earn, on average, 34 percent more than graduates of other liberal arts colleges ten
years into their careers.[3] The news media jumped all over this study
as proof that the college-brand skeptics were wrong. The *Wall Street
Journal* reported, "Where people go to college can make a big difference in starting pay, and that difference is largely sustained into mid-
career, according to a large study of global compensation." One of my
colleagues at WalletPop.com triumphantly announced in a column,
"Where you go to school DOES matter."

What's terrifying to me is that otherwise normally intelligent
people would draw such a definitive conclusion from a study that is
anything but. When I started to learn about science in third grade
from Ms. Lash—the best teacher I ever had in my life by far—one of
the first things she told us was, "In order to be able to draw conclusions from an experiment, you have to have your variables controlled.
If you don't control the variables, there's no way of saying which factor caused the result." So armed with "everything I need to know
about studies I learned in third grade," I started to think about the
results of this study. Doesn't it seem likely that there are other factors
influencing the differences in pay? For instance, Ivy League graduates tend to be smarter and more ambitious than graduates of schools
like the one I go to. That's the whole point. That's how they get into
the Ivy League schools in the first place!

So all that the study really tells us is that students who get into
Ivy League schools are likely to earn more money than those who
don't. But that seems obvious. In order to show that there is a benefit
to attending an elite college, someone would have to demonstrate the
marginal value of a diploma from an elite institution: How much
more would a certain person earn if he went to an Ivy League college
versus going to a less elite school? Unless we can establish a causal
relationship (an if-then statement: *if* you go to an elite college, *then*
you will earn more money), the study is about as useful as the one

I did this afternoon where I found that people who sleep in cribs weigh far less than people who sleep in beds.

Alan Krueger and the Study That Changes *Everything*

The problem of selection bias is where the whole argument that "where you go to college does matter" falls apart, thanks to an incandescently clever study conducted by the Princeton economics professor Alan Krueger. Krueger and his colleagues sought to quantify the marginal impact of a diploma from an elite institution. To control for the obvious differences between students accepted to prestigious and less prestigious universities, they surveyed 519 students who were accepted to both prestigious and less prestigious schools, some of whom attended the Yales of the world and some of whom attended Rutgers and other colleges of similar selectivity. The results were startling: students who were accepted at schools like Yale and Rutgers but who chose to attend Rutgers over Yale (most likely a financial decision) earned, on average, just as much as Yale graduates twenty years into their careers. The title of Krueger's 2000 article describing his findings tells the story: "Children Smart Enough to Get into Elite Schools May Not Need to Bother."[4]

Krueger offered this advice to prospective college students: "Don't believe that the only school worth attending is one that would not admit you. That you go to college is more important than where you go. Find a school whose academic strengths match your interests and which devotes resources to instruction in those fields. Recognize that your own motivation, ambition and talents will determine your success more than the college name on your diploma."

Warren Buffett echoed these sentiments when he commented, "I don't care where someone went to school, and that never caused me to hire anyone or buy anyone's business."[5] Warren Buffett is one of the wealthiest people in the world, and has done that by acquiring businesses at great prices and hiring talented people to manage them. What does the admissions officer who comes to visit your child's high school know that he doesn't? What does your neighbor who took out a home equity loan to send her kid to Bowdoin know that he doesn't? If a state university—Buffett went to the University of Nebraska—is good enough for Buffett, maybe, just maybe, attending one won't ruin your kid's life either.

The best part of Krueger's study is that it looked at the differential between schools like Yale and Rutgers. Even if you don't believe that there really is no earnings advantage to going to Yale instead of Rutgers, the study is still important. That's because the truly elite schools have enormous endowments and use extremely generous financial aid packages to make sure that anyone they want will attend. So if you can get into a top school, you probably won't have to take out loans. In fact, there are essentially two kinds of schools that made *US News & World Report's* 2006 list of schools from which students graduate with the least debt: extremely elite schools and large public universities. Take a look:

Students Graduate with the Least Debt

1. Princeton
2. California Institute of Technology
3. Harvard
4. Howard University
5. Utah State University
6. University of Massachusetts–Amherst
7. Louisiana Tech University
8. SUNY–Albany
9. University of Hawaii–Manoa
10. University of California–Irvine
11. Clark Atlanta University

12. University of Central Florida
13. University of Colorado–Denver
14. Florida State University
15. Yale

In other words, no student will ever have to choose between attending Harvard and taking on debt or attending Rutgers and graduating with none. But think about it: if the study shows that attending Yale over Rutgers does not correlate with increased earnings, what about the University of Massachusetts over Northeastern? Or the University of Connecticut over Connecticut College? To give you an idea of the schools that you'll have to forgo in the pursuit of cost control, take a look at the schools where graduates leave with the largest debt loads (also from *US News & World Report*).

Students Graduate with the Most Debt

1. Seton Hall University
2. New York University
3. Worcester Polytechnic Institute
4. University of North Dakota
5. Pace University
6. Iowa State University
7. Pepperdine University
8. Nova Southeastern University
9. Drexel University
10. Hofstra University
11. University of St. Thomas
12. New School
13. St. John's University
14. George Washington University
15. University of La Verne

DEBT-FREE U

At the risk of offending anyone reading this who went to any of these fine schools, it's worth noting that none of these institutions is likely to stand out on a résumé to the extent that Yale, Harvard, or Princeton might. If students who graduated from Rutgers fare just as well as those who go to Yale, it's unlikely that there is anything to be gained by attending one of these institutions (all but two of which are private).

Where Do the Most Successful People Go to College?

Here's a list of where CEOs of the top 20 Fortune 500 companies for 2010 got their bachelor's degree (compiled based on publicly available information):

Company	CEO	College
WalMart	Mike Duke	Georgia Institute of Technology
Exxon Mobil	Rex Tillerson	University of Texas at Austin
Chevron	John Watson	University of California at Davis
General Electric	Jeff Immelt	Dartmouth College
Bank of America	Brian Moynihan	Brown University
ConocoPhillips	James Mulva	University of Texas at Austin
AT&T	Randall Stephenson	University of Central Oklahoma
Ford	Alan Mulally	University of Kansas
JPMorgan Chase	Jamie Dimon	Tufts University
Hewlett-Packard	Mark Hurd	Baylor University
Berkshire Hathaway	Warren Buffett	University of Nebraska at Lincoln
Citigroup	Vikram Pandit	Gannon University
Verizon	Ivan Seidenberg	City University of New York, Lehman College
McKesson	John Hammergren	University of Minnesota
General Motors	Ed Whitacre	Texas Tech University
AIG	Bob Benmosche	Alfred University

Cardinal Health	George Barrett	Dartmouth College
CVS Caremark	Thomas Ryan	University of Rhode Island
Wells Fargo	John Stumpf	St. Cloud State University
IBM	Samuel Palmisano	Johns Hopkins University

As you can see, elite universities hardly have a monopoly on the nation's top CEOs. In fact, only three of the nation's top twenty CEOs went to colleges that could be considered elite: twelve of the top twenty CEOs went to public colleges, including Warren Buffett—who transferred from Wharton after deciding he hated it!

A few caveats. Krueger found that the one group of students who did seem to reap a material benefit from attending highly selective college were those who came from low-income families. But this is also moot in the context of financing college. If you are a low-income family and your brilliant child gains admission to a highly selective college, he will likely receive heaps of financial aid, and will also qualify for a number of third-party scholarships.

Krueger also found a fairly strong correlation between the amount a college spends on instruction and the amount students earn, on average. But interestingly, the correlation with tuition is very weak. Why? Because tuition tends not to be a particularly big determinant of how much money a school spends per student. Some schools charge a lot of tuition because they have weak endowments or receive little or no state aid—but that often does not lead to higher spending per student compared with schools that receive more aid or have larger endowments. For instance, students at private colleges and universities pay an average of 75–85 percent of their costs of education, compared with around 50 percent at public research universities—meaning that attending a public college allows students to earn a return on someone else's money. In addition, private colleges generally have high spending per student in part because they are generally smaller than public research universities and miss out on the economies of scale associated with having more students on one campus—so the spending per student goes up even though the access to resources is lower.

To get an idea of how spending breaks down, take a look at this table from the *Chronicle of Higher Education*:[6]

Median Spending per Full-Time Enrolled Student, 2005, by Sector

Sector	Direct Instructional Costs	Non-Educational Costs	Other Educational Costs	Total
Public community college	$4,051	$1,092	$3,976	**$9,119**
Private bachelor's institution	$6,655	$1,208	$10,598	**$18,461**
Private research university	$14,134	$11,214	$8,940	**$34,288**
Public research university	$7,255	$4,416	$9,393	**$21,064**
Private master's institution	$6,577	$693	$8,520	**$15,790**
Public master's institution	$5,064	$1,734	$4,620	**$11,418**

The first thing that is striking about this data is the fact that public research universities spend far more on instructional costs than private bachelor's institutions—in spite of the huge differences in tuition and fees. What of the huge discrepancy in "other educational costs"? It seems fair to chalk that up to differences of scale. For example, let's say that a school with five thousand students invests $10,000,000 in a new laboratory. Then let's say a school with twenty thousand students does the same thing. The small school has increased its spending per student by $2,000, while the larger college has increased its spending per student by $500. Both schools still have the same new lab. Incidentally, these economies of scale generally allow large research universities—public and private—to bid more aggressively for new faculty, facilities, and other resources than small private colleges.

When I talk about the benefits of attending a less expensive public college, many people roll their eyes and say, "Well, you get what you pay for." But the truth is that, to the extent that's true, you don't get what *you* pay for. You get what *is paid for.* Isn't it better to earn a return on taxpayer dollars rather than your own?

But in a larger sense, 99 percent of students fail to take advantage of the wealth of resources available at any college. So why go deep into debt to attend one with slightly better resources? Why not just maximize the value at the college that is affordable enough to give you life options? Think of college as a car. Most college students drive twenty miles per hour. Some cars go a hundred miles per hour and some go two hundred miles per hour. But if you're not going to make use of it, why bother? This is a point that Krueger drives home in his commentary on his study, which I repeat here: "Find a school whose academic strengths match your interests and which devotes resources to instruction in those fields. Recognize that your own motivation, ambition and talents will determine your success more than the college name on your diploma."

As I explain in Chapter 6 on why community colleges are a great option, the first two years of college are unlikely to be devoted to your child's field of study. At the vast majority of colleges, he'll mostly be fulfilling general education requirements, checking off boxes in subjects that don't really interest him. So cross off "devotes resources to instruction in those fields" for the first two years of college. That's a good way to avoid wasting money.

So which schools devote more resources to what? Here again, the economies of scale argument comes into play. Large universities have far, far more professors than small ones. As a student, all of them are at your disposal for networking, mentoring, instruction, and possibly research opportunities. There is scant evidence to suggest that class sizes are an important factor in what students get out of college, and my experience—and the experiences of the many students I've talked to—tells me that professors at large universities who have hundreds of students are more than willing to make a personal effort in the education of ambitious students. All they have to do is ask.

Maybe There's an Advantage to Attending a Lesser School

Krueger's study also found, not surprisingly, that students who are accepted to more selective colleges but attend less selective ones tend to graduate with higher GPAs than comparable students who attend more selective colleges. Krueger writes, "The improvement in class rank for students who choose to attend a less-selective college may help explain why those students do not appear to incur lower earnings; employers (and graduate schools) may value their higher class rank by enough to offset any effect of attending a less-selective college on earnings." Krueger points out rather obviously that "a student who goes to Penn State instead of the University of Pennsylvania is more likely to end up near the top of the class. Employers and graduate schools may not adequately adjust for the competition." Krueger's research found that students who graduate seven percentile ranks higher in their class earn about 3.5 percent higher earnings, "which may largely offset any advantage of attending an elite college on earnings."

Stop and think about this, because the idea is actually quite revolutionary. The conventional wisdom in picking a college is that students should attend the best college they can. "Be all that you can be!" "Reach for the stars!" But there may actually be an advantage to shooting lower when selecting a college. Students who find colleges where they can distinguish themselves as stars may be better positioned for success in the workplace than students who max out on their selection of a college and have nowhere to go but down once they get there. Groucho Marx said that he didn't want to be a member of any club that would accept him, but for college applicants, the better maxim may be, "Don't go to any college that rejects a lot of students who are less talented than you."

Then there's the motivational aspect to attending a less selective school. I was telling a friend who went on to become a major-league baseball player about Krueger's study, and he said that being rejected by Stanford actually may have been instrumental in propelling him to greater achievement. He was the valedictorian of his high school class, and as a star athlete, he was recruited by more schools than most kids would ever dream of. His first choice was Stanford and he thought for sure he'd get in with a full scholarship. Guess what? He didn't get in at all. The baseball coach told him—and the admissions people—that he was too small to make it beyond the high school level. Instead he attended a less prestigious college and quickly emerged as a star of the baseball team. A few years into his college career, he was playing a game against Stanford and found himself in the batter's box with the coach who'd rejected him sitting in the opposing dugout. That day he hit the game-winning home run.

He told me that not getting into the elite school of his dreams left him with a chip on his shoulder that drove him to work harder at his game and in the weight room as he sought to prove his doubters wrong, and eventually led to his career as a professional. He believes that had he gotten into Stanford, he might have become complacent and failed to meet his potential.

I'm not saying that going to a less prestigious school will make your child a star athlete or student. But if he doesn't get into his dream school—or does get in but is unable to attend for financial reasons—it may be possible to channel that disappointment and even anger into a work ethic that will prove the admissions officers wrong. Inspiration is a huge part of success, and getting mad may not only be healthy, but also a catalyst for future successes.

What About Graduate School?

So there you have it. Exhibit number one in my quixotic quest to rid Americans of their desire to send their kids to whatever private college strikes their fancy, regardless of the cost. But wait a minute: What if Junior wants to go to Harvard Medical School? Surely then attending an elite college matters? Not nearly as much as you might think. According to Gregg Easterbrook, writing in the *Atlantic Monthly*, "the Gotta-Get-Ins can no longer claim to be the more or less exclusive gatekeepers to graduate school. Once, it was assumed that an elite-college undergraduate degree was required for admission to a top law or medical program. No more: 61 percent of new students at Harvard Law School last year had received their bachelor's degrees outside the Ivy League. 'Every year I have someone who went to Harvard College but can't get into Harvard Law, plus someone who went to the University of Maryland and does get into Harvard Law,' college admissions consultant Shirley Levin says."[7] Author Loren Pope analyzed eight consecutive sets of scores on the medical-school aptitude test. Caltech produced the best results, but Muhlenberg beat Dartmouth and Carleton finished ahead of Harvard.

Again, there's a survivorship bias problem: students who attended elite colleges for their undergraduate education are more likely to get into elite colleges for grad school because they are smarter, more ambitious, more driven, and perform better on the GMAT than students who attend lesser schools. This makes it look as if attending an elite college makes it easier to get into an elite graduate school, but there just isn't good evidence of that. Plenty of students from non-elite universities go on to elite grad schools because they're smart and driven.

And, because they attended less expensive schools and hadn't looted savings or taken on massive debt obligations, they were more able to afford graduate school: according to the Higher Education Research Institute at UCLA's 2009 survey of nearly 220,000 freshmen, 42 percent hoped to attend graduate school after graduating.[8] Of course, many of those students will change their plans, but the fact is that if you want to attend graduate school, you should be more worried about your balance sheet than the name of the institution on your undergrad diploma.

Here again, the data is clear. What you do as an undergraduate—grades, internships, extracurriculars—will have a much larger impact on future success (i.e., getting into graduate school) than the name of the college on the diploma. Students who dream of attending elite graduate schools would do well to stay out of debt so that they have little financial pressure when they graduate and plenty of time to study for the GREs. And remember: to the extent that the name of the institution on a diploma matters, any expert will tell you that the most recent degree is what matters. Get an MBA from Harvard and no one will much care that you did your undergrad at Budget State.

From a return on investment perspective, students interested in pursuing MBAs must stay out of debt to keep their options open for grad school. Unlike at the undergraduate level, where there is relatively little variation in earnings between graduates of different schools, the differences in earnings among MBA graduates are enormous—starting with the first job out of school. To help you understand how important it is to stay out of debt and not deplete cash reserves if your student is planning on attending business school later, take a look at this quick comparison I put together. Let's assume that your student is debating between Harvard/UPenn and UMass Amherst/Harvard for undergrad and graduate school—and has just enough money to do undergrad or grad at Harvard/UPenn but not both. Which should she pick?

Institution	Undergraduate Median Starting Salary	MBA Median Starting Salary
UMass Amherst	$46,400	$81,700
Harvard	$60,000	$114,400
SUNY Binghamton	$51,700	$58,000
Columbia	$57,300	$100,000

As you can see, the starting salary differentials between undergraduate programs are much, much smaller than the gaps between starting salaries for business school graduates. I could list more schools—and I would encourage you to go online and do this research yourself for schools your child is considering—but the message is this: financially, where your student gets his MBA is far more important.

An undergraduate degree from SUNY Binghamton correlates with a starting salary that is $5,600 lower than the median starting salary for a Columbia graduate. For MBA graduates though, the difference is $42,000!

Other Things That Matter More Than Where You Go to College

I've made the case that talent, energy, and work ethic are a larger contributor to success than the name on the diploma, but as it turns out, there are other factors that are, disturbingly, more relevant than your child's choice of college.

For instance, a Federal Reserve Bank of St. Louis study found that beautiful people tend to earn 5 percent more per hour than their less attractive counterparts. Even after factoring out things like education and experience, this "beauty premium" seems to exist across industries. Worse, particularly unattractive people tend to earn 9 percent less than average-looking people. A 1980s study found that obese women earn an astounding 17 percent less than women who are a healthy weight. For whatever reason, that bias does not seem to exist among men.

In other words, there's actually an argument to be made for sending your kid to a cheap college and using the savings to pay for nose jobs, fashion makeovers, tummy tucks, and Weight Watchers. So ditch those SAT prep courses and send your kid to Neiman Marcus with all your credit cards. Just kidding. I'm being facetious, but think about it. The evidence that being in shape and perfectly groomed and coiffed will increase your child's career prospects is actually more compelling than the evidence that attending a dream college will do that.

The point I am trying to make is a very real one. When I was in high school, I knew several severely overweight people who were absolutely obsessed with the college admissions process, living and dying over every A and B as they looked to build the perfect set of extracurriculars to gain admission into the colleges of their dreams. They were convinced that where they went to college would set them up for lives of happiness and success, and looked at the college admissions process as a sort of cure for all their emotional and social issues. It isn't. As a parent, you cannot afford to—and your child cannot afford for you to—play into processes of denial where your student looks to substitute admission to a selective college for other personal and life issues. There is simply too much at stake, and the danger is that college fever will distract him from more important issues that can affect his future—negatively or positively—much more profoundly than which college he attends.

Debunking the College Rankings

"Ah, but wait!" you say. "I've done thorough research on the rankings of the various colleges in the most respected source of knowledge on college in the country: *US News & World Report*'s 'America's Best Colleges.'"

If I had a penny for every thousand dollars in household wealth that was destroyed by college decisions made based on US News's rankings, I would buy a summer house in the south of France. First, a little bit of history. In 1983 *US News & World Report* began publishing an annual list of its top-ranked colleges and, since then, it has become by far the most successful part of the brand. The printed issue incorporating the college rankings sells 50 percent more copies than the regular issues—at more than twice the cover price. According to one former managing editor, *US News & World Report* introduced its graduate school guide because Chrysler was looking for a place to launch an ad campaign for a new car. In a 2007 press release, the publisher announced that within three days of the best-colleges ranking release, the US News Web site received ten million page views, compared to 500,000 average views in a typical month.

So it's big business. The *US News* ranking of the top colleges is media-friendly because it claims to be so definitive, and that makes it quotable and conveys a level of authority. Jay Matthews, who compiles *Newsweek*'s list of the top high schools each year, laments the focus on rankings. "Like most journalists," he says, "I learned long ago that we humans are tribal primates with a deep commitment to pecking orders. We cannot resist looking at ranked lists. It doesn't matter what it is—SUVs, ice cream stores, football teams, fertilizer dispensers. We want to see who is on top and who is not."

People in general, and especially the media, adore numbers. In her book *If You Don't Have Big Breasts, Put Ribbons in Your Pigtails*, the real estate mogul Barbara Corcoran describes the advice a PR person gave her early in her career: "The best way to make your company known is to put out some sort of survey or report on the marketplace. Something with a lot of numbers—the media love numbers." So Corcoran took that advice and typed up a list of her firm's apartment sales over the past six months—eleven units in all of New York City. Then she declared that the average apartment price was $255,000 (this was a *long* time ago) and released it to the media. This BS, totally nonrigorous study ended up making a headline in the *New York Times*, and provided her with more free publicity than she could possibly have imagined. She later sold her firm for $70 million—not bad for a business that started with a $1,000 loan from a boyfriend.

The point is that studies reporting average sales and magazines reporting a ranking of the best colleges attract our attention, even if they're total crap. In the case of the *US News & World Report* rankings, it most certainly is total crap. To make this debunking of the *US News & World Report* easy to follow, I've broken it down by metric.

Average Freshman Retention Rate/Graduation Rate

One significant component of the rankings is how likely freshmen are to come back the next year, and how likely they are to graduate. It's true that private colleges generally have higher retention and graduation rates than public schools, but the explanation for this seems clear: people who achieved better grades in high school and who spent more on college are more likely to stick with college, just like people are more likely to lose a Timex than a Rolex. Rather than pay up for a school with a high retention rate, save your money and just don't drop out! There is little to suggest that any given student will drop out of one school but not another.

Percentage of Classes Under Twenty Students/Percentage over Fifty

This one seems to make sense: small classes are good, right? Yes, but the reality is that large colleges offer a lot more classes of all sizes. At the University of Massachusetts, for example, a student who wanted to take nearly all classes with twenty or fewer students could likely do that. Nearly all colleges have some small classes, and the more classes and sections there are to choose from, the better. If you want small classes, make a concerted effort to pick small classes. You don't need to pick a college based on a desire for small classes.

Another problem with this statistic is that class sizes can demonstrate huge variability based on the popularity of the class and subject. The college counselor Mark Montgomery advises students, "Note to future economics majors: if you really want small classes, go to a college where economics is NOT a popular major."

Percentage of Faculty Who Are Full Time

This one is easy to manipulate because a school can have all full-time faculty hard at work on erudite research papers but still have classes taught by grad students. For instance, a 2005 study found that at Harvard, "undergraduate students often feel neglected by professors, and that they don't have as much fun as peers on many other campuses." This in spite of Harvard's ranking near the top of the list for small classes and percentage of faculty who are full-time. New York University has built itself into a highly regarded college by investing aggressively in big-name stars of academia. But here's the thing: famous professors build their reputations primarily by publishing, and they're not about to jeopardize that by wasting time teaching lowly undergrads. NYU employs 2,700 adjuncts who teach about 70 percent of its undergraduate classes—much higher than at many other universities that are less highly regarded. This raises an interesting question. Who cares about the luminaries a school has on its payroll if you can't interact with them? The six-figure professors should be viewed as just another cost incurred by undergraduates. High-profile faculty hires are a little bit like endorsement deals for food products. D'Angelo has to charge more for its subs in order to pay David Ortiz however much money it cost to sign him. But that doesn't make the sandwiches taste any better.

The really interesting thing about this faculty metric is that there is literally no evidence to suggest that it's relevant. According to a report from the Delta Project, "in higher education, in contrast to K-12, there is no consistent research showing that access to full-time faculty pays off in greater student learning, student retention or degree attainment." Ironically, community colleges, which don't have graduate students, often have extremely accessible faculties. At Cape Cod Community College, which is located in a town popular with retirees, many of the part-time professors retired to the beach after years teaching at Ivy League schools but now want to teach a few small classes on the topics that interest them most. To get a good idea of who is teaching what classes, a student can Google professors before signing up and take a look at their accomplishments. Sites such as RateMyProfessors.com offer "reviews," with professors assessed for accessibility, ease of grading, interest level, and even physical attractiveness.

Here again is evidence of the advantages of attending a big college. If you're signing up for classes at a school with fifteen professors teaching one class, you'll be able to do a bit of research to pick the one who offers the best class. The Internet has made this task, once literally impossible, easily doable with about three minutes of Googling.

SAT/ACT 25th–75th Percentile, Freshmen in Top 10 Percent of High School Class

These metrics really go to the heart of the matter. The rankings list schools that attract a large number of intelligent, ambitious students, and then those schools with higher rankings attract more elite students, and the result is a self-perpetuating positive feedback loop. Some colleges have actually paid students who have already been accepted to retake these tests. Larger colleges and universities attract a wide array of students. At the University of Massachusetts, I have met some of the smartest people I know and some of the dumbest. This metric is indicative of the market acceptance of a college and the ease with which it can handpick the students it most wants, but, alas, tells you little about whether the college is actually good.

Acceptance Rate

This tells you what percentage of applicants the college accepts. In his essay "Let Them Be Students," Vanderbilt University's dean of undergraduate admissions, William M. Shain, calls admissions selectivity a "poor criterion" because it measures "market appeal and the effectiveness of promotion rather than the quality of education." The acceptance rate is also incredibly easy for colleges to manipulate. Many schools have elected to offer free, easy-to-fill-out applications online to attract more applicants to reject, thereby boosting their selectivity score. Other colleges have taken to handing out applications at shopping malls and bombarding high school juniors with mailings asking them to apply.

There's another great way to game this number: don't accept students you know won't be attending. Elite students might apply to ten colleges, tossing in an application to the local state college just for the heck of it. When admissions officers look at the application, they realize that the student is really, really, really overqualified for the school and that she will get into a more prestigious college and go there. So they reject the student, thereby artificially inflating their acceptance rate.

The fundamental question that I have about the acceptance rate metric is this: Why on earth is a school that accepts 51 percent of students more desirable than one that accepts 59 percent? And yet the *US News* rankings look at it that way.

Financial Resources Rank

This one gives you an idea of how well-endowed the school is. This can be useful in understanding how much money is likely to be available for financial aid. But other than that? Not much.

Alumni Giving Rate

I don't understand this one at all. Who in their right mind would choose or skip a college based on the percentage of alumni who send the school's annual fund twenty-five dollars at Christmas? I've heard a number of explanations for why this metric is used: "It gives you an idea of the connection that alumni feel to the school." And "It's an indicator of how nice the facilities will be."

Maybe so. But isn't it also possible that a school would have a low alumni giving rate because its graduates are in tune with the state of world affairs enough to realize that maybe, just maybe, there are better outlets for charitable giving than building a new dorm with a cost of $225,000 per bed as the Massachusetts Institute of Technology recently did?

The alumni giving rate, like every other metric used by *US News & World Report*, is also subject to considerable gaming by the colleges that are responsible for self-reporting their numbers. In his essay "Sanity Check," Pomona College's dean of admissions, Bruce J. Poch, describes the hilarious lengths one university went to. The survey asked the college to report the percentage of "living alumni" that donated to the school in the past year, but had not defined "dead." This particular college decided that "living alumni" meant alumni who had donated within the past five years, and decided that anyone who hadn't donated within the past five years was "dead" for the purposes of the calculation. So the college reported its giving rate as the "number who donated this year divided by the number who donated in the past 5 years" and then invoked the old "we misinterpreted the rules" defense.

But the larger point is that it's hard to understand why a school's alumni giving rate would be a good indicator of institutional quality.

Peer Assessment Score

The peer assessment score is possibly the most bizarre of all the metrics used by *US News*. Basically, this metric asks deans, provosts, and presidents to rate their competitors' programs on a scale of one to five. The biggest problem with this metric is that these deans, provosts, and presidents are at one school, and that school happens to be a different school than the one they're being asked to rank. The result is that the peer assessment score has a way of perpetuating the status quo, and bureaucrats rank their competitors based on vague impressions of reputations. So if a little-known college invests aggressively in brilliant faculty members and new programs, it's unlikely that administrators at competing institutions will know about it. Colleges have been known to bombard each other with brochures and updates in the months leading up to the peer assessment scores (a fantastic waste of students' tuition money), but most deans have better things to do than read glossy brochures from other colleges.

Worse, some schools actively try to sabotage competitors' rankings by giving nasty grades on the peer assessment scores. Clemson University has admitted to doing this very thing, and who can blame them? With so much riding on *US News* rankings—and the peer assessment score making up 30 percent of the ranking—administrators have a strong motive to complete the peer assessment process in a manner that reflects something less than good faith. In large measure, the role of the peer assessment score is to lend credibility to visceral notions about what schools are "good" and what schools are "not good." The status quo in the college selection process is a recipe for disaster, and the peer assessment score plays a role in perpetuating it.

The Admissions Yield

Here's how this one works: you take the number of students who enroll and divide it by the number of students who were accepted. If five thousand people were accepted and four thousand enrolled, the school has an admissions yield of 80 percent. If ten thousand students are accepted and a thousand enroll, the school has an admissions yield of 10 percent. The theory behind including that in the guide is that a school with an 80 percent yield is more successful in converting acceptance letters into enrollment deposits. These schools are more "popular." According to *US News*, "The results—the colleges that, in ways, could be considered 'most popular' among their applicants—were surprising yet intuitive."

But there's just one problem: Who the heck cares? Does the fact that students who are accepted are more likely to enroll make a school better or "best," to use the title *US News* applies to its guide? Of course not. High school students and their parents pick one school over another for an infinite number of reasons. To give you an idea of how incredibly lame this statistic is, Kansas State University has a "yield" of 50 percent, while accepting 95 percent of its applicants. Cornell and Georgetown accept just 21 percent of students but have a yield of 47 percent.

So students accepted to Kansas State are more likely to enroll than students accepted to Cornell and Georgetown. Why? Most likely, many students who were accepted to Kansas State—one of the least selective schools in the country, not that there's anything wrong with that—had limited options for other colleges because of low grades and poor SAT scores. Consequently, they head off to Kansas State. In a way, that school's admissions yield is indicative of a generally weak student body, but that still somehow gives the college a leg up in the *US News* rankings. Completely insane, but that's how it works.

The other problem with this number, like the selectivity ranking, is that it's subject to manipulation. Colleges collect massive amounts of data on prospective applicants: how many times they called the admissions office, whether they visited, what kind of questions they asked, and so on. The result is that they often have a pretty good idea whether they are a student's first-choice school—and will accept students who want to attend and reject those who don't. This is why college counselors often advise students to show their first-choice colleges how enthusiastic they are about attending. Any college that admits a large number of students with few other options is likely to have a high admissions yield. The larger problem is that, like the peer assessment score, it measures a school's popularity in the marketplace rather than the value it provides to students.

The admissions yield statistic is vital to admissions bean counters who have to anticipate how many students will actually enroll when they send out acceptance letters to avoid empty dorms or overcrowding. But using the admissions yield as a reason to attend or not attend any college—as anyone who pays attention to the college rankings does, knowingly or not—is completely inane.

So there you have it. A point-by-point rebuttal of every major metric used by *US News* to formulate its college rankings. I'm not the first person to question the validity of the guide to America's best colleges and there will be many more after me.

Another systemic problem with the *US News* research is that the editors and publishers are too lazy and/or cheap to actually do the research themselves (note to self: cross *US News* off list of magazines to pitch future freelance articles to). Instead, they send questionnaires to the colleges asking them to self-report the data. Because, you know, who would lie or exaggerate about statistics with no chance of getting caught just to gain tremendous national prestige, millions of dollars in donations, an ability to attract a more elite student body, and possibly a more attractive job offer from a competitor?

When I tell people about my beef with the rankings of the top colleges, they usually ask me, "Well, how would you rank them?" Indeed, many other rankings of colleges have been offered in response to the shortcomings of the *US News* numbers. To try to figure out how I would rank colleges, I tried to do some research on what factors really do matter, but I hit a wall quickly, as you'll see in the section below. Telling people which colleges are good and which ones aren't—and especially which one is the right fit for your child— has developed into a not-so-cottage industry. I think this amounts to a lot of pseudoscience: people arbitrarily establishing criteria about what makes a great college without a shred of evidence.

The Real Experts Admit: We Don't Know Which Colleges Are Better!

In September 2005, United States Secretary of Education Margaret Spellings gathered a blue-ribbon panel of nineteen of the top education experts in the country for a "Commission on the Future of Higher Education." Their findings? There was a "woeful lack" of information about colleges' teaching methods and their effectiveness. The report found that the colleges and universities "make no serious effort to examine their effectiveness on the most important measure of all: how much students learn." The report found that there was "inadequate transparency and accountability" and complained that colleges provide "no solid evidence" of their educational value and performance that consumers could use in comparing one college to another.[9]

You hear that? There isn't enough information available to compare the educational merit of one institution over another. Maybe one day there will be, but right now there isn't. This is exactly the reason that you should ignore all the hype about colleges. Real experts—not journalists looking to sell magazines or guidance counselors with little formal training—have looked at colleges and found that there just isn't enough information available to make useful comparisons in determining which institution is likely to provide a higher-quality education. Stepping into that glaring gap, hucksters and opportunists like *US News & World Report* have invented metrics for ranking schools, but the problem is that there's no evidence that any of these metrics are especially useful. And as I just showed, a close examination suggests that they are all deeply flawed to the point of near worthlessness.

In many ways, the argument I'm making here is analogous to the one that the Princeton economist Burton Malkiel made in his landmark 1973 book *A Random Walk Down Wall Street*. In it Malkiel showed—with overwhelming statistical backing—that actively managed mutual funds underperform passively managed index funds over the long term. Professional money managers can only beat the market by taking excessive risk—which will come back to bite them in the long run—or by getting lucky, and those streaks always come to an end eventually too.

Malkiel's book has been criticized for being too simplistic: just buy and hold low-cost index mutual funds and avoid trading? And yet history has demonstrated that Malkiel's strategy would have beaten the vast, vast majority of other trading strategies. I'm making a very similar argument here: the evidence demonstrates compellingly that low-cost college options provide value very similar to higher-cost ones—and that there is insufficient information available to demonstrate one institution's educational superiority over another's. Cost of attendance is the variable that is easiest to measure and there is tremendous evidence showing that overspending on college has a negative impact on a graduate's life.

It isn't just the specifics of the ranking methodologies that bother me. I fundamentally disagree with the notion of ranking colleges. First, every student is different, and, for an infinite number of reasons, the fiftieth-ranked school may be better than the second-ranked college for a certain individual. The idea of saying one college is ranked twenty-ninth and is therefore better than number thirty is just ludicrous—the publishers themselves would probably admit that if you pressed them. But then why rank them? It comes down to numbers. No one wants to buy a magazine featuring a "descriptive list of various colleges." We want rankings! Different colleges offer different programs and different environments, and they all have their own pluses and minuses. But the larger problem with ranking colleges is that it is based on the premise that attending college is like an amusement park ride: a passive experience where the student picks the most thrilling ride he can handle, straps in, and holds on to his digital camera.

College is nothing like that. When students go to college—any college—they take classes. Some of those classes are taught by brilliant professors, some are taught by lousy professors, and some are taught by graduate students. What they get out of their education is a function of the effort they put in. It's possible to go the number-two ranked college and get a terrible education, just as it's possible to go to number 180 and get a wonderful education. In Chapter 4, you'll learn about how your student can make any college an Ivy League college, and how you can help. Families are up against a formidable industry that is trying to convince them that college selection is a hugely important decision, and the consequences of a "bad" diploma can be so dire that you must get your child into the "best" college by any means necessary. The thing that you need to keep in mind as you navigate the college search process is that the people you talk to at a college are there to sell you on their school. While you look to make the right financial decision for your child and your family, there are billions of dollars working toward the goal of sucking up as much of your cash as possible, in addition to as much of your child's future earnings as they can get their hands on.

Choosing a College: What Matters and What Doesn't

So here's where we're at. In Chapters 1 and 2, I showed the devastating impact that overextending yourself or your child to finance college will have on your life and your child's. In this chapter, I've shown you extremely compelling data that demonstrates that students who are smart and motivated enough to attend an elite school will do just as well even if they don't. I went through the list of metrics used by the most respected source of wisdom on college admissions in the country—The *US News & World Report* guide to America's best colleges—and showed why every single metric is hopelessly flawed and useless as a college selection tool. I've also shown that the people who have objectively studied what makes a college great—experts who don't have a ranking guide to sell—have found that there is a lack of available information to show which colleges are better than others. Yet I've found reams of data showing this: if you and your child overextend yourselves financially in the quest to pay for the "right" college, the consequences are likely to be devastating.

For a few students, this problem will solve itself. They'll receive large financial aid packages to attend the private colleges of their dreams. But for an increasing percentage of students, the choice will come down to this: loot my parents' retirement accounts and take on loans to attend the fancy private college of my dreams or head off to a state university. In the current economic meltdown, more families are at least keeping the public college option open. The *Boston Globe* recently reported, "Students are applying to the state's public colleges and universities in record numbers, as the nation's financial crisis forces more families to consider less expensive schools." The paper goes on to report that applications for early admission to UMass–Amherst, the state's flagship campus, are up 29 percent over last year. Bridgewater State College has seen its applicant pool double.[10]

Interestingly, many guidance counselors have given up on the notion that any given college is necessarily "better" than any other college, a good decision because there is literally not a single shred of evidence that that is the case. At more progressive high schools, guidance counselors are looking to downplay the frenzy to get into the "right" schools. This is a step in the right direction, but the alternative that they present is flawed. I still occasionally wake up in a cold sweat with nightmares of my high school counselor droning on about finding the right "fit" and "the college that is right for you!"

In the literature of guidance counselors, their perceived role has changed from getting kids into the best schools to finding the one that is a good fit. This has a nice ring to it, but much of what passes for wisdom about finding the right "fit" is really just barf: mysticism made up with no particular grounding in reality.

The cult of college fit is nearly as dangerous as the cult of college prestige because it is so full of vagaries and just plain bad advice: suggestions that lack any foundation in data, experience, or truth. Nowhere is this more apparent than in the campus tour.

The Myth of "Fit" and the Stupidity of "Campus Tours"

Most college experts will tell you that taking a campus tour is an absolute must. In a fit of generosity, the College Board offers a free online list of things you should check out while you're at a college: "Take a look at this list before planning campus trips to make sure that you allow enough time on each campus to get a sense of what the school—and the life of its students—is really like." Here's a partial list of their suggestions,[11] followed by my obnoxious commentary:

• *Pick up financial aid forms.* Right: Why print them out from the Internet or have the college mail them to you when you can drive to the campus and then wander around trying to find the financial aid office?

• *Participate in a group information session at the admissions office.* Sign up to be subjected to salesmanship that would make a car salesman squirm. Sit around a conference table and listen to an admissions officer drone on about the unique opportunities his school has to offer. If he's likable and funny, you'll probably get excited about the college. If he isn't, you won't. But do you really want to pick a college based on the affability of hucksters?

• *Sit in on a class of a subject that interests you.* My commentary on this one is serious. Colleges have tons of classes taught by lots of different people. Some of them are good, some of them are okay, some of them are really bad. Sitting in on one class subjects your college selection process to tremendous randomness. Maybe it'll be a good class. Maybe it won't. Anyone who has ever been to school will tell you that there are some classes that would make you love the school and some that would make you hate it. Guess which ones the school's admissions officers will pick for you to sit in on? Hint: you won't be attending a lecture with the college's most boring and pretentious professor. Sitting through one class tells you very little about the overall experience you'll have at the school.

• *Spend the night in a dorm.* The dorm has a bathroom and a mattress on which to sleep. You can bring a mattress pad if it's too hard for your tastes. If the people on your floor are loud, the floor will be loud. If you choose a quiet floor, the floor will be quiet.

• *Scan bulletin boards to see what day-to-day student life is like.* At most college campuses, bulletin boards are full of ads for indie rock band concerts, Marxist rallies, and grad students trying to sell their old textbooks. Larger colleges will have a wider variety of activities.

• *Eat in the cafeteria.* Many freshmen gain at least fifteen pounds, so the quality of the food is clearly more than good enough. Healthy menu options? Nearly all colleges have plenty of options that will allow the health-conscious student to stay fit and trim.

• *Read for a little while in the library and see what it's like.* It's like a library. It's like reading. It's like reading in a library!

• *Search for your favorite book in the library.* What? No *Choose Your Own Adventure #179: Ninja Avenger?* I'm outta here! What would looking for a book in the library possibly tell you about anything? If they don't have it, you can always get it on interlibrary loan. And if it's your favorite book, shouldn't you own a copy already?

• *Browse in the college bookstore.* Because it is the bookstore for this college, there is a reasonable probability that the college bookstore will have all the books you will need for your classes. It will also have a selection of pens, soft drinks, and sugar-free gum, along with overpriced souvenirs.

- *Ask students what they do on weekends.* What do they do? They're college students! What do you think they do? I know: the admissions people would like parents to think that students spend their weekends doing research at the local historical society and then carpool to go to the museum of natural history. Visit the local liquor store to find out what students do on weekends.

- *Listen to the college's radio station.* It's a good idea to listen to the college radio station because trust me: no one else is.

- *Imagine yourself attending this college for four years.* Ah yes. Once you fail to eke anything of value out of your time wandering around the college, you can always try the creative visualization approach. Close your eyes, breathe deeply, and imagine: this weekend was not a total waste of time.

Part of the problem with campus tours—especially structured activities with guides—is that they are essentially sales pitches carefully designed to show you things that will impress. In 1789 the Russian minister Grigori Aleksandrovich Potemkin was looking to impress Empress Catherine II during her visit to Crimea. That territory had recently been conquered at considerable expense to the Russian empire, and Catherine wanted to see signs of progress in developing it into a valuable property. Problem: there wasn't much progress. So General Potemkin hired people to construct what amounted to cardboard facades of villages designed to impress Catherine as her entourage was guided through the territory. It all went splendidly and Catherine expressed pleasure with Potemkin's work—and the cardboard villages were taken down as soon as she left. Campus tours are often little more than Potemkin villages, and they may tell you plenty about the slickness of the college's sales force—but little about the college in general.

Taking tours of college campuses has become a cliché, and I may be the first person to suggest that it's basically a waste of time. But I honestly believe that it will tell you very little of importance about choosing a college and, more important, can provide you with a sample of randomness that could sway your child in favor of or against a particular school with no good reason.

In June 2009, the *Daily Beast* interviewed some "college experts" along with students and parents for their tips on college tours, a few of which were actually surprisingly candid. A former admissions officer at a liberal arts college in the Northeast reported, "Of course, we always looked for the most enthusiastic students we could for tour guides. But they also had to be the dullest ones, too. We wanted to present the happy side of campus, nothing controversial at all, and nothing off the script. You learned nothing remotely interesting on our tours."[12]

The president of Earlham College advised families, "Visit a class or two for first-year students, and try not to be steered in your selection by the admissions office. Don't pay too much attention to the person at the front of the room, but look around closely at the students. Are they participating? Are they engaged? Did they do the reading? Because students educate themselves in context, and you have to see if they want to be present in that classroom." This also sounds like reasonable advice—until you actually think about it. Whether students are participating and engaged depends on the class and the specific students who happen to be in that class—and the time of day, whether there was a keg party the night before, and a whole slew of other factors. Of course you should try not to be steered into a particular class, but then you just end up in a random class—which isn't really indicative of much either. Regardless of where your student goes, there will be plenty of hard-working students she can study with—and plenty of lazy ones she can drink beer with.

The other problem with a college tour is that it can set your college decision-making process up for awkwardness, broken dreams, and an overwhelming temptation to overextend. Most families visit colleges before they have filled out applications and gotten acceptances and financial aid packages. But what if you visit a school and your child falls in love with it, and then you get the financial aid package and your contribution is substantially more than you can afford? Are you going to say, "Remember that school I drove you out to visit and you absolutely loved it? Yeah, you got in, so congrats on that. But you're not going." Many parents don't have the heart to say this, and who can blame them? This whole unfortunate situation can be avoided by simply not visiting colleges—or restricting college visits to schools that are well within your price range. If your state has five state colleges and universities, there's probably no real harm in visiting them—but probably no real point either.

The most important risk when it comes to finding a college that's a good "fit" is that this focus often leads families to choose small, private colleges where people toss Frisbees and everyone seems to know each other. In reality, attending a small liberal arts college is more likely to lead to "fit" problems than enrolling in a larger one. As they look to compete with smaller colleges, larger universities have worked hard to develop schools within schools and smaller communities. Go to a school with twenty thousand undergrads and you're sure to find a group of people with common interests and values, as well as extracurricular activities that appeal to you. But at a smaller college, it's more hit-or-miss. It's a lot easier to make a big school small than a small school big.

Please, for the love of everything that is financially prudent and mentally stable, do not mortgage your house and take out a Parent PLUS loan because your kid liked the sushi at one college and was unimpressed by the fried chicken at another.

Even the Best Guidance Counselors Fall for the Myth of Fit

In 2009 the veteran education journalist David L. Marcus wrote a book called *Acceptance: How a Legendary Guidance Counselor Helps Seven Kids Find the Right Colleges—and Find Themselves.* To research the book, Marcus followed a highly respected guidance counselor named Gwyneth Smith Jr., who worked at a public high school in New York. Mr. Smith speaks with a girl named Allyson, who is ranked fifteenth in her class of 109—so we're not talking about someone who is stupid. She is torn between the University of Michigan and Emory, where her sister is a student. Marcus writes, "Allyson had been to classes, meals and parties at Emory. Her sister had found great friends and great professors. Allyson smiled and added: a great boyfriend, too."

Just because your sister found a great boyfriend at a college doesn't mean that you will too. Really, it doesn't. If Allyson was so infatuated with her sister's boyfriend that she wants to enroll at their school to steal him from her, that is perhaps a valid reason to choose Emory. But it's not very sisterly!

The focus on finding the right "fit" lends weight to factors that should not be relevant. The fact that your sister found great friends there just isn't indicative of anything. People find great friends at all kinds of schools and others go to the same schools and don't find great friends. Allyson then goes on to describe other schools she liked based on a brief visit and others she didn't, and Marcus adds: "In a college search, liking the look of a place is a key factor, and can often lead to the right fit. That's why college visits—even brief ones—are essential." And that's it. No explanation of why liking the color of the facade or the architectural style of the campus will make it an ideal institution for higher learning.

Toward the end of that book, a girl named Chelsea is evaluating her college choices. She's been accepted by NYU and Charleston, but "Chelsea's decision became more complicated when Skidmore took her off the wait list and offered her a spot, giving her three options. She visited Skidmore and the found the idyllic college—students tossing Frisbees and lying on greens. She saw campuses through her artist's eye, *and she liked the way the light filtered through the trees at Skidmore*" (emphasis added).

Please, please, please: do not allow your child to pick a college based on the way the light filters through the trees. Really. There is little reliable data to suggest that arboreal luminescence is a good predictor of college success.

Fit has been elevated to a mystical level, almost as though it were a religious experience that can't be questioned. Well, I'm questioning it, because there is not a shred of evidence that it has any validity, and falling into this trap can be financially disastrous if the school that is christened the best "fit" happens not to fit your wallet. Please, please, please don't go into debt over something as silly as a good "fit."

Of course, some parents and students will point out that campuses do come in a lot of different types: some students want to go to college in a city, others want to go to college in the suburbs. Isn't this a valid issue?

All other (mostly financial) things being equal, yes, it is. Most states have at least one public college or university that is located in an urban area, and one that is located outside of a large city. When I was deciding on which college to attend, I could have attended UMass–Boston if living in the city had been important to me.

But for an Idahoan looking for the big city experience, Boise might not exactly be the dream location. My advice? It's only four years. Suck it up. This sounds cold, but let me tell you a story about a friend, which may help with this. "John" grew up on Cape Cod and wanted to go to school in New York City. A lot. So he took out more than $50,000 in student loans, and his parents took out a bunch more so that he could ship off to NYU, which he did. He had a really fun four years, loved the city, and then graduated and was ready to live in New York for a long time.

Then his student loans entered repayment and, because of New York City's high cost of living, he ended up moving back in with his parents. Now he's geographically removed from the industry that interests him, working hard, saving money, hoping to move back to the city. Someday, he might, but the point is this: I would rather go somewhere cheap for school in a less than ideal location and then have the flexibility to live wherever I want after I graduate.

Learning Disabilities

The number of students entering college with learning disabilities has been on the rise for decades, and there are a number of colleges that make their programs for learning-disabled students a strong selling point. However, many colleges with specialized learning disabilities programs are prohibitively expensive. I recently spoke with a mother whose child had serious learning disabilities, and she was concerned that he wouldn't be able to succeed at a college that didn't emphasize its specialized programs for students like her son. The family settled on Curry College in Milton, Massachusetts—a small institution with annual costs of more than $40,000 (and possibly a lot more by the time you read this). The 2007 graduating class had an average debt load of $27,145.

I understand that Curry College prides itself on its strong support system for learning-disabled students, but think about it: If it costs $40,000 and a small state college costs $15,000, couldn't you take half of the difference—$12,500—and hire tutors and/or coaches to help him make it through the state college? I'm highly skeptical of the ability of a college to provide $25,000 in extra value to special-ed students, and it's likely easily duplicated with graduate student tutors who cost twelve dollars an hour at a public college.

Parents also need to know that any college that receives federal money—and that includes every college in the country because of federal student loan programs and the Pell Grant—is required to make accommodations to meet the needs of students with learning disabilities and ensure that they are not discriminated against in education. The Department of Education informs students that "the appropriate academic adjustment must be determined based on your disability and individual needs. Academic adjustments may include auxiliary aids and modifications to academic requirements as are necessary to ensure equal educational opportunity."

Saving Money on Test Prep

Katherine Cohen of IvyWise.com told *Today* that applying for college can cost an average of $3,500, and that's a cost most families don't give much thought to. Admission expenses can include SAT registration, SAT prep courses, college admissions counseling, campus visits, application fees, and Tarot consultations.

My advice is to severely limit your expenditures on college preparation and applications. Most of the expensive SAT prep courses are simply not worth it, and there are plenty of books out there that cost less than thirty dollars that include tips, sample tests, and so on. Many high schools offer free SAT prep programs for their students, and even if they don't, you can help your child in other ways. Have your student work through the SAT practice tests and ask her teachers for help with any concepts/questions she doesn't understand. That costs nothing and is every bit as effective as the $300 per hour SAT tutors. "It breaks my heart to see families who can't afford it spending money they desperately need on test prep when no evidence would indicate that this is money well-spent," William Fitzsimmons, Harvard University's dean of undergraduate admissions, told the *Wall Street Journal* in May 2009.[13]

Studies show that test preparation programs yield very, very minor benefits in terms of increased scores, and a number of test prep companies have been found to exaggerate the improvement by making the preliminary practice tests more difficult than the actual test. Imagine a weight-loss clinic that told you weighed forty pounds more than you actually did at the start of the program. This amounts to nothing less than blatant consumer fraud, but with people desperate for any advantage they can find, it's a fraud that's likely to continue until consumers get smarter.

The most compelling reason of all to avoid these SAT prep programs is that they are a complete waste of time in the larger context of life. Every hour that a student devotes to drilling SAT words with flash cards is an hour that could have been devoted to reading, hiking in the woods, or any number of other activities that young people have traditionally pursued to figure out what interests them.

Avoid Early Decision Admissions

Applying early decision has a certain appeal. You can apply to a first-choice school and find out whether you're in before everyone else. Often it's easier to get in by applying early because the school knows you've made a commitment to it. If they accept you, you might be able to save a bunch of money on applications to other schools. The problem with applying early decision is that it's a fantastic way to guarantee that you'll get very little in the way of nonloan financial aid. If you've already made a binding commitment to attending a school, why would they try to wine and dine you with generous financial aid? No thanks! They'll save that money for students who are on the fence and have other options, thank you very much.

Applying early decision is like telling a real estate agent that you're absolutely in love with a home the first time you see it, that you don't want to look at any more homes, and that you'll pay whatever you have to in order to make it yours. It might be charming and sincere, but it's a lousy, lousy negotiating tactic.

Don't Put Too Much Value on Your Child's Opinion

We live in an age where people are told from birth that their opinions matter because they are smart, important, and independent. Even if you generally subscribe to that Dr. Spock approach to parenting, on the topic of college selection, you might need to go a little more medieval. The problem is that the college selection process is so emotionally charged for students that they have a hard time being rational. The way most students form their opinions about college tends to be extraordinarily capricious. A few years ago the University of Chicago was struggling to attract the students that it wanted to fill its freshman class, and it commissioned McKinsey & Company (the most prestigious consulting firm in the world, which also gave the future Enron CEO Jeff Skilling his start) to propose new marketing strategies. McKinsey reported that the university was unknown to many applicants and some people, heaven forbid, confused it with the University of Illinois. What did the university do? It tripled the amount of direct mail it sent to high school students and became one of the first colleges to begin targeting sophomores with mailings. Historically, the college admissions officers had focused their attention on juniors and seniors.

Why the emphasis on sophomores? Michael Behnke, vice president and dean of college enrollment, believed that by being the first to contact high school students, the school could establish what is known in the business world as a "first-mover advantage." Because the student is exposed to the University of Chicago before any other school, they come to equate college with this one school and favor it above others. The strategy was a success, and the University of Chicago's applicant pool soared, paving the way for the college to move up in the rankings and reestablish itself as a premier university. All the admissions geniuses had to do was postmark brochures a few months earlier. The postscript to the story is that the success of the campaign awoke competing colleges, who also began their mass mailings with sophomores—with the cost of those extra mailings now indirectly embedded in the cost of tuition.

This is just one example of the powerful psychological marketing techniques that colleges have at their disposal. There are any number of factors that can cause your child to develop an affinity for a certain college and a conviction that it's the right choice for him. Often students' opinions are held in such high regard that these beliefs aren't really questioned—and parents spend exorbitant sums that they don't even have to satisfy the whims of an adolescent.

The best way to handle this is to talk to your child in-depth about what is so great about the college(s) that he has his heart set on and to keep in mind the following script of rebuttals to common objections:

YOUR KID SAYS: I want to go to a small school. I'm intimidated by the idea of a massive university and I'm afraid I'll get lost in the crowd.

YOUR RESPONSE: It's a lot easier to make a large school small than it is to make a small school large. What happens if you go to a small college that you think looks great and then don't end up clicking and establishing a good group of friends? At a large university, you'll have several times that number of people to choose from when it comes to your social circle. And don't worry about getting lost. Large universities have so many programs, groups, and clubs that you will always be able to find a way to get involved and meet people who share similar interests. (Then you can give an example of some clubs at a large university—which you found on the school's Web site— that might interest him.)

YOUR KID SAYS: This school has exactly the program that I want.

YOUR RESPONSE: Did you know that the average American has seven different careers—and many, many more jobs? And most students change their majors at some point when they get to college. If you go to a large university, you'll have an enormous number of programs to choose from. What happens if you go to (insert name of college here) and decide that (insert name of major here) isn't for you? I'd hate to see you and us overextend financially for this program and then have you change your mind. I know you're set on it, but so are a lot of other kids, and there's a good chance that you mind will change. Even if it doesn't, there are certainly more affordable alternatives that offer programs that will prepare you for what you want to do. Why don't we go online and look some up?

Your Kid Says: This school has a great reputation and will position me for a life of success.

Your Response: Did you know that a professor at Princeton found that students who get into an elite college earn the same amount of money regardless of whether they attend that college or a less selective public university? What will determine your success is you, not the college you go to.

Your Kid Says: I'm not worried about student loans. I'll be able to pay them off.

Your Response: Do you know what the default rate on student loans is for people who borrow more than $15,000? There's a good chance you don't even know what that is. Twenty percent of student borrowers with more than $15,000 in debt end up going into default in short order—and have their credit ratings ruined as they watch the amount they owe explode with interest and penalties.

Your Kid Says: I want to go to school in Hawaii/Colorado/Idaho (somewhere far from your home).

Your Response: First of all, you should certainly apply to schools in those places if you want to go, and we may be able to find one that offers a particularly compelling financial aid package or scholarship. But if the difference between that a college that is closer to home and tens of thousands in debt—to say nothing of airfare expenses—the smart choice is to stay close to home. College is a great four years, but it's important to leave school with a degree of financial flexibility that will give you greater life options—such as being able to live in a place that interests you and to do the work that you want to do without being shackled by debt obligations. With the money we save on college, we might also be able to help you buy your first home, which, you never know, could be in Hawaii/Colorado/Idaho if you still want to live there after college.

This is an old sales technique: a canned list of responses to every single answer except the one you want, which is that they will go to the college that makes the most financial sense. But as it's extremely likely that your child's opinions are colored by factors that are irrational or unimportant, it's important to have a conversation about that to help your child see the ways her thinking might not be correct.

Be Wary of Colleges That Market Aggressively in Guidebooks with Cleverly Disguised Ads

Not so long ago I came across a book called *Colleges of Distinction.* The back cover said:

> *Colleges of Distinction* is a college guide with a unique approach. Instead of looking for the richest or the most famous schools, selected schools exhibit the four distinctions that make a college truly great: engaged students, great teaching, vibrant communities, and successful outcomes. . . . *Colleges of Distinction* is a complete guide for students entering college, and contains a wealth of information and hands-on materials to help students find their perfect college fit.

At a first glance, this guide would seem like a great resource. It offers in-depth information on schools that don't get a lot of press elsewhere: Unity College, Rollins College, Alma College, Doane College, and many others. The methods used to evaluate colleges are more sub-jective and less constrained by the limitations of statistics. Colleges that are mentioned in the guide are pretty excited about it. In a press release announcing his college's inclusion, Western Carolina Uni-versity's provost Kyle Carter said, "It's gratifying that others are dis-covering the value and quality of our academic programs. WCU is producing satisfied and competent students who are making a posi-tive impact in the world." In a similar item, Bethel College president Barry C. Bartel said, "It is always gratifying when our strengths are recognized by outside groups. We are pleased to be identified in this select group as a 'college of distinction.'"

Unfortunately, Mr. Bartel was misleading students, parents, and guidance counselors. *Colleges of Distinction* is no more an "outside group" than is a marketing firm hired by a car company to produce television commercials: the colleges featured in *Colleges of Distinction* pay for the privilege. But you won't find that disclosed in the compa-ny's book or on the Web site, and certainly not in self-congratulatory press releases issued by university presidents.

As part of my work covering the financial markets for AOL and other Web sites, I keep up-to-date on stock scams and Securities and Exchange Commission enforcement actions. Here's what I know: if an analyst issued a glowing report about a company that had paid it for providing research and didn't disclose the payment in detail—nature of payment, value, and date—the SEC would likely sue the company and the analyst. In egregious examples, the Department of Justice could take notice and people could end up in the pokey.

Student Horizons, Inc.—the company that publishes this guide, which retails for $29.95—won't say how much they're paid. But after about an hour of trying to Google around (one *Daily Collegian* col-umnist said of me, "Bloggers know how to Google"), I found a PDF of a marketing piece for one of the company's other guides, to "service-learning universities." After explaining the stringent quali-fications standards that allow hundreds of college you've never heard of to be crowned "colleges of distinction," the guide drops this little nugget: "For the premiere edition we are asking all included institu-tions to pay $1,400 this fiscal year and $1,400 next fiscal year." The book is published every other year.

That's $2,800 dollars for listing in a book covering a hundred schools: $280,000 before a single copy is sold. If you'd be interested in having your outstanding high school student profiled in my next book, please send $2,700 to . . .

Colleges of Distinction is just one of many guides like it. Even legitimate guides can be influenced by the colleges that purchase advertising in their pages: "We didn't make the list this year? I guess we don't need that $25,000 full-page ad after all!"

I contacted Student Horizons, Inc., multiple times for a com-ment, but they didn't respond to voice mails or e-mails. For that rea-son, I don't know for a fact that it charges the colleges profiled in it—only that its sister publication does. Your child will come across guides like this scattered around his high school. Please don't use them as a resource in your decision-making process.

A Word About "Gap Years"

One increasingly popular option among high school seniors is taking a gap year. Students who do this defer college admission by a year to work or enroll in a special program that allegedly has some life value and then enter as freshmen the following fall. There are two groups of parents and students who might like this idea:

1. Students who are ambivalent about attending college or have parents who question their child's likelihood of making it through

four years. They may want him to take a year to work and have the time to decide whether it's a good idea.

2. Students who are 100 percent sure they're going to college and have parents who agree but, for whatever reason, also like the idea of taking a year off to do something exciting.

For the first group of students, my advice is this: go for it. College is a huge investment in terms of time and money, and the evidence suggests that students who are uncertain about their level of commitment are extremely unlikely to graduate. It's a much better idea to take some time, gain some life experience, and see where you're at. As I discuss in Chapter 6, taking a few classes at a community college while working full-time is an ideal compromise for college-uncertain high school graduates.

For the second group of students—who are often high achievers and are the main target for these "gap year" programs—my advice is just the opposite: I don't think it's a good idea. Some of these students join programs like AmeriCorps or, heaven forbid, for-profit overseas adventure programs that cost tens of thousands of dollars more. Many gap year students do really fascinating, altruistic stuff. If young people want to make a difference in the world, there are more than adequate opportunities for them to do so in whatever community they end up attending college in. I promise. I would rather see a family save its money and let its child help serve food at a soup kitchen, mentor a young person from a disadvantaged background through Big Brothers, Big Sisters, walk dogs at a local animal shelter, or provide friendship to people with intellectual disabilities as one of my best friends did by starting a Best Buddies chapter at the University of Massachusetts. Best of all, students who focus their volunteer efforts in their local communities can send the money they otherwise might have spent on transportation and lodging to a worthy cause—or use it to avoid taking on student loans so that their philanthropic powers will be greater when they're older.

Some gap year programs are frivolous wastes of money. Others are well-intentioned humanitarian efforts. Either way, I'm not a fan because it just doesn't make sense financially. In a *New York Times* piece, Jonathan D. Glater argued that planned increases in federal student loan limits and the Pell Grant (available to low-income families) could make this a good time to take a gap year: "So here is a heretical idea for this year's high school seniors: Take a year off and go out and do something else. Then, when it is available, see if you can take advantage of that aid money—more fixed-rate student loans and bigger grants to the poorest students. The aid increases are not huge, just a few hundred dollars a year in grants and a few thousand dollars more in loans. So this is not entirely about the money."[14]

As I've discussed earlier, taking on additional student loans is really not something you should be hoping your child will have to do. And the few hundred dollars per year in grants is dwarfed by the fact that your child will not start earning a solid post-collegiate income until a year later—and it could be a lot worse if he gets involved in a gap year program that doesn't pay him enough to cover his living expenses. In fairness, Glater adds that "every admissions officer I spoke to about taking a 'gap year' said that students who had made that choice arrived on campus wiser and more mature and had a sense of perspective their younger classmates lacked."

The other financial problem with taking a gap year is that it can mess with your financial aid eligibility. I recently saw a "college expert" on *Today* advise viewers that deferring college admission for a year to work full-time and save money for college is a good way to ease the financial bite. If you qualify for no financial aid, that might be true. But if you are eligible for financial aid, working full-time for a year before applying is a really good way to virtually guarantee that you will receive no aid the next year because of the extent to which financial aid formulas tax student earnings. If money's no object, it's probably something worth giving some thought to. But I also think that students who are active in volunteer work while they attend college—or during high school—would also likely develop the same maturity and perspective that Glater's admissions officers refer to. As a strictly financial matter, you will have a very hard time convincing me that delaying entry into the workforce by a year without any increase in employability or earnings potential is a good decision.

Beware of "Summer Programs" at Elite Schools

College juniors and seniors receive tons of mailings about "summer programs" at colleges—and those mailings continue well into the college years. Here's a good rule of thumb: toss them in the trash. I just got one of these in the mail from New York University today with this enticing ad copy: "Immerse yourself in New York City's vibrant downtown scene—NYU housing rates are as low as $275 per week. Or study abroad and discover the world's cultural centers." Is staying in a dorm for forty dollars per day really that great of a deal?

Of course the mailing didn't include any information on the cost of the program. But these summer programs are generally operated by universities as profit centers, designed to generate cash from facilities that are vacant while the "real students" are on vacation. They are generally much, much less selective than the college's normal programs. Some families naively assume that attending a summer program at an elite school will be a résumé builder. It probably won't be. Employers know what these programs are, and all that attendance at one really indicates is an ability and willingness to spend several thousand dollars on a summer experience.

As a means of gaining college credit, these summer programs are generally extremely expensive. A much, much better alternative is to stay at home, take classes at a community college, and work full-time. Is it as sexy as "Summer in Greenwich Village"? Of course not. But it's a lot smarter.

In this chapter I've shown that many of the factors that students and parents think are important in selecting a college simply aren't. There is highly credible evidence suggesting that the name on a diploma does not lead to enhanced career and life prospects. College truly is whatever the student makes of it. In Chapter 4, I'll show you how your child can, with your help, get the most out of college.

CHAPTER 4

How to Make Any College an Ivy League College

In Chapter 3 I made the case that the impact of college selection on future achievements and happiness is vastly overstated. Graduates of prestigious universities tend to earn considerably more money than the average, but, as Alan Krueger's study demonstrated, this advantage is a function of their abilities and characteristics rather than anything that is learned in college or the name/networking power of the institution.

As a student at a state university with friends at more prestigious colleges like Amherst College, the University of Pennsylvania, and others, I've observed some interesting things about how students at elite colleges conduct themselves. In general, they seem to take their futures more seriously—just as they did in high school when they studied obsessively, which is how they got into elites schools. My friend who attends UPenn is an obsessive networker. He was heading into his junior year when I met him, and was working as an intern at a then-prestigious investment bank (it filed for bankruptcy a few months later, but hey). I asked him about this gig and I came to discover that he makes a habit of attending at least one career event every month: job fairs, meetings, and so on. Every month. Since he was a freshman.

Students who make a conscious effort to emulate the behaviors and attitudes of great students will do exceptionally well.

I've titled this chapter "How to Make Any College an Ivy League College," but in fact it's debatable whether that's even worth doing. Studies have shown that students at elite colleges are often dissatisfied with the level of personalized attention they receive, and nearly every Ivy League grad I know has told me that the institution they attended was vastly overrated. What I'm trying to do here is help you and your child find ways to achieve the idealized version of the Ivy League education at the college he's attending.

I said this in Chapter 3, but it's worth repeating as we delve into the specifics of getting the most out of college. The primary theme of this chapter is this: choosing a college is not like going to an amusement park to find the one ride that looks the most exciting, strap in, and hold on tight. Success at any college requires active participation and, in fact, many of the attractive characteristics of elite schools can be easily duplicated at any college by ambitious students—starting weeks before they arrive at college.

Honors Programs

Many colleges and universities offer honors programs. These are "schools within schools" that offer a special community to students with impressive credentials. Admission can be based on high school GPA and/or SAT scores, and it's also possible to transfer in by earning excellent grades in the first semester at the university.

When you and your child go through the college admissions process, look into the honors programs that schools offer. When she heads off to college, encourage her to participate in the honors program. There are a few reasons for this. First, if you send your child to a state university when he could have attended a more selective college and are worried that his credentials won't signal his intelligence, putting the honors program on the résumé can help alleviate this problem. For instance, the University of Massachusetts honors college (called the Commonwealth College) has a student body with an SAT profile similar to that of a more selective private college like Tufts.

Second, honors classes at colleges are almost always smaller than regular classes. For instance, I took a New England poetry class that had fifteen people in it my freshman year, and sophomore year I took a class on the Vietnam War with sixteen people in it. This is a more intimate setting than most high school classes at a prep school—and they're available at no extra charge for anyone attending an honors college at a public university. If one of your child's goals is to take smaller classes with accomplished professors—a noble goal—the honors college is a must. Ohio University has one of the most unique and exclusive honors programs in the country. The program admits only about sixty students per year and is based on the tutorial method of learning. According to the college, "A tutorial consists of either one student and one professor or a very small group of students and a professor. Instruction is undertaken through dialogue rather than lecture. [Honors program] students are required to take [a] substantial portion of their academic work through tutorials although they also enroll every academic quarter in traditional courses. A tutorial-based education lays the foundation for success in graduate and professional school and career opportunities. It also sets the stage for life-long intellectual engagement." Large scholarships are available for students who get in.

Large scholarship opportunities are a common feature of honors colleges. This can mean that even an out-of-state public college or university can become very affordable for students accepted into their honors programs. For in-state students, acceptance into an honors college can dramatically reduce the cost of attendance. And these are merit scholarships, so they're available regardless of financial need. Here's some information on honors programs at a few large universities to give you an idea of the value that these programs offer:

- **Pennsylvania State University:** The Schreyer Honors College provides an automatic $3,500 scholarship to all accepted students, but more is available. The school has over 250 honors courses to choose from—all limited to no more than twenty students. With that many courses available, you could send your child to a large state university with classes smaller than every class he took in high school. Who knew? Most of the students live together in the honors dorms, which are more upscale than the living quarters of the masses. The students have access to better advising, priority registration, and grants for study abroad. An SAT score of at least 1350 is required, along with a strong GPA.

- **University of Connecticut:** The honors college promises "challenging academics for high-achieving students, a personalized collegiate environment, a community designed for individual, social, and cultural development and engagement and leadership beyond the classroom."

- **University of Delaware:** The honors program enrolls about four hundred freshman each year, which works out to about 10 percent of the entering class. Students can opt to live with other honors students, and the program positions students to compete for academic awards, including Rhodes, Marshall, and Truman scholarships. The Web site boasts "rigorous coursework, comprehensive advising, private music study, [and] smaller classes."

- **City University of New York:** The Macaulay Honors College at City University has long been known as a sort of plebian Ivy. It's rigorous, difficult to get into, and offers a great experience for gifted and motivated students. Students accepted into the Macaulay Honors College receive a scholarship covering tuition (but not fees) and, get this, a new laptop.

- **University of Maine:** According to the University of Maine's Web site, its honors college seeks to provide top students "with the intellectual experience and close working relationship with faculty members characteristic of the best small colleges, coupled with the extensive choice of majors and opportunities for original scholarship available at a nationally-recognized research university." Honors classes at the University of Maine have twelve to fourteen students.

This is just a small sample of honors programs, and isn't meant to suggest that these are the best honors programs or the only ones worth attending. I just provided some information on a few to give you an idea of what is available. Googling the name of any college with the phrase "honors college" will yield information on its program. The strong market acceptance of these programs has led nearly every state university—and even most smaller state colleges and community colleges—to offer honors programs to their students. In addition, state governments have invested heavily in these programs because they are an integral part of attracting elite students to public colleges.

How to Choose a Major: What Matters and What Doesn't

Any number of guidebooks will tell you tons about the different college majors, what they entail, what kind of careers they tend to lead to, and how much money graduates make on average. I recommend *The Princeton Review's Guide to Choosing a Major* for detailed information on majors. Alternatively, your child can log on to his school's Web site for information about departments, professors, programs, and resources available to students. Before choosing a major, I recommend that students schedule a meeting with that department's chair to ask questions and discuss personal and professional goals and better understand how that major might help achieve those goals, or not.

But in the spirit of providing some unconventional wisdom rather than trying to rehash well-worn ground, I'm going to

DEBT-FREE U

provide you with a few things to think about—and tell your kids about—when it comes to the major selection process. The first is this: don't be overly focused on the average earnings of graduates with each major—as I'm about show you, these numbers are largely useless. But since you'll probably be somewhat interested in that data, here's a breakdown of the average starting salaries for 2006 graduates, courtesy of the National Association of Colleges and Employers:[1]

Electrical engineering: $51,372
Accounting: $41,110
Economics/Finance: $40,906
Business administration/Management: $38,188
Marketing: $35,321
Political science: $32,999
English: $31,169
Biology: $28,750
Psychology: $27,791
Journalism: $27,646

The problem is that business majors are shallow, greedy people who are just looking to enlarge their share of the pie, while journalists are civic-minded people who are intent on saving the world, and if that means starving, then so be it. I'm joking! But I'm also exaggerating to make an important point. People who major in business tend to get jobs in business that pay more right out of school, and people who major in political science tend to get low-paying public-service-type jobs. Don't interpret starting salaries as an indicator of lifelong earnings potential. In fact, the people who study this stuff (economists) have found something interesting. The choice of the college major isn't as important as superficial data would seem to indicate. A 2007 study conducted by the consulting firm Payscale,

Inc., found that the choice of career impacts earnings far more than the choice of major: history majors who become business consultants earn a median total compensation of $104,000 a decade into their careers—around the same as business majors who became business consultants.[2]

At the University of Texas, Austin, Dr. Daniel Hamermes looked at the earnings patterns of his university's graduates and found that "perceptions of the variations in economic success among graduates in different majors are exaggerated. Our results imply that given a student's ability, achievements and effort, his or her earnings do not vary all that greatly with the choice of undergraduate major."[3]

Another thing that's important to look at is the career earnings trajectory of a given major. For instance, engineering ranks at the top of the list for starting salaries, but according to Payscale, it ranks at the absolute bottom for career earnings growth. Liberal arts majors see their earnings rise by 95 percent over their first ten years in the workforce, compared with just 76 percent for engineering majors. Ten years into their careers, engineering majors earn an average of $103,842, compared with $89,379 for liberal arts majors. Of course that's still a material difference, but there is tremendous variation in the earnings of liberal arts majors. "With a liberal arts degree, it's what you make of it," says Al Lee, director of qualitative analysis at PayScale. "If you're motivated by income, then there are certainly careers in psychology that pay as well as careers out of engineering."

Still, many parents and students are extremely focused on their child's choice of major. When the future media mogul Ted Turner's father learned that he had elected to major in classics, this was the letter he sent back:

> I am appalled, even horrified, that you have adopted Classics as
> a Major. As a matter of fact, I almost puked on the way home
> today. . . . I have read, in recent years, the deliberations of Plato

and Aristotle, and was interested to learn that the old bastards had minds which worked very similarly to the way our minds work today. I was amazed that they had so much time for deliberating and thinking and was interested in the kind of civilization that would permit such useless deliberation. . . . It isn't really important what I think. It's important what you wish to do with the rest of your life. I just wish I could feel that the influence of those odd-ball professors and the ivory towers were developing you into the kind of man we can both be proud of. . . . I think you are rapidly becoming a jackass, and the sooner you get out of that filthy atmosphere, the better it will suit me.

The coda to that story is that Turner ended up switching his major to economics before he was expelled for sneaking a coed into his dorm room. But that is another matter entirely. For students who really do want to major in things like classics or gender studies because that is where their passions lie, there is nothing wrong with these majors.

With all that in mind about college majors and the effect they have and don't have on career earnings, here are my tips on how college students should go about selecting a major.

Don't Be Cynical About Your Choice of Major

Recognize that your intelligence, motivation, passion, and choice of career path will have a far greater impact on your financial and life success than your choice of major. Don't feel like your career prospects will be hopelessly constrained because of your choice of major, and please, please do not pick a major only or even mainly because you think it will lead to a lucrative job. If you have a real passion for something, major in it. No one should ever go to college and major in something other than what interests them.

Pick Something You'll Do Well In

This goes along with the first item. According to the National Association of Colleges and Employers' "Job Outlook 2005" survey,[4] 70 percent of hiring managers do report screening applicants based on their GPA, and the largest group say they use a 3.0 as their cutoff. Of course, 3.0 may be the cutoff, but a student with a 3.9 will likely have a leg up on one with a 3.02. Labor market studies show that students with lower GPAs have more difficulty in finding jobs out of college and also tend to earn less money. If you pick a major that doesn't really interest you, you're less likely to excel in the classes.

Pick One with a High Average GPA

This one varies from school to school, and it's not a data point that you'll find published anywhere— there's no handy guide to GPAs by major. But if you call or e-mail—probably best to call—departments at most schools will probably be happy to give you some information on the average GPAs of their majors. However, I'm not suggesting you choose or not choose a certain major because of the average GPA. If you're really interested in a field, you'll be excited to devote time to it, and you will do fine. But all other things being equal, choosing an easy major is better than choosing a hard one. This is especially true because employers often look at GPAs when making hiring decisions, and won't know that your school's political science major is a lot harder than the history major. Use this one as a tie-breaker. If your student has it narrowed down to two possibilities, go with the one with the higher average GPA. Of course, don't advise your student to skip out on a major she's passionate about because of a low average GPA. But all other things being equal, this is something to consider.

Pick Something That Gives You Flexibility

I'm not in the habit of ragging on anyone's choice of major, but since the average person has seven different *careers* over the course of his life (and many more *jobs*), it's probably unwise to major in something that's overly specific with the goal of working at one very specific job. For instance, a major in "hospitality and tourism management" or "video game design" might be painting yourself into too small of a corner. Specialization is great for many aspects of the résumé-building process, but for majors, I think it's best to stick with something reasonably traditional and broad. There are some situations where extremely specialized majors may be great, but I think it's generally something to avoid. It's also extremely questionable whether some specialized majors—like Emerson's bachelor of arts in writing, literature, and publishing—really open more doors than traditional majors like English or creative writing (especially when combined with a management degree). I asked one friend who had enrolled in Emerson's publishing program what made it superior to an English major, and his response was classic: "It's a private college! It's $40,000 per year. If you want your English major to be called publishing, you got it!" Don't let any college's "great program" in an obscure field—especially a college that isn't particularly well-known—lure your child there. If you're really interested, ask to speak with graduates of the program and find out where they work and how much they make—better yet, ask for statistics on average earnings and employment statistics.

To help talk a friend out of enrolling in an über-expensive program that specialized in video game design, I asked Cindy Nicola, vice president of talent acquisition at the video game giant Electronic Arts, for her thoughts on these programs. "Less than 10 percent of hires come from courses identified as specific gaming degrees. EA has found that students who pursue traditional degrees and take a variety of coursework in subjects like math, physics, computer science and business studies are well-prepared to have rich careers at EA." She added, "Our advice to new grads is if gaming is your passion, a broad-based degree can open doors to many types of careers."

Do a Double Major

Unless there's a really great reason not to, I'm a big believer in the idea of double-majoring. It gives students an opportunity to explore two interests and build a résumé that may be more flexible in the job hunt. Plus, it demonstrates a willingness to take the initiative and go above and beyond the mandatory minimum—both things that most potential employers will find sexy. This is a really good idea for students who have one very practical interest and one that interests them greatly, but who are worried that their interest is not practical as a career. For example, I have a friend who is majoring in finance and art history. He dreams of a career representing great artists as an agent, but knows that a background in finance may make getting his first job easier in the art world or elsewhere.

Develop Strong Verbal Skills

It's possible to do this regardless of your major just by taking a strong concentration of communications classes (or simply reading more), but here are some facts: the "Job Outlook 2004" report from the National Association of Colleges and Employers found that "unfortunately, the skill employers value most—communication skills—is the skill employers think students most often lack." A recent government study found that less than a third of college graduates are "proficient" in basic reading tasks, and the numbers got worse from 1992 to 2005. Another study found that college graduates who are highly literate earn 67 percent more than college graduates who are less literate.

Recognize That the Most Challenging Majors Have the Highest Attrition Rates

Quite a few students are attracted to majors like chemical engineering because of the high starting salaries graduates with these degrees can look forward to. If math and science are your student's passions and he has tremendous aptitude in these fields, that's fantastic. But students who pick these majors for the wrong reasons—and, worse, students who rationalize aggressive borrowing because they chose engineering—are in for a rude awakening. A 2010 study conducted by the Higher Education Research Institute at UCLA found that among white and Asian American engineering and science majors who started college, only 33 percent of whites and 42 percent of Asian Americans (the numbers were worse for African American and Latino students) had graduated with a degree in those fields within *five* years. About 73 percent of white students who skipped the sciences graduated within five years. A large chunk of these students jumped into less rigorous majors once they found out just how hard higher-level science classes are.

One of the most common misconceptions about choosing a major is that employers will expect students to be proficient in tasks related to their field of study once they enter the workforce. The reality is that chemistry majors won't be expected to know everything about chemistry once they start work and finance majors won't be expected to leaf through SEC filings for signs of shady accounting: all companies expect—and want—to train their workers for the specific tasks they want them to perform.

Finally, the best reason of all not to obsess about the choice of major is that it is extremely likely to change, very possibly more than once. According to Julia Barlow Sherlock, director of career services at Central Michigan University, students change majors an average of three times during their college careers. As I'll explain in Chapter 5, this is a great reason to opt for a large public university.

Arguments in Favor of Majors That Are Generally Thought to Be Poor Choices

To play the devil's advocate, here are my defenses of a few classic "You'll never get a job!" majors.

Theater

I have quite a few friends who are or were theater majors, and they all have one thing in common: their parents had absolute conniption fits when they found out about their child's choice of major. But when it comes to developing strong communication skills—again, the number-one thing employers are looking for and find lacking in most students—what could be better than a major that involves tons of public speaking? Sure, the average earnings of theater majors tend to be low, but that's because so many are pursuing the pie in the sky of a career in Hollywood or on Broadway. For graduates who pursue "more realistic" options, theatrical training can offer a number of competitive advantages that are rare in most professional fields. Packaged with the right internships and a solid cover letter explaining the value of a degree in theater, an ambitious and intelligent theater major could likely do very well in a number of fields. Obviously this major only works if your child is really interested in theater, but if he is, do not discourage him!

English

Again, this major develops communications and critical thinking skills. Combining an English major with work experience and internships in other fields—including business—and a high GPA can make an applicant look very attractive. The former Disney CEO Michael Eisner majored in English at Dennison University—and never earned an MBA either! The astronaut Sally Ride—the first woman in space—also majored in English in addition to physics.

History

"If you major in history, all you can do is teach it" is what one friend was told by his parents when he announced his choice of major. A few college history majors who would disagree: Carly S. Fiorina, the former CEO of Hewlett-Packard; ESPN broadcaster Chris Berman; former Speaker of the House Newt Gingrich; George W. Bush (insert your own joke here); TV personality Bill O'Reilly; Supreme Court Justice Antonin Scalia; Martha Stewart; and comedians Conan O'Brien and Sacha Baron Cohen.

Arguments Against the Business Major

The Harvard economists Claudia Goldin and Lawrence Katz looked at majors and career choices and their correlations with happiness and work-life balance and found that careers in finance and consulting—two of the most sought-after careers in the world—rank at the bottom of the barrel. Worse, free-spirit types who might want to take a year off now and then suffered the greatest hit to their earnings in these careers.

It's not that there's anything wrong with working seventy-hour weeks with no vacations, but students need to know going in that either their career goals must to some extent dictate their lifestyles or their lifestyles must dictate their careers. But it's very, very hard to have it both ways, nifty little books like *The Four-Hour Workweek* aside.

But the best argument against majoring in business is that it is such a common major—the most common major in the world. The only thing a business major really says about someone is that they entered college with the goal of earning a lot of money. This can make it very difficult for graduates to differentiate themselves from their classmates when they enter the job market: no one is likely to see it as a special asset. For students who do major in business,

I think it's important to pick another major as well—something interesting to make the résumé stand out.

How to Pick Classes: What Matters and What Doesn't

At nearly all colleges, students will have to choose classes based on a combination of general education requirements and major requirements. However, if your child attends a large college, he'll have a wide range of classes to choose from in fulfilling these requirements. So the first thing to do is to look through the student handbook and the course catalog, and determine what classes he'll need to take to graduate on time. Do not procrastinate!

In their book *Getting the Best Out of College*, a professor, a dean, and a student suggest that there are really six factors that matter when selecting a course—in order of most important to least important:

1. Reputation of the professor as a teacher/scholar

2. Reputation of this particular course as a course

3. Your intrinsic interest in the topic

4. Level of difficulty so you can balance out your schedule

5. Any graduation/distribution requirements

6. The applicability of the time slot for the course

These are all important factors, although I don't agree with the order. Taking a class from a highly respected professor in a topic that a student has no interest in or aptitude for is unlikely to be a good experience. Similarly, picking classes with little regard for graduation/distribution requirements is a really good way to end up with graduation problems—especially in this era of too many students chasing too few classes—making it difficult to fulfill graduation requirements in a timely manner.

As I mentioned in Chapter 3, RateMyProfessors.com can be a great resource for finding out about faculty members. Curricula vitae are valuable (and also something that should be looked at), but a great researcher is not always a good teacher. Instead, consider following Dr. Marty Nemko's advice on picking professors: call up the department secretary and ask which professors are the best. The secretary will know and will probably be happy to tell you. One thing to avoid in picking classes is graduate students. I know this is a generalization, but it's a really good rule to go by. Grad students generally have relatively limited knowledge of the subject they're teaching, and there's also a good chance this is the first time they've ever taught anything. Even if you're following my advice and your child is attending the most affordable option you could find, you are still paying far too much to take history classes run by people who are not qualified to teach high school history.

I was contemplating signing up for one class until I looked up the professor on RateMyProfessors.com and found nuggets like this: "Fat old man that is bitter at the world. Will take life out on the students." "Extremely offensive man." "Biggest Jerk I have ever met." "We get it. You're old. And grouchy. WHATEVER. Just teach the freaking class. This guy gets an F-." "Other than—'s notes being terrible,—himself is pompous and rude. . .—was the worst professor I've had at umass and would take this class with someone else if possible." "—is an awful professor and a hypocrite. He treats students like 5-year olds and administers half-baked exams . . . Completely squashed my interest in Greek Myth which was my sole reason for enrolling in this class. He's a washed-up hack who should probably retire." "He is a jerk who thinks too much of himself. Enough said."

Enough said indeed! I saved myself a lot of aggravation and signed up for a different class. So the first rule for signing up for classes—other than those that are absolutely mandatory for a major or other core requirements—is to do the research on the professors. Before the Internet, this was nearly impossible. Now it can be done thoroughly and discreetly in ten minutes or less. Sure, any professor can have a student who develops a grudge and posts something nasty about him on the Internet. But when half a dozen students from different classes are complaining and the professor has no defenders, it's hard to write off.

An important point here is that when it comes to picking a college, you don't need to pay too much attention to professor ratings. All that students have to do is pick a college with enough professors so that they can comb through the course catalog and find enough classes with highly rated teachers. Here again, size is an advantage.

Always take classes that interest you, partly because those are the ones you'll do well in and partly because they may help students explore career possibilities that they hadn't thought of. Here again, don't be cynical and try to pick classes that employers will think are sexy. Good employers will be more impressed by a student who has a passion for learning, not one who tries to be all things to all people.

Do Independent Study Options When Possible

Many colleges offer opportunities for independent study projects for course credit. This is something that students should do, even though it will in all probability require far, far more effort, direction, and creativity than classes that come complete with a neat syllabus, homework assignments, and tests. The reasons for this are varied:

- It will give your child an opportunity to explore a special interest in depth and develop research skills that you really don't develop in the course of normal classes.
- Doing independent research work can lead to opportunities for recognition that you can't get in a regular lecture-based class. Students who embark on in-depth projects may have an opportunity to present their work or gain local media attention and this

can lead to internship opportunities, scholarships, and perhaps even job offers.

- Independent research generally involves more one-on-one interaction with a professor. This can be a great source of references and letters of recommendations, and may lead to important connections that can help with postgraduation careers.

One friend worked with the highly regarded head of a department on an independent study project. He was then able to parlay that experience into a highly personal letter of recommendation for an elite internship at a museum that was normally only available to graduate students. But the name on the letterhead was enough to allow him to bypass that system and score a big leg up on the competition—he'll be the only undergrad applying for jobs with that internship on his resume.

Graduate in Four Years!

Nationally, only about 36 percent of students graduate from college in four years.[5] Why? They take partial course loads, take random classes, fail classes, study abroad, and generally just goof off.

Graduating on time is a fantastic way to make sure that you don't end up wasting money on college. The expert on this topic is Angelica Kalika, whose book *How I Graduated from Berkeley in Two Years* is a worthwhile read for especially ambitious students. Here are a few strategies I recommend to make sure your child graduates on time:

1. Take summer classes at a community college. Avoid taking summer classes through the four-year college because this will cost just as much as taking regular classes there. It may help students graduate quickly, but a better strategy is to fulfill general education requirements with summer classes and then use traditional classes to take coursework in your major.

2. Make sure you take a full course load each semester. Ideally, take as many classes as possible.

3. Don't fail any classes!

4. Don't do study abroad programs. In addition to costing a lot of money, these programs can make it very hard to fulfill course requirements while studying abroad. A better idea? Graduate on time, save money, and *then* travel.

5. If changing majors will require your child to stay in school for an extra semester (or two or three), discourage her from doing this—especially if it's a relatively similar major. I have seen students switch from journalism majors to English majors and stay in school longer. This is an unnecessary waste of money with a very limited upside.

Do I Really Need to Go to All These Classes?

In her book *The Snowball: Warren Buffett and the Business of Life*, Alice Schroeder describes how the world's greatest investor got through his first year at Wharton—before deciding he hated it and transferring to the University of Nebraska. Before classes had even started, he skimmed through all of his textbooks and then, according to his roommate, never looked at them again. He had a good enough grasp of the material that he was able to devote the rest of his studying time that semester to sitting in his chair mimicking Al Jolson's "Swanee" at the top of his lungs while his roommate was trying to work.

Of course, few of us are blessed with Buffett's tremendous intellectual powers or memory, but the point is this: the more students prepare for their classes, the less likely it is that they'll need to go to them. At any college, there are a number of classes—especially large ones—whose lectures consist of little to nothing that isn't already in the book, on the syllabus, or on the Web site. Cliff Mason, a Harvard grad and reporter for TheStreet.com, wrote the following in a column providing advice to college students:

> You're at college to get a degree and make connections, and if you keep that in mind, you'll have a lot more fun. The rational strategy in that situation is to accomplish that goal at the lowest possible cost, which in this case would mean effort. The more time you spend getting an education, which is not what you're there for, the less time you can spend doing what you want. So what else should you know in order to wring the most free time out of your college experience? At some schools, you really don't need to attend classes, or at least lecture classes. As long as they don't take attendance, I found that most people I knew either went to the lectures or did the assigned reading, but rarely both. Find out if you can get away with not attending class. Everyone says that doing well in college is all a factor of learning how to make effective use of your time, and I agree. Start by making better use of your class time.

If you're a parent reading this, you might be extremely hesitant to show it to your child. Don't worry: he'll figure it out on his own. The question of whether students should attend all their classes comes down to opportunity cost. Let me be the first person to tell you that there have been a few classes I attend rarely. At my ethics class sophomore year, a professor came up to me on the third to last class and shook my hand and said, "Nice to meet you!" in a mocking tone. I was busy enough with other stuff that I decided I could do well enough in that particular class without attending it, and that it wasn't worth the extra effort of schlepping myself across campus in the middle of winter. I ended up getting something like a B or a B-, which was fine for a mandatory class outside my major.

None of this is to say that students shouldn't attend classes. For the first month or so of every semester, it's good for students to go to every single class—that's more than enough time to figure out which classes are worth attending and which ones you can learn just as much from (and still get great grades) by staying home and following along in the textbook. Many classes, especially at large universities, have an online component that makes this more practical than it ever has been.

Bottom line: students should attend classes because they get something out of it, not out of a compulsive need to be good. What's more important than attending every single class is getting the most out of the college experience.

How to Deal with Professors

A lot of students coming out of high school are a little bit unclear about how the professor-student relationship should work. In many cases the classes are much larger than high school classes, and considerably more structured. PowerPoint presentations and hour-long lectures without pause for questions are common. It all can seem intimidating, and the result is that most students decide to just sort of pass through their classes without getting to know the professor or making any particular impression. Many students finish a semester without a single professor knowing their names. This is *not* the way to go. Having good relationships with as many professors as possible is important for getting good grades and the networking that can lead to internships and perhaps even full-time jobs. So how can students get started? I have a few ideas.

In classes that are of special interest to the student—classes where she'd like to get to know the professor in order to pursue future opportunities—it's worth making a bit of extra effort to reach out. One way of doing this is to ask questions about material that is related to the classroom material but comes from outside of class. Show that you're able to look at the coursework in the broader context of the world, especially in humanities classes. If your student sees something in the news that ties in with coursework, visit the teacher during office hours and ask him about it. What? Your student doesn't read the news everyday? It's time to get started. Obviously it's good to be an informed citizen, and it's great for making it possible to have intelligent grown-up conversations—it can also generate tremendous ideas for career possibilities. When a student is reading CNN.com, the *New York Times,* or an aggregator like the *Daily Beast* every day—which he should do every day anyway because it's good for him!—he'll have no problem finding articles that are related to courses. Trust me on this. Sending an e-mail every once in a while with a quick "It reminded me of our discussion about . . ." is a brilliant way to network. And of course ask a question to demonstrate interest and curiosity and respect for the professor's brilliance. Everybody loves flattery, but don't be too obvious about it.

In my freshman year I took a class on the global hunger problem and, midway through the semester, found an article in the *Wall Street Journal* about the rapidly falling levels of grain stores. I e-mailed my professor the article and asked her what she thought about it: Should we be concerned that less grain was in storage than before or elated that the food was being used to feed hungry people instead of being stored? She sent me an e-mail thanking me and, the next day, used the article in her PowerPoint presentation to lead into a discussion. From then on she knew my name, and was inclined to give me the benefit of the doubt when I missed the occasional class. Now when I see her around campus, she always says hi, and I have no doubt that if I needed her to help me with career networking, she'd be more than happy to. Her reaction to my e-mail was not unique: I know many people who have had similar experiences with many other professors. Most students display considerable apathy about their classes and only talk to professors to find out how they can raise their grades. Demonstrating your ability to integrate outside material into your coursework will make professors excited.

The plan here is to encourage your student to do whatever she can to gain the attention of the professor, as long as it's in a positive way. Professors have a lot of students, but most students aren't interested in making connections—leaving more than enough opportunity for an ambitious student who is. Professors at most colleges are required to hold weekly office hours, but often, no one shows up. Students who do show up to ask a question or discuss the material will score major brownie points. It doesn't require that much effort and can lead to improved grades and networking opportunities. Again, don't be cynical about this: it must come from a place of genuine interest and enthusiasm.

Extracurricular Activities

When I talk to recent graduates, the most common regret I hear is not having taken part in more of the extracurricular and cultural opportunities that they had while in college. I've yet to meet one who wishes he'd spent more time binge drinking. It's possible that that will be one of my regrets—since I've spent exactly no time binge drinking—but I somehow doubt it. Every college has plenty of interesting concerts, performances, sporting events, and guest speakers, but the opportunities are especially good at large universities.

For college freshmen, it's a good idea to commit to attending one extracurricular, nonparty event each week: sporting events, concerts, lectures, art gallery openings, and so on. This is a great way to meet new people and develop new interests. College Web sites and student newspapers generally have information on most of the activities on campus.

It's also a good idea not to bring video games to colleges—not buying the games in the first place or selling them if you already have them is also a good way to save money. Some students may be reluctant to give up their Xbox Live, but if they're unwilling to sacrifice video games to help pay for their education, that's a problem. Some experts warn that video games are correlated with weaker academic performance and decreased studying time, but the greater concern is that video games can discourage students from getting out in the world and taking advantage of all the opportunities that college life has to offer.

CHAPTER 5

Why Large Public Universities Are Better Than Private Colleges

I'm biased. I attend a large public university and love everything about it—with the exception of the dilapidated campus and usual administrative bureaucracy (it took me forty-five minutes on the phone to get approval to stay in the dorm for an extra day to attend my brother's graduation). However, some small private colleges have gained popularity, and a new wave of once relatively obscure small liberal arts colleges has become downright chic.

The journalist turned college administrator turned college guru Loren Pope has sold over 100,000 copies each of his books *Looking Beyond the Ivy League: Finding the College That's Right for You* and *Colleges That Change Lives*. Much of the advice in his books is spectacular: don't obsess over the name brand, and don't think that the only college worth going to is the one that won't accept you. Where we part ways is in our views on college size. Pope doesn't like large public universities. In *Looking Beyond the Ivy League*, he writes, "The big university may have two thousand courses, but they're all filled. If you do get in, it will probably be all lecture, and your grade will depend on one or two multiple-choice exams. In the small college, the professor is your friend and mentor, and there is no limit to the breadth or depth of your collaborative explorations." Later, he boldly states, "It is nonsense to think that bigger is better, especially in education. The good small liberal arts college will give you the best and most challenging education."

As you can guess from the title of this chapter, I think this argument is absurd. I believe the quality of education is almost entirely up to the student, so it's ridiculous to paint with such a broad brush. One of the problems with Pope's arguments is that they rely too heavily on anecdotal evidence and interviews with students who had great experiences at certain colleges. You may have noticed that unlike many other authors of college books, I don't do that. Here's why: I think it's disingenuous. There are over four thousand degree-granting institutions in the United States, and according to the 2000 United States Census, there were 14.4 million Americans enrolled in undergraduate education, and many times that many alumni floating around in the workforce. Given that, you can find anecdotes and student interviews to say that any college is great or horrible or that any type of college is great or horrible. Anecdotal evidence simply presents too much of an opportunity for data mining—starting with a thesis and then gathering testimony to support it. For every student Pope finds who transferred from a large university to a small college and liked it, he could have easily found another student who transferred to a large university after a lousy experience at a small college. People have told me that I should include more anecdotes about students who had good experiences at public colleges in this chapter, but I don't. Anecdote mining might be a good way to put together an emotionally compelling argument, but it's intellectually dishonest and can lead to bad conclusions.

So back to the question at hand. Do private colleges do a better job of meeting student needs and expectations than public ones? The answer is simply no. They don't. A 2000 Noel-Levitz survey interviewed 423,003 students at 745 institutions of higher learning and reported the following:

- Two-year institutions are outperforming their four-year counterparts in meeting student expectations.

- Four-year public and private colleges and universities exhibit performance that appears to be in a "holding pattern," with the public schools maintaining a slight edge over the private.
- Four-year private colleges—typically the nation's most expensive— are losing ground in meeting student expectations.[1]

A 2007 study from Noel-Levitz asked students at different institutions whether they were satisfied with their college experience and how likely they would be to reenroll "if you had it to do all over again"; note they were not asking students whether they planned to return to the school for the following semester. Here were the results:[2]

Institution	Percent Satisfied	Likelihood to Reenroll
Four-Year Public	53%	56%
Four-Year Private	52%	59%
Two-Year Community Colleges	59%	69%

You can find students who report having their lives change for the better anywhere. The data suggests that satisfaction numbers for four-year public and four-year private colleges are very comparable.

Arguments for Attending a Public University

But, as I see it, these are the main advantages to attending a large public university over a private school. They allow students and families to

- Take advantage of subsidies
- Get a higher return on their investment

- Choose from a wider array of courses and majors
- Live among a more diverse student body
- Enjoy a college-town atmosphere that offers a variety of events and activities
- Draw on the support of a larger alumni network

Take Advantage of Subsidies

No matter where you live, a significant chunk of your tax dollars is being funneled into your state's higher education system. Why not use it? Frank Knight, one of the greatest economists of all time, once said that the key to success for young people is to "Take Advantage of All Subsidies!"

Remember that one of the findings of Alan Krueger's research was that the amount that a school spends on educating each student has a fairly strong correlation with later earnings success. By sending your child to a publicly funded institution, you allow him to benefit from instructional costs borne by state taxpayers, not just by your child and you. Earning a good return on your own investment is important, but earning a great return on someone else's investment is downright awesome.

Get a Higher Return on Your Investment

College is the second-largest investment most people will ever make, and it needs to be evaluated as such. That means taking a hard look at the numbers and making a decision based on rational thought, not fancy dining halls, elaborate marketing campaigns, or *US News & World Report* rankings.

In March 2009 *BusinessWeek* took a look at the return on investment of various undergraduate business programs and proclaimed, "While the top-ranked private schools such as No. 2 Notre Dame and No. 3 Wharton get all the attention, it's the big state schools (and their lower tuition costs) that fare the best on this measure."[3] To calculate the return on investment *BusinessWeek* divided the average starting salary for the college's business major graduates by the school's tuition and mandatory fees. The results are telling: for every dollar they spend on tuition and fees per year, public school grads took home $5.98 upon graduation, compared with just $1.87 for the private school grads.

Brigham Young University scored the best on that metric of any private school, but only because of its cut-rate tuition offered to Mormon students, who make up 95 percent of the student body. Cornell placed second at $2.70—still less than half the ROI of the average public university. Cornell's business school offered a high return in part because it receives some public funding. On the public university side, *BusinessWeek* found that North Carolina's Kenan-Flagler Business School was the best value, with students earning ten dollars for every dollar they invest in tuition. That was followed by SUNY Binghamton ($8.52) and James Madison University ($7.18). It's important to note that those strong returns only applied to in-state students. Out-of-state students who paid out-of-state tuition and fees earned returns comparable to what they would have received at private colleges. In other words, trying to pick the private college or university with the highest ROI is likely to be pretty futile. The best return will come from attending an in-state institution, unless your child hits the financial aid or scholarship jackpot.

While *BusinessWeek* looked exclusively at business schools, the *Wall Street Journal*'s *SmartMoney* magazine used a similar metric and reported, "For parents fretting about sending their kid to the University of Washington versus, say, Columbia or Brown, they can rest easier knowing that Husky alums recoup their tuition costs, on average, twice as fast as grads from those two Ivies." Not unlike *BusinessWeek*, *SmartMoney* found that not a single private college even made the top eighteen on its list of colleges offering the highest return on investment.

But there's one critical flaw with the data from *BusinessWeek* and *SmartMoney*: it fails to take into account selection bias, just like every other study (with the exception of Alan Krueger's) comparing earnings based on college attended. When you combine that data from Krueger with the data from *BusinessWeek* and *SmartMoney*, the conclusion is clear: for most students, paying up big to go to a brand-name college will not generate a high ROI.

When looking at college as an investment, there's one key economics phrase that I want you to keep in mind: the law of diminishing marginal returns. Remember that the first dollars spent on college tend to generate the highest return. Sending your child to community college for two years followed by two years at a public university offers a better average ROI than sending your child to a public university for four years. Similarly, sending your child to a public university for four years offers a better average ROI than sending him to a private college.

The word *average* in that line is key, because the difference between *average return* and *marginal return* throws off a lot of people. For instance, an admissions officer at any college will likely tell you that education is a great investment. The financial aid officer will echo this sentiment when he assures you that signing up for student loans is a prudent decision. Guess what: they're both right. Sort of. The Harvard economists Claudia Goldin and Lawrence Katz looked at the "labor-market premium to skill"—the amount that college graduates earn in comparison to non–college graduates—and found that over a lifetime, a 2007 college graduate will earn about $800,000 more than a high school graduate. "With college as an investment, you're looking at 15 to 20 percent annual rates of return over your lifetime," Katz says.

That's a pretty good return on investment—in fact, it's considerably better than what Bernie Madoff was promising, and only Warren Buffett has been able to put together a better long-term average annual return in the stock market. There has been some debate about the validity of this number, but most people will agree: college is a good investment, on average. College dealers will try to confuse you with this statistic, but remember: when you're picking a college, you're choosing between colleges, not between going to college or getting a job at Wal-Mart. So the dichotomy that you should be looking at is "College X versus College Y." Don't let them fool you with "expensive private college versus no college."

On the topic of college as an investment, there's a little bit of a tangent that's worth following. College is interesting in that many families incorrectly believe that the more they pay for college, the better return they'll get. As I've shown above, that's the exact opposite of the truth: the more you pay, the *lower* the marginal return you'll get. This is what economists call declining marginal returns— high returns on the first dollars spent on education (a community college and then transferring to a public college) and low returns on higher dollar amounts (private colleges, interest on student loans). And before you give me that soft crap about a good education not being about money, consider that surveys and studies show that higher earnings potential is the number-one reason that most students enroll in higher education in the first place.

The metaphor that I find helpful in explaining the concept of lower marginal returns for increased college spending is this: Imagine that two people offer you different diet products. One is really, really expensive but highly respected and generally considered to be the crème de la crème of miracle diets. We'll call this one Harvard. The other has a solid but unspectacular reputation—we'll call that one the University of New Hampshire. Which one would you pick? For most people, the answer would depend on (a) how badly they wanted to lose weight and (b) how much money they could afford/ were willing to spend on the endeavor.

But in this case, it's more complicated than that, because, you see, these diet products aren't traded in ordinary dollars and cents. You pay for these diet products in pounds. That's right: the more expensive diet bar won't subtract a nickel from your bank account, but it will add ten pounds around your midsection. The less expensive diet bar only adds two pounds. Now which one do you pick?

In this case, you need to calculate whether the eight pounds extra that you'll add by choosing the "better" bar will be outweighed by the benefits of that bar.

This is exactly the scenario that you enter when deciding how much to invest in your child's college education: your investment is made in the same currency as your expected return. But as Krueger's study demonstrated, the answer to the college conundrum is this: spending tens of thousands of dollars more to send your kid to a "better" college is highly, highly unlikely to generate a good return, if it generates any return at all.

Here's how it works when you look at it on the margin:

In 2007 *BusinessWeek* broke out the data in an easy-to-understand spreadsheet, so I'm using that data for the purposes of this illustration: The University of Florida (Warrington), Gainesville, charged its in-state students average tuition and fees of $2,968, and they reported an average starting salary of $42,000, for an ROI of $14.15. That is, in their first year of work, graduates earned $14.15 for each tuition dollar they spent per year. At Boston College, students paid $33,000 for an average starting salary of $51,000, an ROI of $1.55—which is pretty dismal.

The math is about to get just a little bit more complicated here, so hold on to your seat. We are about to calculate the marginal return on investment of a Boston College degree compared with the next best option—a University of Florida degree (just for a random comparison).

So we do $51,000-$42,000=$9,000: that's the marginal return of a Boston College degree over a University of Florida degree. Then we do $33,000-$2,968=$30,032: that's the marginal cost of a Boston College degree over a University of Florida degree. So when you look at it like this, the ROI of a BC degree is not really that dismal $1.55 figure that *BusinessWeek* reported. It's actually much, much worse. To be precise, it's $9,000/$30,032, or $0.30. The *BusinessWeek* data—which has been a major source of pro–public college opinion—actually exaggerates the value of a degree from a private college by failing to separate out the same returns that could be earned by attending a public college. That is, it doesn't look at the marginal return. The Boston College return appears to be higher than it really is because it doesn't take into account the increased earnings that come from attending any college.

That 30 cents in additional earnings is really 7.5 cents, because most students go to college for four years. At that rate, it will take you more than thirteen years to earn enough money to recoup the cost of a Boston College diploma—and considerably more if the adventure was financed with debt, because you'll also have interest payments to take into account. By comparing the return on investment of a Boston College grad to zero instead of the earnings of a public university grad, *Business Week* vastly overstates the value of a BC education.

And remember: the value is also overstated because Boston College is a far more selective college than the University of Florida—remember the Alan Krueger study. More likely than not, a huge chunk of that marginal return for attending Boston College would be wiped away if it were adjusted for selection bias. Interestingly, the University of Florida versus Boston College comparison is not as atypical as you might think. Many, many public colleges offer their graduates better starting salaries than many, many private colleges, meaning that the marginal ROI of some private colleges is actually negative: less than zero. For instance, Penn State grads ($46,500) earn more than Babson grads ($46,050). Rutgers grads ($52,500) earn more than grads of Baylor, Marquette, Northeastern, Lehigh, Bentley, and Villanova, all of which are substantially more expensive.

Choose from a Wider Array of Courses and Majors

Here's reason number three to go with a large public college. Let's say that your child spends months visiting colleges and browsing through Web sites and college guidebooks to find the college with the best program in Latvian literature. You send him off and then, presto! He decides he wants to study journalism instead. Guess what? Chances are that something like that will happen. "About 80 percent of students who start college switch their major at least one time," Louie Bottaro, academic adviser for the College of Liberal Arts at Oregon State University told *CareerWorld*. "Many students will change their major three or four times over the course of a college career."

In other words, there is a roughly 80 percent chance that choosing a college based on a specific major or program is likely to end up being a waste of time. So one strategy is to pick a college with a wide range of programs that will provide options and latitude for when your child changes her major—for the first, second, third, and fourth times. Not surprisingly, this route will nearly always lead to attending large research universities, which are, in most cases, public and more affordable than small private colleges.

Most guidance counselors will encourage students to evaluate colleges like this: think of the field of study that interests you, and then look at schools that have "strong programs" in those areas. That's exactly the advice that one student took—advice that she lived to regret, as she told me in an e-mail response to a column I had written.

Alexandra took out $35,000 in loans for her first three semesters of college at the University of Maryland as an out-of-state student, which she chose largely based on her interest in the journalism program—the Philip Merrill College of Journalism is a well-respected program. But after a couple semesters at the school, she realized that journalism wasn't the right major for her, deciding that she wanted a "more worldly background"—and the whole reason she'd selected that college no longer applied. She left Maryland after her third semester and transferred to the University of Massachusetts, Amherst. "One of the things that stressed me out was that I felt like I was getting the same experience I would have had at UMass but I was paying $20,000 a year more for it," she said.

Given the frequency with which college students change their interests, majors, and career goals, Alexandra's story is hardly unique—and represents a cautionary tale about the dangers of picking a college based on a single program. The good news for Alexandra is that her parents are using the savings from attending UMass to help her pay off the $35,000 in loans she's already taken, but many students won't be so lucky and will have their career and life prospects hampered by student loans taken out to attend a school prior to transferring.

Another added expense she said most families don't factor in when selecting a college that's far from home: flying back and forth for vacations. If a student goes home for Thanksgiving, winter break, and spring break, and then goes to school in the fall and back home in the summer, you're talking about a total of sixteen round trip flights over the course of a four-year education: at least $500 per year in additional expenses, even if you do sit up late at night on Travelocity, clicking reload in the hope of finding better prices.

Live Among a More Diverse Student Body

I attended a high school with little diversity among its students. For a bunch of reasons, a more diverse student body was a priority for me when choosing a college. At a large public university, you'll have a wide variety of students: many people who are the first in their families to attend college, minorities, people of different religious and cultural backgrounds, a larger LGBT community, and so on. If your child had trouble finding the right social group in high school, a large college is probably the way to go. There are so many people that it's impossible not to find a group of friends. For some students, this is especially important. Gay, lesbian, and bisexual students can often feel isolated in high school, where they may feel like they're the only one in their class. Large universities generally have large, active gay communities and opportunities to meet people with similar interests. If religion is important to your child, a large college will have plenty of student groups devoted to whatever god he happens to worship.

Don't underestimate the importance of a diverse student body. At public universities, your student will have the opportunity to be exposed to many different cultures and ideas that he simply wouldn't meet at a more provincial small college. Exposure to a diversity of cultures and worldviews is a vital component of a liberal arts education, and one of the reasons that so many experts believe that semester abroad programs are so important. Nearly all colleges trumpet a diverse student body, but the fact is that an affordable school with a large student body will always be more diverse than an expensive school with a small one. By enrolling at a large school with students from all walks of life, your child will gain a big piece of the multicultural experience.

Enjoy a College-Town Atmosphere That Offers a Variety of Events and Activities

Don't be fooled. Any college admissions officer worth his salt will be very convincing in his argument that there is a ton to do at the college he's representing. Keep in mind that the vibrancy of a college campus is likely to be a function of the size of the college, the diversity of its student body, and its geographic location and proximity to other institutions. Colleges located in large college towns and big cities are a good choice for students. Small and isolated stand-alone colleges are probably not.

I know what you're thinking: Your kid is going to get an education. Who cares about the nightlife and weekend activities? But the Harvard education professor Richard J. Light interviewed 1,600 undergraduates for his book *Making the Most of College*, and here's what he found. "I assumed that the most important and academic learning goes on inside the classroom, while outside activities provide a useful but modest supplement," he said. "The evidence shows that the opposite is true: Learning outside of classes, especially in residential settings and extracurricular activities such as the arts, is vital. When we asked students to think of a specific, critical incident or moment that had changed them profoundly, four-fifths of them chose a situation or event outside of the classroom."

Jay Matthews of the *Washington Post* adds, "It is risky, unless a student is very sure of what he wants or very uncomfortable on a large campus, to go to a small school." But what if your child falls into that "very uncomfortable" group? Talk to residence life representatives at the college and find out what kind of programs they have for freshmen who are insecure about the transition from high school to a college many times the size of their graduating classes. Many large universities offer residential learning communities, sometimes known as living learning communities, residential academic programs, or an alphabet soup of other insipid jargon. While the specific programs vary from campus to campus, the basic idea is that students can opt to live on a floor with students with similar majors or interests and take several classes together and participate in group activities. These programs are a perfect example of ways that large universities are providing students who desire a small college experience with the opportunity to have that—without giving up the access to resources that can only be had at a large university.

Draw on the Support of a Larger Alumni Network

The alumni networking opportunities are often one of the best selling points for elite private colleges. But the counterargument to that is that larger colleges have larger alumni networks, and ambitious students can take advantage of that.

Consider: Colby College in Maine graduates about five hundred students each year. The University of Maine graduates something like three thousand. Of course, the numbers of graduates each year have risen over time as the schools expand, but there are probably something like six times as many University of Maine graduates floating around in the workforce as there are Colby College grads. Ask yourself: If your child is looking to make an internship or job connection, do you like her chances better with five thousand prospective contacts or thirty thousand? It's true that many small colleges boast about having exceptionally involved alumni, but a pool of one fifth as many people is a heck of a deficit to overcome. Bigger is better.

Arguments for Private College

Of course, most guides will tell you that there are also advantages to smaller colleges. I'm not sold on this idea. My experience tells me that it is very easy to make a large college small but impossible to make a small college large. In order to provide rebuttals to the pro–small private college arguments, I read up on the topic and found the most common arguments for the private college proposition. These arguments can be found in books by authors like Loren Pope, and in the marketing materials of many small colleges.

Private Colleges Are More Selective and Have a More Motivated and Intelligent Student Body

If true at all, this one is only true for the more elite schools. There are many, many private colleges that are far less selective than many other public colleges and universities. But the truth is that most colleges—especially large public colleges—have all kinds of students with varying levels of ability and drive.

As Alan Krueger wrote, "First, even elite colleges have diverse student bodies, and it is possible for apathetic students at elite schools to find other apathetic students with whom to play Nintendo and guzzle beer. By contrast, a good student can get a good education almost anywhere." This is especially true of large colleges. With a student body of 15,000-plus students, these schools will always have some brilliant, studious scholars who could have gone to far more elite schools but didn't because of financial or other reasons.

As I discussed in Chapter 3, there can actually be an advantage to attending a college with a large number of less able, less ambitious students: a higher class rank. Nearly every large public university in the country—and many state and community colleges—offer honors programs that provide a community of bright, ambitious students for driven achievers to study and socialize with.

Private Colleges Have Better, More Devoted Faculty

Is this one true on average? There's no evidence of that. But as I discussed earlier, many colleges—elite and less elite—offer classes taught by graduate students. And even if a professor is leading the class, some well-respected professors with impeccable pedigrees are simply not the most engaging or helpful teachers. One great way to research professors before signing up for classes is to check out RateMyProfessors.com. The site is visited by hundreds of thousands of students who rate their teachers. At the time of this writing, the site has over a million professors listed and over ten million ratings from students. Professors are rated for easiness, helpfulness, clarity, and the rater's interest in the class. On the front page is a list of the top-rated professors. Here they are (as of April 2010):

1. Robert Citino, Eastern Michigan University
2. Devon Hanahan, College of Charleston
3. Donna Christy, Rhode Island College
4. Chris Legrow, Marshall University

5. Eric Wildman, University of Houston
6. Martin Jones, College of Charleston
7. Melissa Bush, University of North Florida
8. Christine Lottes, University of Pennsylvania
9. Kateryna Schray, Marshall University
10. Jenny Lee, Pratt Institute

How many of those schools have you heard of? Seven of the ten professors who made the list teach at public universities and, interestingly, none of the colleges are in the category that people would bother lying about attending. But wait! Maybe those are anomalies. After all, one good teacher does not a great faculty make. I'm glad you pointed that out. Here are the colleges with the top rated faculty overall (as of April 2010):

1. Brigham Young University
2. Southeastern Louisiana University
3. Christopher Newport University
4. Stephen F. Austin State University
5. University of Houston
6. Texas Christian University
7. Augusta State University
8. University of Central Oklahoma
9. College of William and Mary
10. Grove City College

I know: the methodology is inexact and subject to manipulation. Hey, maybe kids at Christopher Newport University are stupid and therefore easily impressed, just like an infant can sit in a crib and watch a mobile for four hours. Maybe these professors just give easy A's and that's why people like them? With some, that's definitely the case. But reading the comments, it's clear that it isn't always: students at public colleges appear to be satisfied with the quality of the education they receive.

One of the reasons that large public universities attract better faculty could be the resources devoted to research that few small colleges can compete with. One professor at a large research university told me that there's a widely believed myth that more elite colleges attract more elite faculty, when that simply isn't the case. Faculty members work at colleges for a number of reasons—climate/location, resources devoted to research, the reputation of the department, connections to current faculty members, and so on. Often, large public universities provide better opportunities for faculty who are interested in research, which allows them to attract more impressive professors. The notion that more elite universities attract better faculty isn't necessarily true, and the superstars of academia generally have deals that allow them to teach very few courses anyway.

Private Colleges Generally Have Better Facilities Than Public Ones: The Campuses Are Prettier!

This one might be true, but why does this really matter?

Let's perform a quick experiment. Go into your child's room and tell me what you see. If he's like most high school students, you'll find a mess: laundry on the floor, posters covering every square inch of wall, and soda bottles sticking to the furniture. Now ask yourself: Why would you loot your retirement so he can live in a dorm room with hardwood floors instead of linoleum?

Most college books and guidance counselors urge students to tour campuses at colleges they're thinking about attending so that they can see the campus and "get a feel for the place and how they'd fit in." Okay. What does that even mean? Are we trying to find a place to get an education or looking for an assisted-living facility? Because so far the methods for searching sound the same. Is your high school junior a chi master who can, after a fifteen-minute tour of a campus, assess the feng shui and how it will contribute to his career and life prospects? The physical attractiveness of a campus is just not a legitimate reason to pick one college over another, and it is especially not a good reason to fork over tens of thousands of dollars per year. Tell your kid to suck it up and deal with it—and save the money so she can have a prettier place when it's one that she owns, not a place she's staying for four years. Put another way: your child does not want to put himself in a position where he's living in a dilapidated studio apartment in a bad neighborhood in fifteen years, dutifully sending Sallie Mae checks every month to pay for the wonderful dorm room he stayed in.

When you're being told about the importance of fit and similar nonsense about trying the food at colleges to decide whether it's the "right school" for your child, ask yourself: Is it worth the extra money? If you're rational about it and take a long-term view, I think you will conclude that no, it most certainly is not.

Private Colleges Generally Offer Smaller Class Sizes

This one tends to be true. Class size gives small private colleges a big leg up in the *US News & World Report* rankings. But as I discussed in Chapter 3, a student who values small class sizes can, with a little bit of effort, take tons of small classes just about anywhere. This is especially true for students who enroll in a school's honors program.

Another good reason not to fixate on class sizes is this: unlike at the elementary and high school levels, there just isn't any consistent evidence of strong benefits associated with smaller class sizes. Worse, many small classes are just plain bad: tiny seminars of ten to fifteen students taught by a graduate student are extremely common at many colleges—and a great way for schools to lower their average class size numbers for the *US News* rankings. The problem, of course, is that many grad students know marginally more about the subject they're teaching than the undergrads.

The Private College Experience Is More Personal

One of the key anti–large university arguments made by people like Loren Pope is that private colleges provide a more personalized, individual-oriented education; that there are plenty of professors there to keep an eye on students—what some might call a nanny culture that stands in sharp contrast to the laissez-faire, "We have all the resources if you want to tap them" attitude of large public universities.

But I think the laissez-faire attitude is good, and here's why: the most successful people will be those who are self-motivated and independent. True: a student might benefit in the short run from middle-school-style prodding and babying at a small private college, but guess what? That personalized attention stands in sharp contrast to the way the world actually works once you get out of the ivory tower. Students who head off to large, anonymous universities and then develop the skills to make the most of them will have also developed skills that will serve them well in postcollege life.

At large universities, students learn to navigate the bureaucracy, make valuable connections with people who might not seem readily accessible, and research and investigate to find the resources that will help them pursue their career goals. In elementary school, having friendly people guiding you by the hand is important, but in college it can be a detriment because it's so out of line with the way the real, postcollege world works. If college is about developing skills that will serve students well later in life, I would argue that large universities offer a better chance to do that.

Avoid Out-of-State Public Colleges and Universities

At the University of Vermont, 72.7 percent of students come from out of state. At the University of Delaware, the number is 66.2 percent.

At the University of North Dakota, Grand Forks, 54.2 percent of students come from out of state.

With the average public college charging out-of-state students more than $10,000 per year extra compared to what in-state students pay, here's what I have to say about sending students off to out-of-state public colleges: you'd better have a really, really, really, good reason. Public colleges rely on out-of-state students to subsidize their in-state students. Because out-of-state students pay more, the more out-of-state students a college enrolls, the less it can charge in-state students. Whenever public universities run into budget crises, they quickly start scrambling for ways to attract more out-of-staters.

But the disadvantages to being an out-of-state student don't stop there. In February 2009, the *Chronicle of Higher Education* reported that "Michigan residents pay $11,037 in tuition and fees in their freshmen and sophomore years, compared with $33,069 for non-state residents. Furthermore, Michigan has a policy of meeting full demonstrated financial need for in-state undergraduates, but doesn't extend that policy to those who come from other states. As a result, 80 percent of state residents receive some form of financial aid—compared with 52 percent of non-state residents."[4]

Michigan's policy of giving financial aid priority to in-state students is pretty typical, and when you combine that with the $22,000 out-of-state surcharge, it starts to look like attending an out-of-state college will be at least as expensive as attending a private one—and possibly a lot more than a private college with a solid endowment and generous financial aid program. Given that, it's shocking to me how many students attend out-of-state public colleges, and while it would be bad news for in-state students if out-of-state enrollment collapsed, the takeaway for you is this: cross out-of-state public institutions off your list of possible colleges to attend—unless your child qualifies for exceptionally good merit aid.

This can be hard to do because, in light of budget pressure, state colleges are doubling down on their efforts to recruit out-of-state students. This means more postcards, more smiling suits at college fairs, and more unsolicited e-mails. Toss the cards in the trash, walk by the suits, and delete their e-mails and mark them as spam so they don't bother you in the future.

If Your Child Really Is Attached to the Idea of Attending a Small School

Some students are absolutely set on attending small colleges and for those students, it's definitely worth applying to a slew of liberal arts colleges, because you never know: some might offer a tremendous financial aid package or merit award. But if that doesn't come through, small-school-minded students should definitely take a look at the public liberal arts colleges, which most people don't even know exist because there's a tendency to think of large classes and fraternities when someone says "public higher education."

But public liberal arts colleges offer a larger share of small classes and have few if any grad students—and have faculty devoted to teaching rather than research. And it all comes at the same price—and often lower!—as larger public universities. The Council of Public Liberal Arts Colleges' Web site—www.coplac.org—offers more information on these institutions and links to the sites. See if there's one in your state! If your kid wants to attend a small college, he might as well at least take a look at the ones your tax dollars are already paying for.

CHAPTER 6

The Community College Solution

Since I began researching and writing about personal finance, I've learned that if you want to make people really mad, suggest that they send their kids to community college. In my columns and blog posts, I frequently write about the tremendous opportunities that attending community college presents and, inevitably, every single piece elicits at least a few e-mails or comments filled with sheer outrage. Here are a few examples:

"The quality of writing and critical thinking produced even by our top colleges and Ivies is in need of great repair. I cannot imagine what sort of degradation two years of community college education will cause to our entry-level workforce."

"The community college solution will not do the job. I work at a public university where students often take this route; because of it, they are injected suddenly into a more rigorous program but with truly bad training, and become second-class citizens in their own university."

"Have you been to any community college recently and seen the variation between their idea of a 10th grade educational review and an actual college?"

"Community colleges don't beacon [sic] as a guiding light to learning but rather slouch by as a beacon of underachievement and disinterest. Who wants to go there?"

"Zac, it's pretty disgusting to assume that otherwise qualified people should be attending local community colleges if they cannot pay for Ivy League university out of pocket."

As I looked into some of the vitriol that is spewed when people start talking about community college, it became clear to me that this chapter needed to be much more than just a guide to why community college can be a great option and how students can make the most of it. What is needed is a spirited defense and a busting of myths: real information based on statistics. Logic!

But first, a few caveats: if you *really* have enough money (see Chapter 1!) to send your kid to a four-year college for four years, it's probably worth doing. There are a number of very real trade-offs that come with the huge financial savings of community college. One of the most exciting things about going off to college is going off to college—leaving home, abandoning your parents, and moving into a small room with a stranger and then getting drunk and throwing up in the elevator together (no, I've never actually done that). If you suggest to your college-bound student that he start out by living at home and attending a community college to save money, he's likely to do one of three things: (1) storm out of the room, (2) start screaming at you, or (3) begin to cry.

His arguments against attending community college will likely fall under the category of "community college myths." I've listed the myths below along with some rebuttals you can use.

The Five Community College Myths

Myth #1: I Just Won't Get a High-Quality Education Attending a Community College

Many parents and prospective students are concerned that the course load at a community college just won't be sufficiently challenging. News flash: Neither will 100-level classes at a public or private four-year college. Nearly all colleges require their students to take a substantial number of general education credits—even business-specific schools like Babson have this. It's part of our university system's grand design of building a well-rounded citizenry capable of looking at complex issues from a wide variety of perspectives.

Anyway, general education requirements are a fact of life at every college, and this means that your child who wants to design robots that can make ramen noodles out of used lightbulbs (just for example) will first have to take classes in humanities subjects including French, poetry, art history, feminism, or modern dance. Why pay $30,000 per year for those classes? Mightn't it make more sense for him to take those classes locally, save an enormous amount of cash, and then transfer to the university of his dreams, where he can take classes in the computer sciences program that interested him in the first place? Think this through carefully before you spend five times as much money on gen-ed art classes at a school your child chose because of its computer science program.

The argument that community college classes are especially easy just isn't backed up by any particular evidence. They're college classes and the schools that offer them require accreditation. Four-year colleges accept transfer credits from community colleges (although some work overtime not to, as I'll discuss below) because they recognize that the work required is comparable to that of one of their courses. In addition, the level of individual attention is likely to be far better at community college than it is at larger four-year colleges. Community college classes average between twenty-five and forty students. Of course, average class sizes at a four-year college vary tremendously from college to college, but keep in mind that freshmen and sophomores are likely to be enrolled in classes larger than the school's average as they stock up on 100-level courses to satisfy general education requirements.

As one *Daily Beast* reader so eloquently put it: "The truth is that a motivated student can get a better education at a junior college than an unmotivated student can at the most prestigious Ivy League school. Parents need to realize that no college can remake your slacker child into a motivated successful adult. Colleges don't raise kids and shape their personality, parents do. If parents want to waste money sending their precious little mush-brain to Yale or Harvard then there is little we can do to stop them. Stupid runs in families unfortunately." Ouch! I wish I had some way of finding out who exactly this brilliant (and funny) commenter was, but I don't. But he or she is exactly right.

Another nice thing about the quality of instruction at community colleges is that there are no grad students there to teach classes. Community college classes are taught by real live professors, an increasing percentage of whom hold doctoral degrees. At Cape Cod Community College, the institution I mulled over attending and even took some summer classes at to meet gen-ed requirements and free up my time for more interesting classes, the level of instruction is fantastic. Part of this is a function of the location: Cape Cod is a popular retirement destination and many of the professors there had long careers at more prestigious four-year institutions, teaching a few classes locally to stay sharp and supplement their pensions. Given the tremendous apathy that so many community college students bring to the classroom, professors will likely be delighted to shower an ambitious and dedicated student with attention. For students with learning disabilities or other special needs, the small classes and dedicated faculty community colleges offer can be excellent preparation for a larger college.

Based on data from the National Survey of Student Engagement, Kevin Carey of Education Sector, a think tank, wrote in a column that "more than two-thirds of the community college students ask questions in class or contribute to class discussions, compared to only half of the four-year students.[1] Student-faculty interaction is also better—the community college students are more likely to get prompt feedback on performance and to interact with their professors during and outside of class. And the level of academic challenge is more than comparable—the community college students were more likely to work harder than they thought they could to meet their professor's expectations. The first concern of the research university is, unsurprisingly, research. Community colleges, by contrast, are far more focused on teaching, and some are doing it better than even the most esteemed four-year institutions."

Paul Glastris, editor in chief of *Washington Monthly*, adds: "Prestige simply isn't synonymous with good teaching. Some unknown community colleges offer more challenging educations than do certain well-regarded four-year universities."

For students who are willing to work hard and want to learn, there are plenty of opportunities to be had at a community college. I recently interviewed a student named Brittany Blackburn for WalletPop.com. She had started her academic career at Shawnee State Community College, Columbus State Community College, and Ohio State University—and was able to graduate from college without any student loans, with the help of scholarships and her choice of budget-conscious schools.

Now she's a student at Yale Medical School, where she also has a full scholarship that actually *pays her $50,000 per year to take classes*—in exchange, she'll work at a hospital in an underserved community for several years after her graduation. She interviewed at many top medical schools, and was never even asked about the community college credits for science classes that appeared on her transcript. In fact, she told me, all of her recommendations for medical school came from the professors at community colleges.

Still, there was a lot of peer pressure to avoid those schools, so much that she "almost listened" to the people who told her four-year colleges would frown upon her tenure at community college. "But I got here, so I don't think they look down upon me too much," she notes.

Myth #2: Financial Aid Is Harder to Get at Community Colleges

This one is completely false. The reality is that the FAFSA form calculates an expected family contribution the same way, whether you attend Pepperdine, the University of Idaho, or Bunker Hill Community College. Attending a community college will still allow you to qualify for the federal Pell Grant if you come from a family of modest means, and all the other federal financial aid programs are still available. According to the College Board, full-time students enrolled in public two-year colleges receive an average of $1,800 in grants and tax benefits from the federal and state governments along with institutions and private sources of funding.[2] The average cost of tuition and fees at a community college is $2,360, so you need to come up with an average of less than six hundred bucks for your child to live at home while taking community college classes. Wow!

Remember: in order to qualify for the maximum tax credit available for higher education spending—$2,500—you only need to spend $4,000 on education. In other words, the federal government kicks in 60 percent of the first $4,000 you spend on college, but gives you no help after that. This is yet another reason that affordable college options are so great.

Myth #3: Transferring to a Four-Year College Is Very Difficult to Do After Attending a Community College

This is a myth that could charitably be referred to as bull crap. Recognizing that kids who are savvy and practical enough to start at a community college before transferring are pretty freakin' smart, a lot of "elite" colleges are making a concerted effort to attract these students. You might be surprised to read these statistics:

- In the fall of 2007 Amherst College (rated the number-one liberal arts college in the country by *US News & World Report*, for those of you playing along at home) visited twenty-two different community colleges to recruit top students. That year, nine out of eleven transfers to the school came from community colleges, according to Amherst admissions statistics.[3]
- In 2006, nearly half the University of Virginia's five hundred transfer students came from in-state community colleges. That number increased to 60 percent in 2007. The University of Virginia also has a program in place guaranteeing admission with junior standing to any community college graduate with a GPA of 3.4 or higher.[4]
- In 2006, 26 percent of transfer students accepted to Stanford came from community colleges.[5]

Clearly some of the most selective colleges in the country are believers in community college students. Markus A. Besselle, who graduated from Harvard in 2008, transferred from a California community college after two years. Among the other schools that accepted him: Yale and Stanford. He was the first person in his family to attend college, and he worked full-time as a computer salesman to save for school while he was at community college. Now that's what I'm talking about.

Myth #4: Even If I Am Able to Transfer to a Four-Year College, I'll Be Unprepared for the Rigors of Tougher Classes

Studies have shown that community college graduates who transfer to four-year colleges tend to earn better grades than students who have been there the whole time. My theory is that students who went through the purgatory of working and attending a community college while living at home have a greater respect for educational opportunity and are more inclined to make the most of it than their more entitled peers. The University of California system, which is renowned for using its community college system as a feeder for its highly regarded four-year programs, reports on its Web site, "Academically, our transfers can compete with any UC student. Studies show that transfer students are well prepared to succeed at UC. Community college students who enter the University as juniors perform just as well academically as students who entered UC as freshmen. Their graduation rates are comparable, too: Nearly two-thirds complete a bachelor's degree within three years of entering UC."[6]

One of the themes of this book is that college is what you make of it, and nowhere is this more true than at community colleges. The small class sizes and underpaid but dedicated faculty present ambitious students with an opportunity to challenge themselves and prepare for a successful experience at a four-year school.

Myth #5: If My Child Attends a Community College, He Is More Likely to Drop Out

The truth is that, if your child is a candidate for dropping out of college, he'll drop out of a four-year college just as he would a two-year college—and you can save a lot of money and a lot of heartache by giving it a test run at a community college first.

According to data from the United States Department of Education—not exactly a foe of higher learning—among college freshmen who graduated in the bottom 40 percent of their high school classes, 76 percent won't earn a college diploma within eight and a half years. Read that last line again, please. If your child has taken the SAT and scored below average—or has a GPA that is only fair—you absolutely should not fall into the trap of starting him at a four-year college. And you especially shouldn't loot your savings or put him in debt to do that. What if your child is an underachiever and falls in that 24 percent of poor high school performers who will experience success in college? He can start at a community college, transfer after a year or two, and be none the worse for the experience. Think of it as a hedge.

But what about the suspicion of low graduation rates among community college students? Just like the data showing that Harvard graduates earn more money than Rutgers grads, this one appears to be superficially true. Community colleges do have very high dropout rates. But that seems much more likely to be a function of what community colleges are than their effect on any given student. Community colleges have open admissions policies, meaning that they accept *anyone*. The costs of attendance are low, you don't have to uproot and move to a dorm to attend one, and most community college students come from that lower echelon of high school students who are unlikely to graduate no matter what school they attend. These factors make community colleges a frequent outlet for people who are lukewarm at best about the idea of attending college, and they drop out quickly. There is, however, no data to suggest that students of similar abilities and backgrounds are more likely to drop out of a community college than a four-year college. Bottom line: don't spend $40,000 to avoid dropping out. Just don't drop out! I realize that you can't control what your kid will do—but you can't influence his future likelihood of dropping out by sending him to a different school.

As long as we're on the topic of dropping out, there's another thing that needs to be said about community colleges. Government statistics show that of students who enrolled in four-year colleges in 1996, only 54 percent had earned a degree within *six* years. (A word of warning: citing this stat to a fellow parent in a café is a good way to get a smoothie thrown at you.) That means 46 percent of parents who send their kids to college effectively end up wasting whatever money they invested. Most people are astonished by this high attrition rate at four-year colleges, and there are a number of possible explanations, but the most compelling one is this: a societal shift toward higher education for all has led more marginal students into the halls of America's universities. The result is that a large chunk of these students were not prepared or committed to their education, and their failure to graduate might have been predicted from the outset. At best, their parents are out tens of thousands of dollars that they had kickin' around anyway. At worst, the student drops out with tens of thousands of dollars in student loans and is unable to make the payments out of his eight-dollar-an-hour job bagging groceries. The parents who cosigned the loans find themselves on the hook, and spend decades faithfully sending 30 percent of their Social Security checks to Sallie Mae while they cook ramen noodles on a hot plate. I'm not being dramatic. Okay, yes I am.

Before you expose your family to a potentially serious financial loss, you really owe it to them to consider the benefits of community college. In a recent report, the Education Trust warned that "hundreds of thousands of young people leave our higher education system unsuccessfully, burdened with large student loans that must be repaid, but without the benefit of the wages a college degree provides." If your child is a B- or C+ student and you are concerned that she might not make it through college, community college is a fantastic trial run. Give her a few semesters to prove herself where the financial stakes are lower, and if she demonstrates commitment, you'll be able to send her off to a four-year college with confidence that your investment is a good one. Students who transfer from a community college to a four-year college typically have a very, very low dropout rate, because they've paid their dues, proven themselves, and developed the work ethic that so many students lack. This work ethic will also, by the way, serve them admirably when they enter the job market. And if your student completes just two years at a community college, he can be awarded an associate's degree, and studies have shown that associate's degree holders earn more than dropouts from four-year colleges.

Bottom line: it's entirely possible that your kid will drop out of college because he is unprepared or uncommitted. But—after adjusting for selection bias-related factors—there is really no evidence that any given student is less likely to drop out of one college than another.

Selling Your Kid on the Idea

When I was going through the college selection process—knowing that my family wouldn't be able to contribute much if anything to my educational expenses—I seriously considered the community college route. Ultimately I decided not to, because I wasn't willing to give up the experience of going away to school and because I was fortunate enough to be able to pay for it myself. However, most kids don't plan to pay for college without your help. If your kid is one of them, and you discover that the four-year-college-straight-out-of-high-school route will put you in a world of financial hurt, here is one way to convince your kid that it's a good idea: *show him the money!* Take a portion of the cash you'll save, and bribe him with it. Tell him that if he helps you save $30,000 by starting at a community college, you'll use $5,000 to buy him an amazing wardrobe or a car. This method tends to be more effective than the spreadsheets mentioned above. It's one that I learned from my Jewish social worker mother, who offered my brother a hundred dollars not to play Pop Warner football when he was six because she was afraid he'd get broken in half. (My dad's response: "What kind of thing is that for a therapist to do?" Mom: "I don't know, but it's a fine thing for a Jewish mother!")

Stay Away from For-Profit Colleges

A chapter about two-year colleges would not be complete without at least mentioning for-profit institutions. Run by large public companies like the Apollo Group, for-profit colleges such as the University of Phoenix and DeVry have been taking market share away from community colleges and even four-year institutions for decades. Especially in rough job markets, their promises of a career-oriented degree without that highfalutin liberal arts stuff has a certain appeal. Let me be clear that my reason for not endorsing for-profit colleges is not ideological. With very few exceptions, nonprofit colleges and universities in the United States are bastions of financial waste and poor cost control. But if a for-profit college can come along, cut the fat, and offer a compelling value proposition for students and their families while also making shareholders rich, I'd be all for it.

So far, though, that just hasn't happened. The University of Phoenix charges students $325 per credit for its online classes—more than what most public universities charge. Cape Cod Community College, for example, charges about $130 per credit. One of the reasons that I'm skeptical about the ability of for-profit institutions to ever become anything more than entities on the periphery of higher education is that they pay taxes—35 percent of their earnings—and that puts them at a considerable disadvantage to their untaxed nonprofit counterparts. A disadvantage that they charge their students to subsidize?

In 2007, *SF Weekly* took a detailed look at the California Culinary Academy (operating with the name Le Cordon Bleu as part of a licensing deal), a culinary education college that had recently been acquired by large for-profit companies. What *SF Weekly* found was a culture focused on increasing enrollment. The magazine reported, "The students claim admissions reps said it was a prestigious school that they would be lucky to gain admission to, when it actually admits anyone eligible for a student loan. The graduates say they were misled about the terms of their loans; many have since realized that by the time they finish making payments, they'll have paid more than $100,000 for just 15 months of school. Finally, the students and graduates we spoke to were told that a CCA degree virtually guaranteed them a well-paying job at an elite restaurant. In fact, the majority went on to low-paying kitchen jobs—and many soon left the food industry entirely in search of salaries that would pay off their student debt." Former admissions representatives at the school described a high-pressure, *Glengarry Glen Ross*–style work environment where admissions people were expected to enroll fifteen students per month—and say whatever it took to get them to sign and take out loans.

To be fair, you'd be hard-pressed to draw a principled distinction between the unethical marketing and bait-and-switch tactics used by for-profit colleges and their nonprofit counterparts. The real problem is that for-profit colleges are at such a competitive disadvantage that they are simply too expensive in comparison to nonprofit institutions. The differences in costs can be absolutely startling. An associate's degree in culinary arts from a for-profit institution can easily cost ten times as much as a comparable nonprofit program—and that difference can be much, much larger when you take into account the effect of interest payments on student loans.

For students interested in pursuing career-oriented education with a very specific goal in mind, there may be a role for for-profit colleges—although I'm still skeptical of how they could possibly provide anything so much better than community college options that they're worth the extra money. For anyone planning to transfer, make use of your local taxpayer-subsidized community college, because many of the credits from the for-profit programs do not transfer.

The Emotional Obstacles to Community College

Even though I'm usually able to convince people that, logically, community college might be a good option for the student in their lives, it's another thing to get them to actually seriously consider it. One of the hardest parts about making the community college leap is the perception of a social stigma attached. At least subconsciously, many parents dread the following dinner party conversation with an uppity friend or relative:

"Jeff just started at Pepperdine, and he's just absolutely loving the surfing. He barely has time to make it to class! Oh, by the way, where is Sam going?"

"Sam is living in the garage and going to Rising Tide Community College. He should be back from bagging at the grocery store around nine, but his boss is a real jerk so it might be more like nine-thirty. Can I offer you some more Easy Mac?"

I fully understand that societal expectations and peer pressure—for parents and students—often trump the more calculated approaches to investing in education. But, just as I said in Chapter 1, the thing that you have to keep in mind is this: the Joneses are broke. Getting into a college-spending arms race with people who are spending money they don't have is a dangerous game and, however alluring it might be, it's one that you absolutely must avoid, for your own future and your child's. When discussing your decision to send your kids to a community college with friends, feel free to make it clear to them that it was a choice your family made collectively because it was the best option, not because it was the only option. If you want to make them feel stupid, use phrases like, "We looked at all the data and the latest research, and we really concluded that this was the best investment decision."

Once You Make the Decision: How to Help Your Child Get the Most Out of Community College

Because the cost of community college is very low, it's important that your child work as much as possible—and save money—while she's taking classes there. This leads to the double whammy of financial success: saving money *on* the cost of the first two years of college and saving money *toward* the cost of the last two years. Once she's enrolled, it's a good idea to focus immediately on the transfer process that will come two years later. First, this will keep her attitude and confidence up. Second, while transferring to a four-year college is certainly doable, it requires some pretty careful planning. In order to make sure that your student will receive credit for all the classes she takes, she'll want to keep the guidance counselor at her community college and admissions officers at four-year colleges she's considering in the loop as she selects classes.

If your child is planning to transfer from a community college to an in-state public college, however, this process is often easy. Nearly all community colleges have articulation agreements set up with their state colleges and universities that spell out which credits transfer and how, and map out a path in black and white for students interested in certain majors on what classes they should take while at a community college. As I mentioned above in the case of the University of Virginia, many articulation agreements also include guaranteed admission to students who meet certain GPA requirements. Better still, some colleges offer special deals on tuition and fees to their community college transfers.

But be careful: it can get ugly. Like other businesses, colleges are always looking for ways to increase their revenue. One way they do this is by inventing clever methods for denying transfer credits, thereby forcing students to take additional classes and, if possible, keeping them there for an extra semester. This really does happen. Kay McClenney, a professor at the Community College Leadership Program at the University of Texas, Austin, told Jay Matthews, a *Washington Post* reporter with a specialty in higher education, "Universities are just expert in playing this game that says, 'Well, sure, you completed English composition, but you didn't take my class,' and sort of cheating students out of transfer credits by insisting that they retake essentially the same classes." If this seems diabolical and manipulative, it is. The best advice is to be extremely proactive and vigilant in your quest to transfer to a four-year college. Make sure your child is in touch by phone and via e-mail with admissions people before he's signed up for his first community college class, and that he stays in touch, keeping a detailed record of all e-mails with them. That way if they try to deny credits they had previously approved, your child can tell the admissions/registrar folks that he knows a really obnoxious writer who would love to do a story with the headline "How the University of X Rips Off Its Students."

As your child progresses through a year or two at a community college with the intent of transferring, he has a chance to continue to develop an impressive résumé. In addition to good grades, it's important to work on internships, gain job experience, and develop other résumé-builders just as a high school student looking to apply for college would. Honors programs within community colleges have become increasingly common, and it's certainly worth looking into those as they may provide opportunities for better classes and a chance to impress admissions officers.

Special Scholarships for Community College Graduates

While some colleges like to find ways to make life miserable for transfer students, many more go out of their way to make it easier. Here are a couple of examples:

* The University of Maryland University College offers $3,300 per year scholarships to community college transfers on a first come, first served basis. Tuition and fees for in-state students are just $5,760 per year, making the Maryland community college for two years followed by two years at UMUC a fantastically affordable option for Maryland residents.
* Graduates of Michigan community colleges with GPAs of 3.75 or higher are eligible for a $3,000 per year scholarship to Western Michigan University.

Many, many state colleges and universities have similar scholarships available as part of their articulation agreements with in-state community colleges. Check with community college transfer advisers for information on that.

The Compromise: Take Summer Classes at a Community College and Graduate Early

Let's say that you have a motivated ambitious student and are looking to save money, but just can't convince him to give up two years of the "college experience" to save cash.

This is the stuff summer classes are made for. For a much smaller amount of money than it would cost at a four-year college—less than $400 for a three-credit class, sometimes a lot less—students who are enrolled at four-year colleges can take community college classes over the summer. This is a fantastic way for students to knock off general education requirements that are ancillary to their majors, save a ton of cash, and, if they play it right, graduate a semester or more early.

The summer after my freshman year, I took a course on human sexuality through Cape Cod Community College. It costs $300 and was online, saving me the hassle of attending class and the awkwardness of sitting in a lecture hall learning about gonorrhea from an old man. Another important point on community college classes is this, and it's worth repeating to your student: if you have trouble with math but have to take a math class or two to fulfill major requirements, community college is the best place to do it. The classes are smaller and the instructor is likely to be more prepared for students who are lousy at the subject. The same is also true for other classes: if your child has to take a class that he isn't good at, community college is a good option.

There are some major mental and social obstacles to attending community college, but my research into the subject has made me incredibly confident in this: attending community college before transferring to a four-year institution will not harm your student's career prospects and will likely leave both you and her far better off financially. As college costs continue to skyrocket, I believe that more students should consider the community college option, including A and B students who traditionally would thumb their nose at these institutions.

CHAPTER 7

Make Money, Prepare for a Career

Nearly all colleges and universities pitch themselves as something far nobler than institutions of career education devoted to helping their avaricious pupils attain wealth. But guess what? For the most part, that's what kids are interested in college for. The 2007 Cooperative Institutional Research Program Freshman Survey collected data on over thirteen million college students at 1,900 institutions and found the following breakdown for priorities considered "essential" or "very important" by incoming college freshmen: "Raising a family" was number one at 77.5 percent, just barely beating out "being very well off financially." "Helping others who are in difficulty" was number three at 68.3 percent. Farther down the list were the things like "influencing the political structure" and "becoming a community leader."[1] Who cares about that?

In other words, my generation is pretty far removed from the values of our hippie parents. But I don't think there's anything wrong with that. If you want to make the world a better place, becoming financially self-sufficient is a really great place to start. But this leads to an interesting paradox. Many families spend a lot of time thinking about the collection selection process out of a belief that the right school will open doors to career success, but then once the student is in college, they don't really do the work that should start at the beginning of freshman year to make that dream career a reality.

To begin planting the seeds for a great career, young people should start by exploring some of the negative stereotypes that are giving Gen Y-ers a tough time in the job market. In January 2009, the unemployment rate among the under-twenty-nine crowd was 11 percent, compared with an overall unemployment rate of just 7.2 percent—that's more than 50 percent higher. The work-place consultant Lindsey Pollak advises young college-graduate job seekers to become aware of the stereotypes that surround our demographic. For her book *Getting from College to Career*, Pollak asked a handful of baby boomer and Generation X hiring manag-ers to give her their impressions of Gen Y workers. Here are the responses:

- "They feel a sense of entitlement, but they don't have the skills to back up their confidence."
- "They don't seem to build a career."
- "They're lazy."
- "They want instant feedback and instant gratification."

What better way could there be to proactively combat these stereo-types than by paying your own way through a public college while working multiple jobs? Some students—and well-intentioned adviser types—complain that working while in college can hinder academic performance, but I think it's a great way to stand out from the pack and quickly establish yourself as someone who isn't entitled, cares about building a career, isn't lazy, and is willing to put in long hours toward a long-term investment.

But still, there are a number of factors that complicate working while in college, starting with the financial aid equation.

Financial Aid and Working: How to Balance It

As I mentioned in the very first chapter of this book, the bureau-cracy of the FAFSA form tosses a real wrench into students' plans to work their way through college. Of a student's earnings, 50 percent over $3,000 per year is deducted from any financial aid he would otherwise receive. That's stupid, un-American, and hypocritical, but that's the way the system works, at least for now. I've written letters to just about every influential person I can think of begging them to change a system that provides more assistance to students who play video games than those who work, but it is what it is until some-one wakes up and changes it. So if your child is in a situation where he qualifies for a huge amount of need-based aid, it might be that it doesn't make sense for him to earn more than the $3,000 per year. If, however, he only receives, say, $2,000 per year in grant aid, it probably makes sense for him to work hard and earn more money—even if that means forgoing some financial aid.

Generally speaking, the more financial aid your child receives, the less it will make sense for him to work. On the other hand, if most of his financial aid comes in the form of student loans, it is much better to work and pay cash and give up low-interest loans. It should also be noted that even though 50 percent of earnings over $3,000 are subtracted from financial aid eligibility, that still leaves another 50 percent—meaning that for every ten dollars a student earns toward college expenses, he still comes out five dollars ahead. For this rea-son, the advice that students should "limit" the amount of work they do to avoid messing up their financial aid eligibility—advice you'll read in most books and guides—is wrong. It's like saying that you shouldn't work too much because you'll have to pay more taxes. The more you earn, the more you keep, and the more your child works, the more money she'll have to put toward college.

The thing to watch out for here is this: if you are like most American parents and your child works during the summer but doesn't contribute toward his education, this is very bad. Your financial aid eligibility will decrease without any increase in the cash you have to pay for college. So if you're committed to not requiring your student to make a financial contribution to his education—and if you're in that camp, you probably put this book down a long time ago—make sure he doesn't earn more than a couple of thousand dollars per year. Then head to a doctor to figure out why you're slaving away and expecting nothing from the most direct beneficiary of your investment.

Why Working During College Won't Hurt Your Kid's Prospects

The average college student wastes an enormous amount of time. I don't have a study to prove that, but I've spent enough time on a college campus to know that that's the case. To quote *Calvin and Hobbes* creator Bill Watterson, "There is not enough time to do all the nothing we want to do." Consider that according to Nielsen, college students watch an average of 24.3 hours of television per week.[2] That's far, far more television than the average American watches, and in 2006 Nielsen decided to start including college students in its television ratings, believing it would provide networks with the greatest advertising revenue. Watching repeats of *Gilmore Girls* does not qualify as a valuable use of time, and students will be much better off if they have less time for such trivialities. Tell your kid that if you're going to help him attend college, you expect him to sacrifice some television time to help pay the bills. According to the American Psychiatry Association, 40 percent of college students "drink heavily." The notion that you or your child should go into debt so that he has more time available to watch sitcoms while drunk is just absolutely appalling. Trust me: success in college requires hard work, but there is still plenty of time left over students to be gainfully employed.

The need and opportunity to work a part-time job to help pay for college can cut down on the amount of time that students waste, and help them develop strong time management skills that will serve them well throughout their lives. The key is to find a job that will allow your student to schedule his hours around classes. You are spending far too much money for him to have to pass up taking classes that interest him (or are important for fulfilling graduation requirements) in order to earn eight or ten dollars an hour. Happily, the vast majority of companies that employ college students are very accommodating when it comes to class schedules.

Dave Ramsey, who paid his way through college selling real estate, summed up his attitude this way: "As an employer if you come into my office out of college and you want to be hired and you tell me you worked three part-time jobs to get yourself through college, that is as impressive as the fact that you have the college degree, because I know that not only are you smart, but you know how to work. If you walk into my office and go, 'I've got six degrees and seven million dollars in student loans and I've never worked a day in my life,' I'm not interested." This is a key reason that working during college is important: it gives students a chance to build their résumés and demonstrate the time management and work ethic qualities that employers so badly want and so often find lacking in young workers.

Determining How Much Your Child Can and Should Work

Most college experts suggest that students work "at most" ten to fifteen hours per week, with vague warnings that working more will harm student performance and very possibly a student's chances of graduating in four years. According to a study commissioned by UPromise, Inc., "Working a limited number of hours (e.g., 10 hours a week) at an on-campus job appears to have positive impacts on student performance, while working a significant number of hours (e.g., 35 hours or more per week) has adverse consequences. It is unclear at what point student employment moves from being beneficial to being counterproductive. . . . However, full-time employment may impair student performance. For example, 55 percent of those students working 35 or more hours per week report that work has a negative effect on their studies. Students working full-time also reported the following liabilities: 40 percent report that work limits their class schedule; 36 percent report it reduces their class choices; 30 percent report it limits the number of classes they take; and 26 percent report it limits access to the library."[3]

"College Student Employment," a 1993 report published in the *Journal of Student Financial Aid*, shows a table illustrating GPAs of students based on their employment status. Here's a shocker: students who worked eleven to twenty hours per week reported a higher average GPA (2.75) than students who didn't work at all (2.69). Weirder still, students who worked forty-one-plus hours per week reported the same average GPA as students who didn't work at all!

A narrow majority of students report that working more than thirty-five hours per week has a negative impact on their studies, but that number could probably be ameliorated somewhat with better study skills and, let's face it, less partying. Maybe thirty-five hours would be too much for your child to work, so it might be a better idea for him to start out by working twenty hours per week, and then toggling that number up or down based on his perception of stress. But even working just fifteen hours per week can have a huge positive impact on your family's ability to pay for college: if she works fifteen hours per week and earns eight dollars per hour, that's $120 per week and approximately $500 per month. Multiply that by the eight months a year she's in school and you have $4,000. She can pay for her living expenses from her summers, when she works at least forty hours per week (ideally quite a bit more).

That $4,000 is enough to cover at least a third of the cost of attendance at most public universities—working just fifteen hours per week, not including any summer earnings. This leads me to one of my main contentions in this book: a public university education is basically very affordable for hard-working students who are willing to make sacrifices. I broke it down for you in Chapter 1, showing that a student who works reasonably hard and gets a few hundred dollars per year in parental help can easily come up with the cash to pay for a public education.

But there's more. The study showing that students who work thirty-five hours or more per week find their study time constricted conflicts with another study, one that rings truer with young people who have been through the college experience. Outside the Classroom and Student Affairs Administrators in Higher Education surveyed 30,183 college freshmen from seventy-six colleges and universities. Nearly 70 percent reported that they had consumed alcohol in the two weeks before the course began. Students were asked to report how long their drinking episodes lasted, how many drinks they had, and how long it took them to finish each drink. The organizations then used that data to estimate how much time the average college student spent drinking each week. The answer: 10.2 *hours*. Just for fun, Outside the Classroom and NASPA also asked students to estimate how much time they spent each week on a handful of other activities. Here are the results:

Studying: 8.4 hours
Exercising: 5 hours
Online social networking and video games: 4.1 hours
Working for pay: 2.5 hours

So by eliminating video games and Facebook and cutting drinking time in half, I just found 9.2 hours of newly available free time that can be used for working for pay. Cut the amount of television watching in half and you have another 12.15 hours per week, and pretty soon you have a student working twenty-one hours each week—while taking a full course load, drinking regularly, and watching twelve hours per week of *Full House* reruns.

All the guidelines, studies, and logic aside, the best way to find out how much work is too much is to have your child start working and see what happens. It's also a good idea to keep some sort of informal diary of time devoted to various activities. I considered myself high-functioning until I did this and realized that, even while taking a full course load, working on a book, investing in real estate, and working as a writer and editor with *AOL Money & Finance*, I was still wasting at least a few hours each day surfing the Internet mindlessly or watching stupid TV shows.

I'm not saying that people should have absolutely no downtime to read *US Weekly*. I'm a subscriber myself! But the notion that being a full-time student is such a full-time job that students can't possibly be expected to work too is nonsense.

A Word About Work-Study

If you fill out the FAFSA form and demonstrate financial need, your child may qualify for the Federal Work-Study Program. If so, he should absolutely take them up on it. Work-study funds do not count against your child when he goes to apply for financial aid the following year. Better still, it's guaranteed work, so you don't have to worry about not being able to find a job. So if he receives work-study, he absolutely must take as many hours of that as possible before looking for other jobs. Of course, if he has an extremely lucrative non-work-study position he may not want to give that up, but honestly, with the way FAFSA penalizes non-work-study earnings, it's unlikely that his other job will pay enough to make it worth forgoing the free money of work-study. Work-study hours are assigned with an extremely conservative eye toward the student's college needs, and the various places that employ work-study students are very accommodating. So there's no excuse not to take work-study hours if they're awarded based on your financial need.

And yet many students do just that. National data is hard to come by on this subject, but at the University of Minnesota, the financial aid office normally awards approximately double the amount of work-study hours it can actually assign because about half of students fail to take advantage. Not taking advantage of work-study is one of the biggest college financing mistakes that people can make. Your child absolutely must work every work-study hour he qualifies for.

Don't Get a Job at the Dining Hall!

The problem with work-study is that, at many colleges student-workers are often pushed into menial tasks with very limited networking and career-building prospects. Students who qualify for work-study should talk with the office at their college that handles work-study and get an idea of the full range of options available for work-study jobs. It may be possible to score a job working on research with a professor as part of work-study. There's nothing wrong with getting a job stamping books at the library, but students may be able to do better with a little bit of extra effort and inquiry. The work that students do during college can be every bit as important in their career prospects as the majors they choose and the classes they take, so it's worth doing some digging to find interesting opportunities.

After work-study hours have been completed, it's time to get a little bit more creative in the search for part-time work. My experience is that most students don't put nearly enough energy into finding low-paying part-time jobs, and deprive themselves of opportunities to meet interesting people, network, and explore possible career paths that they otherwise never would have been exposed to. Here are a few jobs that are worth looking into that most students overlook—even though most students could probably get them.

Caddying

Think about it. You spend the day on the golf course, carrying clubs for rich people while making small talk. You can get big tips (in cash, so an unethical person might forget to report them on the FAFSA form) and possibly network your way into some great opportunities. You'll learn about golf and country club etiquette, and be well on your way to joining the ruling class that divides up the rest of our lives during leisurely strolls alongside the cart path. If there's a golf course near your student's college—which there probably is—this can be a fantastic fall and spring job, and possibly even year-round depending on the region. Your kid just might find his next job on the links!

Bartending

This is a great skill to learn in college, partly because it can make your student an exceptionally desirable host or hostess—and save him thousands of dollars because he'll be proud to entertain at home instead of hitting the bars with friends. And twenty-four states don't even require bartenders to be twenty-one years old. By gaining training as a bartender, college students will have a skill that is in demand and not held by most of their peers. They can also earn a lot more than waiters and waitresses and meet people in the process. Plus it is, I'm told, a fun and somewhat glamorous line of work. And if times are tough when your child graduates and enters the workforce, she can find a job as a bartender on nights and weekends without having it conflict with her day job. If you think this is something that might interest your college student, a quick Google search will turn up a lot of information.

Personal Training

Personal trainers can earn twenty-five dollars an hour or more when working with clients—and if you're good and develop a strong clientele, it can be considerably higher. But the best reason for college students to seek this certification—and it only makes sense if health and fitness are a passion—is that it can give you a big leg up in getting desk jobs at local gyms. Even if it only pays ten or fifteen dollars an hour, it's a steady job and you'll have a competitive advantage in getting it. The American Council on Exercise is the leading certifier of personal trainers in the United States. The test for certification costs about $250 and the exam training materials cost $150. It's a fairly low price to pay for a pretty good shot at a decent-paying college job. And, like bartending, it can also be a good moonlighting job for those tough financial times that so many students will face after graduation. Or it can be a great way to save up for the down payment for a first home.

Selling on eBay

Before I was old enough to work legally, I went to yard sales with my mother every weekend and bought stuff for resale. By browsing through listings, I developed strong niches in a few areas and developed a knowledge of what was worth buying and what wasn't. I specialized in used video games and modern first-edition books and made more money during the summer when I was in sixth grade than most kids a few years older made slaving away as busboys. And I bet I had more fun! If your student has reasonably good computer and organizational skills, he may be able to make some extra money by offering to help friends and friends' parents sell unwanted items on eBay in exchange for a cut of the money. Now that I'm in college and working more than full-time between my various writing gigs,

I don't have time to sell stuff on eBay myself. But when I went to decorate my new condo, buying everything at yard sales, I started buying for resale again with the help of a college friend who agreed to do all the listing and shipping for a percent of the proceeds. Guess what? I've been able to decorate the condo without spending any of my own money.

Delivering Newspapers

This one is not for the faint of heart, but if your student opted to bring his car to school, a newspaper route could be a great job. And since he'll be done by seven a.m., it won't interfere with classes. Incidentally, delivering newspapers—and eventually hiring other people to deliver newspapers—was how Warren Buffett built up the capital that formed the basis for his empire. The newspaper industry is in decline, but if you look through the ads, you'll notice that they are almost always trying to hire delivery people.

If It Sounds Too Good to Be True . . .

I was leaving a class in the building that houses the University of Massachusetts's school of management when I saw this sign on a bulletin board: "ATTENTION ALL STUDENTS. Prepare Mailings in Your Spare Time: Weekly Paychecks. Up to $938.00 Possible Per Week." To my horror I saw that a great number of students had already ripped off the tabs containing the Web site address. Wanting to spare my classmates future heartbreak and wasted time and money, I ripped the flyer off the wall and took it back to my dorm so I could write a warning about it.

But the reality is that college campuses are a hotbed for financial scams. You have large numbers of naive, impressionable people who lack life experience and are desperate for cash but also, on average, not particularly interested in working hard. So I logged onto the Web site for this great work-from-your-dorm-room opportunity and found about what I was expecting. StudentWorkNow.com wasn't really offering anyone jobs—or maybe it was. But to find out more, you had to pay $29.95 plus a five-dollar "one-time processing fee." I'm sure you can see where this is going.

The point is that there are a ton of unscrupulous people looking to take advantage of college students who are hard up for cash. Here are a few "opportunities" you should warn your college student to steer clear of:

• "Work from your dorm room doing menial tasks for a lot of money." Anyone who needs envelopes stuffed or Web sites browsed can find someone in Bangladesh to do it for far, far less than your kid would ever dream of working for. Don't pay a dime to learn more about "opportunities" like this.

• Anything that involves an up-front investment. If you have to "spend money to make money," it should mean that you're starting your own business. Anyone who offers you a job that consists of giving them fifty or a hundred dollars first is most likely ripping you off.

• Multilevel marketing. This is largely a regional phenomenon. Companies like Amway, Usana, Herbalife, and Pre-Paid Legal Services have strong organizations in place in the South but are much less influential in New England for a combination of reasons. These "network marketing" systems, as they are sometimes called, closely resemble pyramid schemes, and most objective research shows that over 99 percent of participants lose money. Any "business opportunity" that involves buying products and recruiting other people to do the same is probably something that should be avoided. Sure, there are a number of people who have earned large incomes with companies like Mary Kay—but selling stuff to your friends or trying to recruit them into a business opportunity is a good way to become a pariah.

The Benefits of Sales Jobs

As great as it would be for your student to use his undergrad years to launch a successful start-up or gain valuable work experience in a field he can take by storm upon graduation, this isn't going to happen for a large chunk of people. Only a small minority of college students are cut out for entrepreneurship, and many others simply lack a clear enough idea of what they want to do for a career to aggressively position themselves in that field.

For that large group of students, I think that commissioned sales jobs have a lot to recommend them, for a couple reasons:

- You will *always* be able to get a job in commissioned sales. A student who generates revenue for the employer gets paid. If he doesn't, he doesn't. It's low-risk for the company.
- Sales skills are important in almost any job—especially in the "new economy," where an ever-increasing percentage of the workforce is freelance and drumming up new business is a constant part of life.

I'm not the only person singing the praises of sales experience for young people. In an op-ed piece for the *New York Times*, the writer, actor, and economist Ben Stein recently wrote about his experience as a small-town shoe salesman in his teens: "Lawyers and doctors and dentists and politicians and accountants and actors—all of us sell something, every day and every time we meet someone. For me, it all goes back to Shoe Giant, 47 years ago, and I wish that every

17-year-old I know could have that experience. It takes some ability at sales to believe in your own future, no matter what that future may be."[4]

The "Job Outlook 2004" report from the National Association of Colleges and Employers reported, "Unfortunately, the skill employers value most—communication skills—is the skill employers think most students often lack."[5] Sales experience can certainly help to build strong communication skills, which is another reason it can be a good choice for college students. Shy students might not be naturally born salespeople, but the experience might help them gain confidence and prepare them for the postcollegiate job hunt, which is, as the cliché goes, really just about selling yourself.

Student Fellowships and Grants

For college students who earn strong grades and are willing to do some extra work, there are a number of paid student fellowship opportunities. Students should check with career services offices at their colleges, along with professors, department chairs, and department secretaries for more information about these opportunities. One of the best tips for ambitious college students is this: when you pass a bulletin board in a building at your university, take a second to scan it for fellowship, internship, scholarship, and job opportunities.

Participate in Experiments

One of the most commonly overlooked ways to earn extra cash in college—especially at large research universities—is participation in academic research and experiments. Participation in clinical trials tends to lead to the largest paydays, and can have other side benefits as well: some studies focus on nutrition, diet, and weight loss, and I have one friend who lost quite a few pounds participating in a diet and exercise study—and got paid for it. But it's also possible to develop a nice side income participating in mundane but noninvasive experiments in departments like psychology, linguistics, and anthropology. Harvard University's psychology department pays ten dollars an hour for participation in its experiments. Of course there's the off chance that you could end up scarred for life by a modern-day Stanford prison experiment, but hey: ten dollars is ten dollars, and there's always the chance of hitting the class-action jackpot if something goes wrong.

If you're looking for a quick buck by participating in research, here are some links to help get you started:

- The cleverly named ClinicalTrials.gov offers the definitive searchable database of clinical trials.
- TheHairTrader.com is *the* place to sell your hair online.
- BloodBanker.com (which is, I'm told, different from Countrywide Financial) has a searchable listing of plasma donation sites.

Entrepreneurship

This money-making venture definitely isn't for everyone, but quite a few hugely successful businesses have been started by full-time college students: Microsoft, Facebook, Napster, Dell, Wing Zone, and many, many others. Need a more recent, accessible example? In 2008 Susie Levitt and Katie Shea were juniors at New York University and they were tired of trudging around the city in painful heels—but according to their Web site, they "simply were unwilling to (totally) give up on these beloved wardrobe staples. And yet, corporate internships, subway dashes, dinner dates, the NYC social scene . . . all of the above led to too many moments of hobbling, near tears, back to their Union Square apartments. The front door never seemed to come soon enough." So they created CitiSoles, a line of foldable ballet-slipper-style shoes that also—and this is pretty cool— expand into a fully functional tote bag. They launched the business with virtually no money, and conducted extensive research online to find out how to outsource the manufacturing of the product. Citi-Soles are now sold in seventeen boutiques all over the country.

Of course, the best stories and the most money will come from students who have brilliant ideas. Don't have any of those just yet? Here are a few ideas for "dorm-based businesses" that students can start:

• A cleaning service: Most dorm rooms are pretty messy, which is, as you'll remember, yet another reason that you shouldn't let amenities dictate your child's college choice. But could an enterprising student make a few bucks by offering to vacuum, Windex, decontaminate, and deodorize the dorm rooms of people who live in his building? Perhaps. I once mulled over starting a dorm room cleaning business called Dust Bunnies that would consist of coeds in Playboy bunny costumes cleaning dorm rooms to techno music, but never got around to it. If you think it has potential, tell your kid about it. No need to thank me!

• Tutoring: As an ever-increasing percentage of high school graduates enroll in college, an increasing number of college students are ill-prepared for the rigors of undergraduate coursework. According to the latest ACT results, 75 percent of incoming freshmen have at least one area where they're unprepared for college. If your student was an academic standout in high school—and has the SAT scores/GPA to prove it—she may be able to make a good amount of money tutoring her peers or helping younger students prepare for college.

- Editing: This one is similar to tutoring. Have you ever read the absolute garbage that students hand in for term papers in college? If your student is an exceptionally good writer and has a knack for turning literary pumpkins into horse-drawn carriages, he may be able to make a nice side income helping classmates improve their grades by editing their term papers. Just tell him to make sure that he doesn't actually write the papers for people, which, in addition to being sleazy, can also lead to expulsion and a slew of other nasty consequences.

- Professional note taker: In his book *Confessions of a Street Addict,* Jim Cramer describes how he made it through Harvard Law School. He and a group of classmates formed a note-taking ring where each student went to one class per semester and took incredibly copious notes and then distributed them to the other members of the ring. The result was that everyone was able to do well in the class while only actually going once. I'm not suggesting that anyone participate in this, but if your student is the anal-retentive, write-down-everything-the-professor-says type, he may be able to make a few bucks selling notes to less ambitious classmates.

Temping

The temporary labor market is seen as purgatory for recent grads who can't find full-time jobs in their fields, but for college students, it may be worth applying for work with temporary employment agencies like Office Team, Kelly Services, and Manpower. Web sites like Craigslist can also be good sources for local jobs in a wide variety of industries. A variation of temping is freelancing, which can be an excellent opportunity for students who have an interest in and an aptitude for writing and/or Web design. Here are a few Web sites that can help the enterprising student get started.

Suite101.com

This Web site has a network of over two thousand freelance writers, and explicitly states that it likes to work with journalism students. Payment is based entirely on advertising revenue for your articles: if more people click on your post, you'll make more money. You won't get rich with Suite101, but it does provide an outlet to get your work published and, equally important, get your name up there when people Google you. Suite101's pieces tend to rank very high in Google search results. This is a great site for trying to develop a niche area of expertise and possibly parlay it into bigger and better things. The site is looking for content on an enormous range of topics. Suite101 has grown very well of late and currently boasts an Alexa ranking of 1,641, making it one of the most trafficked Web sites in the world.

Elance.com

This is the largest online marketplace for freelance writing, editing, and Web design gigs and operates as an auction. People who need freelancers post the jobs online and the freelancers bid for the job. The lowest bidder generally gets it (unless the site/business hiring decides someone else will do a better job). The problem with this site is that there is always going to be someone who values their time less than you value yours. Overseas writers generally work a lot cheaper, and I've heard stories about people bidding $2,000 to ghostwrite an eighty-thousand-word book—not a good deal! It's not at all uncommon to see people writing five-hundred-word articles for two dollars. Elance is a meat market, and most of the jobs probably won't lead to bigger and better things because they're for small businesses and/or Web sites that aren't going anywhere. However, students may be able to earn some money and possibly make contacts that can lead to better things if they are selective and do great work. This site can also help build a sizable and varied portfolio.

Network Like a Pro: Send E-mails

The best career advice you can ever give to your kid—aside from the usual clichés about hard work—is this: *Send e-mails to people you respect and admire. You never know what will come of it.* Reaching out to people is always good advice, but it's especially good now. Here's why: back when you were growing up, you probably had a hero, someone you looked up to and admired, and would have loved to receive some career advice from. Let's say it was Andy Rooney. So you want to get in touch with Andy Rooney. What do you do? You send him a letter. Now because it's Andy Rooney, he gets lots of mail, and doesn't get to open most of it himself. It gets sorted through by secretaries who forward him the important stuff—your letter probably doesn't make the cut. But let's say it does. Let's say that Andy Rooney personally reads all his own mail. He gets to your letter and decides he'll humor you and send back some tips. But wait: that involves calling a secretary over to dictate a typewritten letter, who will then have to put it an envelope and write your address, and spend a couple cents on postage. Guess what? That's probably not going to happen. Today, it's different. Most people in the business world read their own e-mail and, with a couple of clicks of the mouse, they can send back an e-mail. It takes less than two minutes to send a fairly detailed response to a young admirer.

Even with old-fashioned letters, this can work out spectacularly well. When he was still in high school, the aspiring musician Bobby Lopez wrote a letter to Stephen Sondheim, a legendary composer he looked up to. He met an acquaintance of Sondheim's who agreed to pass on the letter. Sondheim wrote back, and a few years later, Lopez had won a Tony Award for cowriting the music and lyrics to *Avenue Q*—with Stephen Sondheim.

During my senior year of high school, when I was busy blogging for AOL from my school's library (much to the chagrin of the librarian, who made a habit of yelling at me for using the computer for something other than schoolwork), I decided to send a post I wrote to Andrew Tobias, a bestselling financial writer and treasurer of the Democratic National Committee. I wasn't really expecting a reply, but thought I'd toss in a little bit about how much I admired his work and how it had influenced me. Long story short, he replied, we ended up talking, and he invited me to New York City to meet him and be his guest at a fund-raiser for then-senator Barack Obama. He seated me next to David Kuhn, a literary agent, and I pitched him on the idea for this book. That's pretty much how the whole thing happened. I sent an e-mail.

The connectivity of the Internet has flattened the barriers between the "connected" and the "unconnected"—which is, perhaps, further eroding the supposed value of the networking opportunities that come with attending a prestigious school.

Using the Internet to Attract Employers

My generation is the first to have the Internet playing a major role in the career-search process—for good and for bad. The Internet can help your child land the job of his dreams, and it can also scuttle any chance he has at getting hired. It all depends on what happens when the human resources manager types the student's name into Google.

A 2005 survey of 102 executive recruiters by ExecuNet found that 75 percent used search engines to uncover information on job applicants, and more than a third of those report having eliminated an applicant from contention because of information found on Google.[6] Those numbers have likely increased since 2005 and seem likely to continue to do so for the foreseeable future. The ease with which human resources people can do research online adds a new dimension to the job-search process. For instance, it is against the law for an employer to ask an applicant whether they have ever been arrested—they're only allowed to ask about felonies. But if they do a search for the candidate on Google and find out that he was arrested for urinating on a sidewalk during a frat party freshman year? It's technically illegal to discriminate based on that, but let's be realistic: your kid will probably be eliminated from the hunt for that position, and will have no way of proving it was because of that Google search.

And what about Facebook and other social networking sites? At least 80 percent of college students use Facebook—and one CareerBuilder survey found that 45 percent of hiring managers use Facebook and other social networking sites to screen job applicants. Thirty-five percent have lost interest in a candidate based on information found on that Web site.[7] That number is also expected to rise over the next few years as social networking sites gain in mainstream popularity. One lawyer told me that he had been interviewing recent law school graduates for a position at his firm and thought he had found the perfect one until he checked him on Facebook. Under "interests" he found "Lubin' Yo Mama." The guy was quickly eliminated from the hunt. "It's indicative of a lack of professionalism and bad judgment—neither of which are character traits I want in my practice."

One way to get over the Facebook problem is to simply make the profile private. But that seems like a cop-out. When your student applies for jobs, chances are that at least one hiring manager will be looking him up on that site: Wouldn't it be better to just make sure that the Facebook page is classy and use it as a kind of guerrilla-marketing tool—a way to gain a leg up on the competition? It's very easy: if the student is under twenty-one, he shouldn't post or allow himself to be tagged in any pictures that feature underage drinking or general sloppiness. Under interests and hobbies, emphasize more upmarket pursuits instead of "Beirut" (a drinking game) and "Lubin' Yo Mama."

Beyond merely purging Facebook of objectionable content, here are two other steps that can be taken to give employers a good impression when they Google:

• Write occasionally for your college's newspaper (assuming it's published online). Even if writing and journalism aren't a passion, most students have (or at least should have) some interest that drives them and might impress potential employers. Does your student have a social conscience? Is he interested in raising awareness for some social justice issue? Encourage him to get involved and get press—it'll come in handy when employers Google him. Incidentally, this "Google effect" is a fantastic reason students should avoid any chicanery that could get them a write-up in the police briefs. Years ago, the incident would have been quickly forgotten and something you could laugh about with friends. Today, though, it may very well live on in Googleable police briefs. Even if he doesn't end up with a record, the bad press could easily dissuade prospective employers.

• Let's say that your child is a history major—how can he distinguish himself from the pack? He could start by reading a lot of history books, because if he doesn't like reading history books for fun, he's in the wrong major. Then he can post reviews on Amazon.com and read some books and essays on book review writing to get good at it. Do this for four years and by the time you graduate, you're one of Amazon.com's top-ranked reviewers. That's got to impress prospective employers and graduate schools.

Above all, my message for working during college is this: students should view their work experience as being as important as their formal educational experience. Of course making money is one primary objective, but ambitious students should look to summer and weekend jobs as an opportunity to explore passions, make connections, and build resumes. And I've said this before, but it's worth saying again: a student who works her way through college is also constructing a personal narrative that employers will find incredibly impressive.

CHAPTER 8

How Your Child Can Save Money While He's in College

The financial well-being of a college student as he walks across the stage at graduation is generally measured in terms of just how negative his net worth is. The average debt load is over $21,000, and most students will spend years toiling away in a cubicle, living in an apartment, and eating ramen, counting down the years—and sometimes decades—until they can achieve a net worth of zero.

As I've shown in previous chapters, it is possible for your child to graduate from college with little or no debt through the savvy selection of an affordable college, hard work, and frugality. Now I'm going to show you how you and your son or daughter can go medieval on college costs. If your student elects to attend an affordable public college, textbooks and living expenses will make up a large chunk of his overall college bill—probably more than half, so it's important to look for ways to minimize these expenses whenever possible.

We'll start by talking about textbook costs, because this is one category that really makes me mad.

The Great Textbook Rip-Off

One of the greatest rip-offs in the world of college is perpetuated by the textbook cartel. Hard data is difficult to find, but the average student spends somewhere in the vicinity of $400 per semester on textbooks, although a portion of that can be recouped by searching around for the best deals on used books. The reason I say that the textbook industry is a cartel is this: it is! Textbooks are updated regularly, often for little or no reason. My favorite example—mainly because it's so obviously absurd—is *Wheelock's Latin*, which was updated in 2005, after having been updated ten years earlier as well. What could possibly have changed since 1995 in the introductory instruction of a language that no one speaks? Here's what changed: most students who take a course have no need for the book after the class is complete and, being cash-strapped college students, they head off to the bookstore to swap their old books for cash. The result is that after a few years on the market, there is a huge surplus of used books (unless the book's popularity is growing exponentially), which means, of course, no money for the publisher. The result is that, to stay in business, publishers have to update textbooks as frequently as they possibly can. The growth of the Internet and the ease with which used textbooks can be located will make this even worse in the future. The high prices on the books—and the captive audience of students literally required to buy the books—make texts extremely lucrative for publishers. Case in point: in light of the weak economy, Houghton Mifflin announced in November 2008 that it would no longer be acquiring any new books until further notice. The only division of the company that wasn't affected? Textbooks, because they're so low-risk. Here are a few ways to save money on textbooks:

* Rent textbooks: This method gets mixed reviews. Textbooks have such a short useful life because of constant updating

that the rental prices are not nearly as cheap as you might think. For instance Chegg.com—one of the top textbook rental sites—offers Marilyn Stokstad's textbook *Art History* for $51.87 per semester. You can buy it used on Amazon.com for $82.99 as I write this, but then you can sell it back to eCampus.com for $46, meaning that the rental is actually about $5.87 more expensive. That's not a big difference and of course there's some variation from book to book. Bottom line: renting textbooks might shave a little off the cost of college and is worth exploring, but be sure to take into account the money you can get back when you sell books at the end of a semester.

• Get them at the library: It may be possible to simply get the required textbooks out of the library, but it's important to check them out before someone else comes up with the same idea. In literature courses for which students are required to use a number of books for short periods of time, this is a good approach. And if the college library doesn't have it, check the local library and various interlibrary loan systems.

• Buy old textbooks: In the fall of my sophomore year of college, I wrote about my plan to save money on textbooks on WalletPop.com. "I already have my course schedule, so I went online to look for my books. One of them—*Before the Law*, a requirement for my Introduction to Legal Studies class—comes in two editions, both available used on Amazon. The 8th Edition will cost me a minimum of $41.54 used but, if I'm willing to settle for 2001's 7th Edition, it'll cost me 1 cent. That's a savings of 99.9759268%!" I bought the old edition and had literally no problem. . . . It was all the same material. There was some minor variation in pagination but certainly not enough to justify spending 4,154 times as much money. I know that in some cases this won't work: the new edition truly will be different. But I've used this method in a number of classes and never had a problem.

Why Students Should Move Off Campus ASAP

Yet another advantage to attending a large state university is the opportunity to save money by living off-campus. Many private colleges require students to live on-campus for all four years—often at inflated prices. At public colleges, policies vary. Some allow students to commute for all four years while others require students to live on-campus until they are sophomores or juniors. Most public colleges have some policy for commuter students but many private colleges don't. All other things being equal, a college with the least stringent requirements for on-campus housing is best.

A big part of the reason that the right to live off-campus is so important is that the college arms race of luxury has made eating at the dining hall outrageously expensive. As a freshman and sophomore at the University of Massachusetts, this irritated me to no end—perhaps more so than most, because I was paying my own way. "I could go to Ihop for breakfast, Wendy's for lunch, and Applebee's for dinner for the price that I pay to eat three meals a day at this place," I complained to my friend, the manager of one of the school's dining halls. "Well yeah," he said. "But is Ihop all you can eat?" I gave up and walked away, appalled that this otherwise rational human being didn't see the insanity of a meal plan at a public college that was comparable to restaurant dining, which is, as Suze Orman will tell you, a sure recipe for long-term poverty.

Why on-campus food is such a rip-off at the vast majority of colleges and universities is something of a mystery. Given their non-profit status (no income tax!) and the ease with which they can predict demand—most students eat there every night, so there should be minimal waste—college food should be very affordable. Why isn't it? My hunch is that the nonprofit culture leads to a tremendous amount of waste in the form of excess staffing and inflated salaries. With the help of some serious overtime, an assistant manager at one of UMass's dining halls earned over $80,000 in 2008. According to

Salary.com, the median annual earnings for an assistant manager are just $37,717—meaning this individual is likely paid at least double his fair market value.

But the point is that on-campus dining is a complete rip-off. Worse, eating on-campus deprives students of the opportunity to learn cooking and budgeting skills that will help them when they're out on their own in the real world. I know quite a few recent college graduates who eat virtually all their meals at restaurants and convenience stores, wasting a huge amount of money. If they'd had to budget for their own meals in college—when they had minimal access to cash—they likely would have better skills and habits today.

According to the College Board, room and board costs at private colleges were $8,149 for the 2006/07 school year, up 5 percent from the previous year. For public schools, the average room and board cost rose 5.1 percent, to $6,960. At public colleges, room and board is often 50 percent or more of the overall cost of attendance, so it's important to look for ways to bring that cost down. Incidentally, this is another reason to avoid chic private colleges in expensive locales (I'm not going to name any names, but an institution that rhymes with Eww Pork University comes to mind): off-campus housing can be prohibitively expensive. In more rural/suburban college towns, housing expenses fall quite a bit. Katherine L. Cohen, Ph.D., founder and CEO of IvyWise LLC, recently ranked Amherst, Massachusetts, the best college town in North America because of its "great public transportation, easy access to affordable resources and a community that supports a vibrant social and cultural environment." Off-campus housing in most "college towns" is reasonably affordable compared with urban areas.

One of the most common myths about on-campus housing is that it's affordable. It isn't. For the 2007/08 school year, the University of Miami charged its students $970 per month to live in hundred-square-foot rooms. As Marc Scheer points out in his book

No Sucker Left Behind, "Miami students could have rented average 600-square-foot one-bedroom apartments close to the school for $1,000 a month." On a per-square-foot basis, on-campus living is exceptionally expensive. A fantastic way to save on college costs is to rent a house or apartment with a few friends or acquaintances— If you put four people in a thousand-square-foot apartment, you have twice as much space per person as in a dorm and you'll most likely pay a fraction of what you'd pay for on-campus housing.

One word of warning though: when it comes to financial aid, living off-campus presents yet another opportunity for the college to screw you (and yet another reason I am such a big fan of relying on financial aid as little as possible in paying for college). Reed College, for instance, reports on its Web site that on-campus room and board costs $10,250 for on-campus living, and that is factored into financial aid awards. But what if you live off-campus? Your financial aid eligibility will automatically drop to just $6,010.

So what is Reed College saying? That its facilities are such a total rip-off that you can save $4,240 just by living off-campus? More likely, the $6,010 figure is just a protectionist measure designed to preserve demand for the college's dorm space and services. If your child ends up attending a private college and receives a considerable amount of need-based financial aid, you will need to check on the allowance for living expenses offered to students who live off-campus. Some colleges keep the living-expense allowance the same for students regardless of where they live. This strikes me as the fairest and most honest method for financial aid accounting—but that's part of what makes it rare.

Another common perception is that students who live on-campus will perform better in school than students who live off-campus. The reality is more complex: some studies show that living on-campus is correlated with stronger academic performance; others show the opposite; some show neither. Most likely, the exact location of one's abode and its impact on GPA is outweighed by myriad other factors—it's possible to shack up with friends in a house or apartment, eat cheap food, use a landlord-provided washer and dryer instead of spending three dollars per load in the dorm, and take the bus to class—and earn a great GPA.

Why College Is the Best Time to Start a Roth IRA

This is going to sound absolutely crazy, because the notion of saving for retirement while trying to pay for college is so far out of the realm of what most people think is possible. That said, if your child can possibly find a way to put aside even just a few hundred dollars per year in a Roth IRA (any capital gains earned are completely tax-free) and then not touch it until she's sixty-five, it could, believe it or not, dramatically change the course of her life. If your student's working her way through college and you have even a little bit of spare change, I strongly recommend implementing the "Mommy Match" program: every dollar she can put into a Roth IRA, you match. This is a much better thing to do than helping your child come up with the cash to attend her dream school.

Just for fun, let's say that starting freshman year of college (at eighteen years old) your student invests $500 in a Roth IRA and you match it with another $500, investing it in a mutual fund with an average long-term return of 10 percent. When he graduates from college, he'll have a nice little nest egg of $5,105.10—a pretty good retirement account for a twenty-one-year old. Then he lets it ride until he's sixty-five, at which point he has . . . $338,284.73. Alternatively, he could take the money out of the IRA to use it as a down payment for a first home without any penalty after five years. With Federal Housing Administration loans requiring down payments as low as 3.5 percent, a little bit of college frugality and savings could make home ownership affordable while his classmates are still paying off student loans and cackling hysterically at the idea of saving for retirement.

And remember what I discussed at the beginning of Chapter 2: because of the way that compounding works, the extra four years of money growth that accrues for a student who starts saving freshman year of college instead of after graduation means that he has to put aside far, far less money.

Look to Avoid College's Junk/Optional Fees

Most colleges these days, especially public ones it seems, have some optional fees that are used to finance all kinds of programs that are irrelevant to their core missions. For instance, the University of Massachusetts chapter of the Massachusetts Public Interest Research Group—a student-run political advocacy organization—is funded with an eleven-dollar "optional fee" collected by the university from every undergraduate at the school. The good news is that you can request to have the fee removed. Most colleges have some fees like this one, and I always ask for my money back. Not because I'm opposed to the work these groups do, but because if I want to donate my money to them, I should do that on my own. There's no reason for it to be included in the tuition bill, and it's sneaky for it to be charged automatically and then refunded upon request.

This seems like obvious advice, but it's a mistake many people make: before paying any university bills, carefully read through each line item to make sure it's an expense that's absolutely mandatory. Many colleges will automatically enroll students in a costly health insurance program—you can get the money back by faxing documentation that your student is already covered by your own insurance.

Stay Out of Credit Card Trouble

In 2004 the average college student graduated with $2,000 in credit card debt. By 2009 the average student was carrying a balance of $3,173. Eighty-four percent of undergrads have at least one card, and more than half have four or more. Only 17 percent pay off their balances in full each month—meaning that most students are paying the double-digit interest rates that come from borrowing money without an established credit history. The slimy tactics of credit card companies on college campuses have been well chronicled. Media exposure in recent years has reduced these problems somewhat, but here's a brief list of what you'll be up against in your battle to keep your student from being dragged into the life-destroying cycle of high-interest credit card debt, penalty fees, and gotcha tactics:

- Many colleges and universities generate millions of dollars in revenue by selling the names and addresses of their students and alumni to credit card companies. The University of Tennessee made $16.5 million this way, the University of Michigan and Michigan State University earned a combined $14 million, and the University of Oklahoma took in $13 million. Looking at these numbers on a per capita basis should give you an idea of how much money credit card companies know they can make off college students (it's been estimated that as much as 25 percent of credit card marketing budgets is used to target college students). Students who do use credit cards should never, ever, ever, ever carry a balance because the interest rates are so high.

- Other colleges receive money from credit card companies in exchange for allowing them to set up booths to greet students and sign them up for credit cards during the first week of school. It's been estimated that the 250 largest colleges in the United States will reap over $5 billion in revenue as a result of these deals over the next few years.

• Credit card companies entice students with offers of free pizza, T-shirts, and Frisbees. Eight out of ten students who have signed up for credit cards on campus say that they sign up just to get the gifts. Of course, once you have four digits of spending power available wherever Visa is accepted, the temptation can be too much to resist. The recently signed Credit CARD Act cracks down on these practices quite a bit, but there are always loopholes, and the best thing to remember is this: never sign up for a credit card at a table on-campus, in a mall, or at a similar location.

Tell your child that he should never, ever, ever, ever sign up for a credit card at a booth, sign up for a credit card based on an unsolicited mailing, or sign up for a credit card based on any sort of advertisement. The only way to sign up for a credit card without virtually guaranteeing a lousy deal is to go to either CreditCards.com or BankRate .com and browse through the deals and apply for a card online. There is really no reason for a college student to have more than one credit card to keep track of. Both of these sites can recommend cards that are appropriate for college students. In general you will want three things: (1) a card with little or nothing in the way of credit history required for approval, (2) a card with no annual fees, and (3) a card with no gimmicks like frequent flier miles or rewards points.

The argument for students carrying credit cards is that they're valuable for establishing a credit history and developing a high FICO score that will help qualify him for low interest rates on mortgages, car loans (please God, no!—see below), and future credit cards. The downside is that because your college student won't have much if anything in the way of a credit history when he signs up, the interest rate on the card he has while he's in college will make Vinny the loan shark from the boxing gym squirm.

So here's the deal: if your student has a track record of being conscientious, conservative, and responsible with money, go ahead and urge him to get one credit card to use for expenses like gas and textbooks—food should never be charged to a credit card! If your student is not mature in his attitude toward money, the consequences of racking up credit card debt in college will be far more severe than the consequences of entering the adult world without a FICO score. You can always wait.

In the summer of 2009, Congress passed and President Obama signed the Credit CARD Act of 2009. The bill made significant changes in the way credit cards are marketed to college students. The most significant changes are these:

• Starting in 2010, credit card companies will be barred from offering free Frisbees, pizza, and so on to college students in exchange for filling out applications—but only when the offer is made on or near a college campus or at a college event.

• Anyone under the age of twenty-one will need "financial information . . . indicating an independent means of repaying any obligation" in order to sign up for a credit card. Failing that, they'll need someone (most likely a parent) to cosign.

This second item is extremely important. By cosigning on your student's credit card, you will take on all the responsibilities as though you yourself were the borrower. If she misses a payment, your credit score gets hit. If she goes into default and the company sues her—yes, this does happen—you will be sued too. While the Credit CARD Act was billed as a pro-consumer bill, this is, in some ways, a give-away to the industry. Now they will no longer have to compete with each other to offer loose credit terms and will be able to demand cosigners who have little ability to monitor the student's use of credit. In general, cosigning on loans for people is an absolutely terrible thing that you should never do. But for young people who are very responsible—who will only use the card for textbooks and will pay the entire balance in full every month—having a credit card in college can be a good opportunity to build credit. So I say it's okay to cosign on a credit card for your student provided that the credit limit is $500 or less. If worse comes to worst, you will be out $500 and will have learned a lesson in the danger of cosigning other people's loans. But let me reiterate: this is the extent of the cosigning you should do for your child. Never, ever, ever, ever, ever cosign a student loan or car loan.

It's also worth finding out whether your student can get a very low credit limit without a cosigner based on whatever part-time work he has. Even with a few thousand dollars per year in income, he might be able to get some credit.

Taking Out a Car Loan, or How Your Child Can Throw Away Everything You Learned from This Book

My brother had a friend who made all the right moves while he was in college: attended a state university, got a degree in engineering and a great job offer, lived off-campus with a bunch of friends to keep his rent low, and graduated with a small but manageable debt load. And then he proceeded to buy a $25,000 sports car as a "graduation gift" for himself, taking out a car loan to finance the purchase. And get this: his parents gave him a few thousand dollars for the down payment. When my brother told me about this, I felt a lump in my stomach: "Do they not get that getting a loan to buy a new car is one of the dumbest things you can possibly do? And do his parents really think that they're doing anything good for anyone by giving him the rope to hang himself in the form of a down payment that enabled him to borrow $20,000, which is, by the way, more than enough for a down payment on a house?"

After a Valium smoothie, I remembered the way that young people can be: most of us are insecure and desperate to fit in. Suze Orman has described America's car buying habits as "spending money you don't have to impress people you don't know who pull up next to you at red lights."

Tragically, the U.S. auto industry—the one that has received billions in taxpayer bailouts because of how great it supposedly is for our economy—takes full advantage of that insecurity in its on-campus marketing to college students, setting them up for lives of indentured servitude to GMAC and other outhouses of auto financing (note to agent: cross GMAC off list of companies for possible future endorsement deals). On a recent stroll through the University of Massachusetts business school, I pulled down two full-color glossy posters, one for General Motors and one for Ford, telling students about the special programs they offer for college students and recent graduates. Ford was offering $500 in "student exclusive bonus cash" as "additional savings just for college and trade school students, recent grads and grad students." GM's poster offered a link to the company's "GM College Grad Discount Program."

Here's the absolute smartest thing you can do to help your child get a great financial head start after she graduates: pay cash to buy her a car. When she graduates, set a budget—an amount that you can reasonably afford; something between $5,000 and $10,000 should be enough to buy her a reliable and fuel-efficient used car that will get her to and from work without references to *Columbo* or Herbie more than once per week. Tell her that the money is available only if she opts to buy a car within that price range. *You absolutely should not give her $5,000 toward the down payment on a more expensive car she'll take out a loan for.*

Here's the reason why buying your child his first car with cash is such a good thing to do: it dramatically reduces the odds he'll ever have to take out a car loan. The way it works is this: car loans create a self-perpetuating cycle of debt, making it very hard to ever own a car outright. Because of the rapid depreciation associated with new cars, nearly 34 percent of vehicle trades is upside-down: That is, the person trading in his car owes more than it's worth. So what do dealers do when you trade in a car that you owe more than the value of? They roll it into the new car loan, of course. That's great for now but then it's compounded when you owe even more when you trade in the next car because the loan now includes a good chunk of the car you bought ten years ago too.

The result is that people who buy cars new and take out car loans are required to spend an average of $479 per month on car loans while driving a car that they will get literally less than nothing for when they trade it in. This is a really lousy way to try to get rich. This curbs their ability to save money—$479 per month is a considerable sum—and leads to this problem: *once you take out a car loan, it is extremely difficult to accumulate enough cash to stop taking out more car loans.*

What happens if you're able to avoid spending $479 on car payments from age twenty to twenty-five and drive a cheap, paid-for car instead, investing the money in a Roth IRA? Investing that money at an average annual return of 10 percent, you'll have around $38,600 by age twenty-five. Let that money ride for another forty years until age sixty-five and you have more than $1.7 million. That's a ton more than most people have saved for retirement—and it's all because you didn't get a car loan between the ages of twenty and twenty-five.

What kind of reliable car can you get for a reasonable price? There are quite a few options. In 2005 AutoExtra.com listed the top-ten car options for student drivers:

2000 Chevy Blazer; Edmunds.com value: $2,901

2001 Honda Civic DX: $5,274

2002 Toyota Corolla CE: $5,795

2001 Nissan Altima XE: $4,395

2003 Hyundai Elantra GLS: $5,010

2003 Ford Ranger (Half Bed): $5,299

2003 Suzuki Aerio S: $4,823

1998 Toyota 4Runner: $4,246

2001 Mercury Cougar: $4,329
2003 Ford Taurus LX: $4,819

If you're really strapped for cash, AutoLoanCentral.com lists the best used cars under $4,000: 1999 Hyundai Elantra, 1997 Ford Taurus, and the 1993 Acura. Yard sales and classified ads can also be a source of reliable older cars that have low mileage and will do just fine for getting your kid through college. This isn't the time to try to find the dream car. That will come later.

That's a common theme for money management in college. Stay out of debt, pay cash, and look to have fun in ways that don't cost a lot of money. The college years are all about building the foundation, and a foundation of debt is hard to build on.

CHAPTER 9

Invest in College-Town Real Estate

This chapter might seem to be an anomaly. What the heck does investing in real estate have to do with affording college? Nothing. But here's the thing: one of my messages in this book has been that even if you do have the money to send your kid to the most expensive college on the planet without putting your own future at risk, it's entirely possible and maybe even probable that you shouldn't do that. One of the most important demographics I want to reach with my work is parents who *can* afford to send their kids to whatever college they want, but are questioning whether that's a good idea. Hopefully I've convinced you that that isn't a good idea, and now you might be wondering what you should do with the money that you were going to invest in your child's education.

Here's an awesome idea: Why not take that money and make an investment that will provide a place for your kid to live and cash flow for you during your retirement years—with the possibility for long-term appreciation in value? By making an investment in college-town real estate, you have the potential to achieve all of the following:

- Provide a place for your child to live during and maybe even after college

- Help your kids learn about real estate and investing before most of their peers will have had any experience with either

- Make an investment that can be an important part of your retirement plan, providing the potential for strong cash flow and long-term capital appreciation

- Save you money on taxes

- Lower the cost of college by securing housing less expensive than a dorm, and freeing you from eight-dollars-per-meal cafeteria food

Sound good? It is. I was so convinced of it that I bought a condo myself at the end of my freshman year—and then another one at the end of my sophomore year. There's an argument to be made that, of all the real estate investment opportunities out there, student housing is one of the best, offering low risk and the potential for a strong upside. This is why I've already purchased two condos in Amherst (one of which I live in).

Why College-Town Real Estate Is a Good Investment

Even people who don't have kids in college are realizing that college real estate can be an extremely compelling investment. With the real estate market as weak as it is right now, there are very, very few bright spots, but student housing is one of them. On October 3, 2008, there was one publicly traded real estate investment trust that hit an all-time high. That company was American Campus Communities, which is traded on the New York Stock Exchange under the ticker symbol ACC. American Campus Communities is the largest publicly traded company that invests exclusively in student housing. Since 1996, American Campus Communities has developed more than $1.5 billion in student housing properties and has also acquired in excess of $2 billion in student housing assets. The company owns

54,300 "beds" (spaces for student housing, with units for two students counting as two beds) and manages another 92,100. American Campus Communities provides housing to students at colleges such as Arizona State University, the University of Florida, Minnesota State University, and many, many more.

The ability of student housing providers to weather the perfect storm of plummeting real estate is strong evidence of the value of this investment. It's not surprising. Students will always need a place to live when they're in college, and the number of people signing up for college is growing every year. As overseas competition continues to threaten the job security of low-wage workers, college will only increase in popularity. As college costs continue to rise, public colleges will gain increased popularity, resulting in both increased enrollment and increased selectivity. Even with the number of high school graduates having peaked in 2008, the continued increase in the percentage of high school students heading off to college should ensure continued strong demand for student-oriented housing in college towns.

Even at colleges that have ample dorm space, most students want to move off-campus as soon as possible, and that's also not likely to change. America's stock of dormitories is aging, and with state budgets in disarray pretty much everywhere, renovations and new construction are unlikely to happen any time soon. Many state universities are cutting back on capital expenditures to conserve cash, and the prospect of a large wave of new dormitory construction appears to be remote.

Buy It As an Investment, Not Just As a Place for Your Kid

Many well-intentioned families decide that it's smarter to buy than rent while their kids are in college, and then sell the house or condo after Junior graduates. This is a bad idea! It worked great in the first part of the current millennium, when home prices were appreciating extremely rapidly, but it's unlikely to be a good strategy in a more normal market, let alone a bear market.

The real benefits of real estate appreciation do not show themselves in four years and, in a normal market, there's a high probability that you won't even break even on your sale after factoring in real estate agent commissions, taxes, closing costs, time on the market, and so on. For this reason, it's important to view an investment in college real estate as something that your kid and maybe some housemates will live in while they study, and then you'll rent it out to other college students (or professors, university employees, etc.) after your child graduates.

But I Don't Want to Be a Landlord!

This scenario does involve being a landlord but—relax! It's not as terrifying as it sounds. If you buy a condominium in a large complex near a large university, you will have no trouble in finding someone to manage it—find tenants, collect the rent, deal with plumbing problems, and so on—for no more than about 10 percent of the monthly rent. This is what I do. I simply don't have the time or inclination to be a landlord. For seventy-five dollars per month, I get someone else to handle the whole thing and devote about three seconds per month to each property.

When doing calculations on the cash flows for a real estate property, a lot of people use spreadsheets and calculators. But for small single-family properties, all you really need is this nifty little applet: www.goodmortgage.com/calc_investment_property.htm.

You simply type in the price of the property, how much you'll be putting down on it, the interest rate on the mortgage, the annual property taxes, the rental rate, and any management or homeowner's association fees. More on this later, but remember: it's always good to include the costs of a property manager in your calculations.

Is Your College Town a Good Investment?

Of course, I would never, ever suggest that you allow a town's real estate market to dictate where you send your child to college. But it just so happens to work out that the colleges that will be the best and most affordable option for most families—large state universities— also offer the best opportunities for real estate investment. Many private colleges have enough dorms to house their entire student body, and a large percentage also have a requirement that students live on-campus. In the case of smaller colleges, the housing demanded by students is rarely significant enough to be a driving force in the real estate market. Here are some things you want to look at when evaluating whether the college town your child will be in is a good option for student housing:

• Check into rules governing where students can live. When I bought my first condo toward the end of my freshman year of college, I was planning to live in it the next year, until I found out that there was a requirement that all students live on campus for their first two years at the University of Massachusetts. So I stayed in the dorm and rented it out for enough money to pay all the expenses and leave a nice profit: no big deal. But from an investment perspective, I made a mistake in my analysis, overlooking a requirement that had the potential to curb demand for off-campus student housing. So one thing you want to look at when assessing a college town as a real estate investment opportunity is the college's policy toward where students can live. College towns where students have the option of living off-campus are preferable. Ideally, you want a university that is about to make a decision allowing students to live off-campus. That can unleash a flood of demand for off-campus housing, lowering vacancies and boosting rents.

* Find the beds-to-bodies ratio. In his book *Profit by Investing in Student Housing: Cash In On the Campus Housing Shortage*, the real estate mogul (a real one—not an infomercial clown) Michael H. Zaransky talks about the beds-to-bodies ratio. It's really easy and brilliant. Here's how it works. Take the college's total enrollment and then divide it by the number of beds on campus. The first number will be easy to find on the college's Web site, but you may need to e-mail the housing office for the second number. For instance, the University of Minnesota, Twin Cities, had 50,954 students enrolled in the fall of 2005. But the school only had places to put 6,300 of them, meaning that 87.64 percent of students had to find housing off-campus. Cha-ching!

* Know the vacancy rate. Of course, looking at just the number of beds on campus isn't enough. For instance Michigan State University only has beds for about 38 percent of its student body, but the decline of the Michigan economy and the flight of the state's residents to other parts of the country has put that real estate market in a world of hurt. For this reason, you also want to look at the town's vacancy rate, just as you would with any other real estate investment. This information is readily available on the town's Web site or by asking a real estate agent (note: ask him to send you the information in an e-mail—you don't want spit-balled numbers pulled out of the air by a salesperson!). Often just Googling the town and state with the phrase "vacancy rate" will get you all the information you need. The vacancy rate was a key statistic in my decision to invest in Amherst. According to the town, "Amherst has a very low vacancy rate for both owner-occupied (0.4 percent) and rental housing (1.7 percent)." This compares extremely favorably to the national housing market, where more than 10 percent of homes are currently sitting vacant.

* Look at the demand for rental housing in the area. In a true college town—one where a university is the major employer, not just a large city with a bunch of colleges—rentals will make up a

large portion of the housing market because demand is transient: undergrads and grad students looking for a place to live for a few years with no plans of settling down. The higher the percentage of housing that is rental, the more competitive the property management business is likely to be—that means more options and better prices.

What Kind of Property? Why Condos Are the Best Investment

If I've convinced you that student housing is a good investment and you've done the research and concluded that the market your child will be living in presents a good opportunity, the next question is: What kind of property to buy? My only experience with real estate involves condominiums, and I intend to keep it this way for the foreseeable future. Condominiums get a bad rap in some circles, and a lot of people think that the management fees are a rip-off.

Here's the reality. The management fees are mostly used to cover expenses that you would have anyway if you bought a single-family detached home: landscaping, repairs, water, and so on. In fact, maintenance costs can actually be lower with a condominium because of the economies of scale involved. By buying a unit in a well-managed development with reasonable condo fees, you get professionals to take care of the exterior, landscaping, and common areas and all you have to worry about is what's between the walls. This makes condominiums the ideal investment for absentee landlords. You can hire a property manager to market the property, screen tenants, collect rent, and deal with problems for something in the range of 10 percent of the rental rate, although there is considerable regional variation to that number—in higher-rent areas it will generally be a lower percentage.

Most real estate investors prefer to buy single-family homes or multi-family buildings, but here's the problem with that: you do the numbers and the property looks great and the cash flow positive, so you buy it and then find out that you need a new roof. In addition, you probably won't want to live in a college town in the long term, and condominiums are well suited to absentee landlords in a way that most other real estate investments aren't.

Real estate investment isn't for everyone, and for most families, the upfront costs of investing in college town real estate will make it impractical. But for those with solid incomes, decent capital, and adequately funded retirement plans, it may be a fantastic way to provide a place for your child to live, teach him about real estate and investing, and add to your net worth.

CHAPTER 10

It's Not Just a Personal Finance Issue:
How to Solve the College Crisis

Throughout this book I've addressed the topic of college admissions and college affordability from what might be called a "rugged individualist" perspective: students can make intelligent decisions and, with considerable hard work and sacrifice, get a great education without putting an anchor around their necks as they head into the workforce. The vast majority of people who are talking about the rising cost of college are politically liberal, and focus on what might be called big government solutions: increased public support for higher education, student loan forgiveness programs, more subsidies to bring down interest rates, more scholarships to help high-achieving low income students and minorities attend elite schools, and so on.

There is nothing inherently wrong with any of these ideas, but by themselves they won't fix the college funding nightmare. How do I know that? Because they haven't. Student loan availability has exploded upward even as college becomes less affordable than ever. In fact, increases in financial aid and student loan availability may be fueling an inflation in costs, as the funny money of student loans removes the natural ceiling on affordability that would exist if everyone had to pay for college in cash. The result is that administrative costs and ancillary services that have nothing to do with the undergraduate experience continue to spiral upward, and students are stuck with the bill for the next twenty years of their lives—if they're lucky enough to be able to pay it off that quickly. That isn't just inefficient. It's immoral.

Retool FAFSA to Provide Support and Incentives for Students to Carry the Water Instead of Drinking the Water

As I showed you in Chapter 1, FAFSA is a deeply flawed system for making financial aid decisions. In large part, this is just the nature of its being a formula: it's impossible to incorporate all the different issues that can affect millions of families into one formula. But the FAFSA form doesn't even come close. Here are three changes lawmakers can make to the formula to make it more fair:

- Include the parents' entire net worth in calculating the expected family contribution. People with little in the way of retirement assets or home equity need to save a larger chunk of their income—so it doesn't make sense to expect them to contribute a significant amount of money toward educational expenses.

- Don't include long-term capital gains (assets held for at least one year prior to sale) in the calculation of income. Since capital gains are—for most people—one-time in nature, they can really mess up EFCs. For instance, if a mother sells stock she's held for a long time to pay for college, the capital gain gets added to her income and can artificially disqualify the student from receiving financial aid the next year. For now, the only way to avoid this problem is to find ways to pay for college without the benefit of financial aid, but that's far from being an ideal solution.

- Retool the FAFSA formula to provide financial support to students who work hard and live beneath their means to save money for college: Why should someone who spends summers playing World of Warcraft get financial aid while someone who works sixty hours per week bagging groceries is expected to pay full price?

Be Wary of Unintended Consequences

The Apollo Group is the parent company of some of the largest for-profit colleges in the world, including the University of Phoenix. Because it's a publicly traded company, its Securities and Exchange Commission filings provide a level of insight into its business practices that we often don't get with nonprofit colleges. In a quarterly report filed with the SEC, the company reported that "in May 2008, the Act increased the annual loan limits on federal unsubsidized student loans by $2,000 for undergraduate students, and also increased the aggregate loan limits on total federal student loans." CitronResearch .com, a controversial but often dead-on accurate fraud research Web site, picked up the story, commenting, "This was a bonanza for Apollo. . . . They increased tuition immediately following the government action." In other words, the government's presumably well-intentioned effort to provide more money to students struggling with the cost of college did nothing but burden them with debt—and pumped more money into the coffers of the Apollo Group, which is, incidentally, the single largest recipient of student loan funds in the country.

The important point for lawmakers and voters to keep in mind is this: the relationship between college costs and the availability of tuition funds is reflexive. That is, there is a partially circular relationship between cause and effect. The federal stimulus package of 2009 raised the maximum federal Pell Grant award from $4,730 to $5,550 per year. Because the Pell Grant is available only to students who demonstrate considerable financial need, it's not likely to have the effect of driving up tuition prices: it offers targeted help to needy people.

But increases in the federal Stafford loan limit will almost certainly have the effect of lifting the natural cap on college affordability—because everyone can receive an unsubsidized Stafford loan. Efforts to make college more affordable need to be targeted at the people most in need of help. Policies that artificially inflate the amount of money families can spend on college by making loans more available will just drive up prices. See also: real estate bubble.

Radically Redefine What Students Can Expect Out of College

In 2002 Princeton embarked on an ambitious plan to build a five-hundred-bed Gothic-style dormitory at a cost of $100 million—that's $200,000 *per bed*. The *New York Times* reported that the undertaking would "require skilled masons to cut thousands of pieces of stone on the site."[1] What exactly does this have to do with education? Absolutely nothing. Of course, that's okay because Princeton has a boatload of money (albeit less than it used to because of massive endowment losses), and it also provides among the best financial aid programs in the world.

The problem is that many other colleges are embarking on similarly lavish vanity projects, often at the expense of affordability. In 2006 UMass blew $11.2 million renovating—not building—a single dining hall, at a cost of $14,000 per seat. The school's decision to borrow money to pay for the renovation effectively forces future classes of UMass students to pay interest on granite countertops and high-end pizza ovens. And since most students borrow to pay for college, "investments" like this actually lead students to pay (a decade or more after graduation) interest on interest on granite countertops and high-end pizza ovens that they had when they were in college. This is not a way to get rich!

We must ask ourselves: At what point are we going to say enough is enough, and stop allowing schools to blow money on vanity projects that have no impact on core educational missions, other than raising costs so much that education is unaffordable to the people who can most benefit from it?

At most colleges, a portion of student fees is diverted to fund various programs that only a tiny percentage of students benefit from. When the track team flies across the country to participate in a tournament, the students aren't charged any extra fee for it. Instead, that expense is simply divided among all the other students. Why should people have to pay for services they don't benefit from?

Some colleges are already experimenting with this model. The Advantage Program, a service offered by Southern New Hampshire University, a private college, offers an education at less than a third of the cost of the regular program at the college's main campus—by stripping out services like campus dining, dorms, expensive gyms, sports teams, and other staples of most colleges. SNHU's president, Paul LeBlanc, described the Advantage Program as a "low-cost airline equivalent" in higher education—"a high-quality academic experience, but not a whole lot else."

To be sure, this isn't without its disadvantages. What about the college experience? Some rationalist students, though, have simply decided that the high cost of the traditional college experience outweighs its benefits. And looking at the rising cost of college and the tragic consequences of student loans, it's easy to understand why.

One innovative start-up in the college industry is StraighterLine .com, which allows students to take classes at a wide variety of colleges for ninety-nine dollars per month plus thirty-nine dollars per course. If it catches on, StraighterLine could provide an invaluable way for students to meet general education requirements by assembling credits from dozens of different schools. The site is too new and doesn't yet offer the variety of courses that would make it a valuable resource for students. But if it catches on and grows, this could be a true game changer in the world of affordable higher education.

Stop Stigmatizing Financial Prudence

While I've gone to great lengths to demonstrate that attending the most affordable college option is extremely unlikely to harm your child's financial and life prospects, there is still—in many social circles—a significant stigma attached to options like state colleges and community colleges.

This absolutely needs to stop, because it is making everyone broke. The best advice I can give to parents who are worried about this "cocktail party factor" is to ignore it—that's the only rational thing to do. I recognize that's hard for many people, but my hope is that as college costs continue to become increasingly unaffordable, this stigma will disappear by necessity: it will just be too expensive to keep up. Eventually a tipping point will be reached, but here's my question: How many students will have their lives destroyed by college debt before we realize that what we've is done wrong and undergo a radical shift in values?

A shift toward community colleges and public institutions by better students will encourage politicians to invest more money in public education.

Consumer Education: Let People Know What They're Getting Into

Throughout my work on personal finance issues, I've always maintained that most people will make sound financial decisions if they have access to engaging and easy-to-understand information. This may be naive, but the evidence that private student loans are bad, that college prestige is overrated, and that credit card companies would be prostitutes if they had more self-respect is so overwhelming that I think people would see the light if it's shown to them. Put another way: let me write a one-page disclosure statement that must be signed by students and parents prior to making any of the financial mistakes that I've discussed in this book and I think we could cut down on the number of people overextending themselves for life when they're eighteen years old.

Most important, we need to take a serious look at whether high school students are being equipped with the financial acumen necessary to determine how much student loan debt is prudent, and whether any student loan debt represents a good long-term investment. At most high schools in America today, there is no requirement that students receive any kind of financial literacy training. In an era where the average student is borrowing close to $25,000 to pay for college, this absolutely has to change. Young people are making huge financial decisions with long-term consequences, and the public schools have a responsibility to make sure that they are equipped with the education to understand the decisions they're making.

The first piece I ever had published anywhere was an op-ed piece in the *Cape Cod Times* when I was a high school student. In it, I called for statewide financial literacy training for all high school students. I wrote that "The failure of the schools to teach kids about money has done more to perpetuate the status quo than any lobbyist in Washington could ever dream of doing."

I strongly believe that with access to fair, unbiased, and authoratative information, consumers will make smart financial decisions. That's why I wrote this book, and I hope that you and your student will prove me right—and get a fantastic education at a great price, preparing him for a fantastic life free of so much of the stress that is impacting the hearts and minds of students all over America who are collapsing under a burden of excessive debt.

CONCLUSION

In this book I've tried to convince you of four things:

- You shouldn't sacrifice your own financial security to help your child pay for college.

- Your child should take out absolutely no student loans if possible and if he does take out loans, it should be done as a last resort in the last year or two of his education—and only after all cost-cutting measures have been explored. If you still have any furniture left in your house and have eaten anything other than ramen in the past two months, you should not take out student loans.

- Attending college is far, far more important than attending a certain college. Students who attend a less expensive college will not be at a disadvantage.

- The effort that a student puts into her educational experience is far more important than where she goes to school. A student who's willing to work hard and work smart can do well at any school.

Spurred on by the Great Recession, exploding college costs, and student debt nightmares, a number of pundits have questioned whether college is really worth it at all. In October 2008, the *Chicago Tribune* asked, "Is College Worth It?" The answer is still an unequivocal yes—even more so now as jobs that could once be had with high school diplomas now require bachelor's degrees, and industrial jobs are shipped overseas. But putting aside the financial benefits, the intangible good that comes from higher education also makes it a worthwhile venture. The problem is that all the bad things about college in twenty-first century America threaten to overwhelm all the good things about it. When I began this project in 2008, a majority of American undergraduates were borrowing money to pay for college. Now, just two years later, a supermajority are doing so, and the percentage of those students who are using dangerous private loans has more than doubled.

Make a list of the reasons your child wants to go to college—and the reasons you think your child should go to college. Chances are that you'll come up with something like this:

• **Increased income and job security**: Studies have shown that a student who attends the average public college and pays the entire cost of attendance with student loans will need to work for decades before the missed work time and interest payments are outweighed by the increased earnings that come with a bachelor's degree. Only by keeping college costs to a minimum and avoiding interest expenses can you avoid this fate. It used to be that a bachelor's degree was a no-brainer as a financial investment. Rising college costs mean that's no longer the case, the way that most people are paying for college. The solution? Spend as little money on college as possible, and *pay as you go*. Otherwise, the interest charges on education financing will eat deep into the returns. As I demonstrated amply in Chapter 3, spending more on college will not increase the return on investment—it will destroy it.

• **A chance to build wealth**: A survey of the Forbes 400 found 75 percent reporting that getting out of debt and staying out of debt is the best way to build wealth. That's what the richest people in America say. It's possible that your neighbor and the financial aid officer and the guy at the gym know something about wealth-building that the richest people in America don't—but do you really want to bet your child's future on it?

- **The ability to pursue dreams:** What education giveth in terms of freedom and opportunity, student debt often taketh away. In extreme cases, students who default on student loans can be denied the renewal of professional licenses—student loans can get in the way of becoming a doctor, lawyer, accountant, or engineer, even though they're sold as the products that can make those dreams possible.

- **Attending graduate school**: According to surveys, a majority of college freshmen report an interest in attending graduate school. However, large debt obligations can make this dream difficult. Students who are able to defer their loans for graduate school continue to accumulate interest while they study, and for students interested in expensive graduate programs, the combination of undergraduate and graduate debt may put the dream out of reach. As I discussed earlier, attending a less elite school does not hurt your child's chances of getting into graduate school, especially for students who work hard and get good grades.

- **A wonderful and memorable four years:** This is one of the few areas where it's hard to rebut the claims of the "college fit" crowd. If your child likes the idea of attending college in Malibu, attending a state university in Kentucky won't offer the same environment or experience. The question is whether the cost is high enough that it's worth "settling" for a lesser locale for a few years. I would argue that the answer is an unequivocal yes. If your student is very particular about where he wants to live, or particular about the quality of living space he prefers, then he should not subject himself to life in a cramped studio for twenty years so he can live in an oceanfront dorm for four.

• **Happiness:** Money problems are the number-one cause of relationship woes and the number-one cause of divorce. Entering relationships with a clean financial slate dramatically improves the odds of success, and student loans do nothing good for marriages. Outside of relationships, there is a vast body of research showing a connection between depression, anxiety, and stress and financial concerns—especially large debt loads.

The reality is that doing whatever it takes to send your child to the college of his (or your) dreams will very likely lead to disaster—and at best will lead to an outcome no better than the one that could have been had by attending a less expensive college.

For many parents, the challenge will be selling their kid on these ideas—and explaining to her that you cannot afford and are not willing to make horrible long-term decisions so that she can attend her dream college for a few years. The societal pressure to send kids to the "best colleges they can get into" is intense and it won't be easy to resist. But the consequences of not resisting that pressure are so catastrophic that you must do whatever it takes. If you do, your kids will thank you in the long run.

THE DOS AND DON'TS OF PAYING FOR COLLEGE

This book has been full of dos and don'ts for the processes of selecting a college, financing that selection, and attending it. In case you forget some stuff, here is a quick guide to the dos and don'ts of college.

1. **DO** recognize that the amount your kids' friends' parents will be contributing to their educational expenses is likely far higher than it should be.

2. **DO NOT** allow the expected family contribution calculated by financial aid formulas to determine how much you contribute. There is a very good chance that the EFC will be far higher than you can really afford—especially if you do not have a large quantity of retirement savings and substantial home equity.

3. **DO NOT** let someone tell you that student loans are not that big of a deal. We simply don't have a long-term track record of debt loads of the size students are taking out now, and therefore anyone who says it will be okay doesn't know what he's talking about.

4. **DO NOT** allow your child to take out any student loans in the first year of college. Some students may need, for a combination of reasons, to take out a small loan in their last years of college. If loans are needed in the first year, STOP! You need to consider more affordable college options.

5. **DO NOT** fall in love with a college based on its name recognition, campus, or a few professors you happen to meet, and do not allow your child to fall in love either. Every college is a combination of great professors and lousy professors, cool students and not so cool students.

6. **DO NOT** let anyone tell you that one college will provide better earning power than others. There is no evidence of this. What will determine your child's success will be his talent, determination, and work ethic, and the career path that he elects to pursue.

7. **DO** expect your child to be *the* major contributor to his educational expenses—starting NOW! If your student can clear an average of $1,000 per month—less during the school year and more during the summer—that's enough for him to pay for four years at a state university on his own! If your kid's still in high school, make sure he's working and saving money.

8. **DO** allow and even encourage your child to apply to expensive and selective private colleges. There is always the possibility that she will receive a large financial aid package or merit-based scholarship. Most likely, these large merit awards will come from schools where she is in the top 15 percent of the student body.

9. Most of all: **DO** look at college as a rational investment, not a coming-of-age ritual where money is no object. Skip expensive college guides, and don't obsess over reputations, specific programs, and locales. You're picking a college, not a resort.

RECOMMENDED READING

College in General

No Sucker Left Behind: Avoiding the Great College Rip-Off. The former professor Marc Scheer looks at many of the same topics I look at here, and also has a wealth of data. He takes a more conspiratorial tone, and explains how colleges operate as glorified businesses, ripping off their students at every opportunity. This is a fantastic book and an incredibly valuable source of research on the finances of college.

Scholarships and Financial Aid

Sallie Mae: How to Pay for College; A Practical Guide for Families. Okay, I included this one as a joke. Why would you ever, ever, ever, rely on a company that earns money from fees on student loan defaults for information on the best ways to pay for college? What's next? *The Philip Morris Guide To Healthy Smoking?* This book contains the usual descriptions of the various loan programs and similarly brilliant advice, like scholarships are better than loans because they don't have to be paid back.

How to Go to College Almost for Free. This is Ben Kaplan's book on how he paid his way through college by winning more than twenty-four merit-based scholarships, good for $90,000 in funds that could be used at any school. The problem is that he ended up going to Harvard, so he's clearly a very bright kid. The statistics show that the vast, vast majority of kids won't be able to pay their way through college with scholarships, which makes the title and its implicit promise highly suspect. But scholarships are still worth pursuing—especially if your child attends an affordably priced college with minimal need-based financial aid—and this book has great tips on how to go about it.

Getting Financial Aid 2009 (College Board Guide to Getting Financial Aid). This book is literally a thousand pages long, and contains information on how to fill out the FAFSA form along with a detailed directory of financial aid at every major college in the country. Just keep in mind the significant problems associated with paying for college with financial aid (go back and read Chapter 1 if you don't remember!).

http://nces.ed.gov/collegenavigator. This is a really handy government-provided guide to researching financial aid at just about any college in the country. It's provided by the government, it's free, and it's more objective and reliable than the information you'll find in any of the guides that cost money.

Making the Most Out of College—While You're There

There are very, very few good books on this topic. They range from the patronizing to the banal, and tend to be full of obvious advice about how to deal with annoying roommates and great tips like "Don't binge drink when you have a final exam at eight a.m.!" It's not that the advice is bad—it's just that it's intuitive and your kid probably won't read it. Therefore, I recommend that you not waste your money on those nifty little "getting the most out of college" books.

Career Advice

Getting from College to Career. The career coach Lindsey Pollak offers wonderful tips on how any college student can make the transition from student to entry-level worker to mogul.

The Brazen Careerist. This is a fantastic book by Penelope Trunk. It includes forty-five detailed tips on how young people can find career success, some of it quite counterintuitive and different from the conventional wisdom most parents will provide. It's by far the most readable career advice book I've ever seen.

The Element. Ken Robinson's book is more conceptual than the others above. Robinson is a former college professor and an expert on creativity, and this book is all about how you can unlock your passion to achieve success and happiness. In an era where too many college students are forgoing passion for profit, Ken Robinson's book shows how short-sighted and counterproductive this is.

48 Days to the Work You Love. Dan Miller's book has been a bestseller for years, and with good reason. He gets beyond the focus groups and Labor Department statistics and shows how anyone can have a wonderful career doing something fulfilling.

Postgraduation Financial Advice

The Money Book for the Young, Fabulous and Broke. My generation faces a number of unique financial challenges, and Suze Orman understands that better than most financial pundits, who seem to view young people as having essentially the same financial issues that older people had when they were our age. If you can convince your kid to follow her advice on cars, credit cards, and investing, he'll thank you in a few years.

The Only Investment Guide You'll Ever Need. I'm biased because Andrew Tobias has been a wonderful friend and mentor to me, but this book has sold over a million copies for a reason (the same reason I decided to e-mail him—it's awesome!). It's packed with solid financial advice and it's funny.

Investing in College-Town Real Estate

Profit by Investing in Student Housing. Michael H. Zaransky's book makes a compelling case for a long-term bull market in rental properties for college students.

NOTES

INTRODUCTION

1. http://www.usatoday.com/money/perfi/columnist/block/2008-04-28-student-loan-consolidation_N.htm
2. http://www.osc.state.ny.us/osdc/3-2010.pdf
3. http://www.insidehighered.com/news/2009/07/09/debt
4. http://www.mindingthecampus.com/forum/2009/07/a_recent_report_from_education.html
5. http://www.cnbc.com/id/30438711/America_s_Biggest_Types_of_Personal_Debt?slide=7
6. http://www.collegeboard.com/student/pay/add-it-up/4494.html
7. http://local.youngmoney.com/Curbing_College_Debt_Tifton_GA-r1211862-Tifton_GA.html
8. http://www.nytimes.com/2008/04/16/business/16leonhardt.html?_r=1
9. http://www.nytimes.com/2004/12/03/health/03mood.html

CHAPTER 1

1. http://www.countryfinancialsecurityindex.com/trendrelease.php?tid=3
2. http://www.imninc.com/Evergreen1/BC_Index.pdf
3. http://www.usatoday.com/news/nation/census/2008-09-23-census-moms_N.htm
4. http://www.bluesuitmom.com/money/dollarstretcher/vacations.html
5. http://moneywatch.bnet.com/saving-money/blog/college-solution/four-crazy-facts-about-college-that-could-save-you-money/603/
6. http://www.nea.org/home/29999.htm
7. http://www.collegeboard.com/press/releases/201194.html
8. http://www.npr.org/templates/story/story.php?storyId=4664568
9. http://nces.ed.gov/pubs2009/2009166.pdf
10. http://www.nber.org/papers/w9228
11. http://money.cnn.com/2005/06/08/pf/college/generous_schools/index.htm
12. http://money.cnn.com/2009/05/04/pf/kowitt_collegeloan.fortune/index.htm

NOTES

CHAPTER 2

1. http://projectonstudentdebt.org/files/File/Debt_Facts_and_Sources.pdf
2. http://www.nber.org/papers/w13117
3. http://www.experience.com/corp/press_release?id=press_release_122226349
   9735&tab=cn1&channel_id=about_us&page_id=media_coverage_news
4. http://www.profam.org/pub/fia/fia_1912.htm
5. http://www.nefe.org/ResearchandStrategy/YoungandInDebtSeries/
   Youngpeoplestruggletodealwithkissof/tabid/147/Default.aspx
6. http://getoutofdebt.org/14740/survey-finds-debt-equals-depression-for-
   many-women-at-risk-to-suffer-with-financial-depression
7. A. Minicozzi, "The Short Term Effect of Educational Debt on Job Decisions," *Economics of Education Review* 24 (2005), no. 4:417–30.
8. http://www2.ed.gov/offices/OSFAP/defaultmanagement/cdr.html
9. http://www2.ed.gov/about/offices/list/oig/auditreports/a03c0017.doc
10. http://www.rebuild.org/news-article/student-loans-considered-a-good-kind-
    of-debt/
11. http://www.schoolchoices.org/roo/fried1.htm
12. http://www.filife.com/stories/ways-to-get-loans-for-college-now-in-tough-
    new-climate-it-pays-to-ask-your-school-for-help-find-yourself-a-cosigner
13. http://projectonstudentdebt.org/files/pub/private_loan_facts_trends_09.pdf
14. http://www.nelliemae.org/library/research_10.html
15. http://www.mcclatchydc.com/2009/06/25/70788/recessions-toll-most-recent-
    college.html
16. http://moneywatch.bnet.com/saving-money/blog/college-solution/did-the-
    value-of-your-college-degree-just-drop-350000/1448/
17. http://pewresearch.org/pubs/536/working-women
18. http://www.gocollege.com/survival/loans-and-taxes/deduct-loan-interest.html
19. http://www.nationalskillscoalition.org/press-room/skills-in-the-news/2009-
    articles/abcnews_011609.pdf
20. http://www.bankrate.com/finance/debt/student-loan-forgiveness-rare-but-
    possible.aspx
21. http://www.nytimes.com/2009/05/27/your-money/student-loans/27forgive
    .html

CHAPTER 3

1. http://www.cgsnet.org/portals/0/pdf/Open_Doors_with_a_Doctorate_
   BW.pdf
2. http://www.cnn.com/2009/LIVING/worklife/01/19/cb.20.big.salary.jobs/
   index.html
3. http://online.wsj.com/article/SB121746658635199271.html

4. http://www.krueger.princeton.edu/04_27_2000.htm
5. http://wsjclassroom.com/archive/06dec/care_coecollege.htm
6. http://m.insidehighered.com/news/2008/05/01/spending
7. http://www.brookings.edu/articles/2004/10education_easterbrook.aspx
8. http://moneywatch.bnet.com/saving-money/blog/college-solution/20-facts-about-todays-college-freshmen/1417/
9. http://m.insidehighered.com/news/2006/06/27/commission
10. http://www.boston.com/news/education/higher/articles/2008/12/23/applications_soar_at_public_colleges/
11. http://www.collegeboard.com/student/csearch/college-visits/101.html.
12. http://www.thedailybeast.com/blogs-and-stories/2009-06-14/how-to-ace-your-college-tour/p/
13. http://www.citytowninfo.com/career-and-education-news/articles/study-says-sat-prep-courses-wont-significantly-boost-scores-09052001
14. http://www.nytimes.com/2009/03/14/business/14year.html

CHAPTER 4

1. http://www.career.vt.edu/Jobsearch/Salaries/NACESurvey.htm
2. http://www.walletpop.com/college-finance/u-of-phoenix/article/looking-for-a-job-study-shakespeare/675359
3. http://usuphilosophy.com/why-major-in-philosophy/what-are-you-going-to-do-with-a-major-in-_____/
4. http://www.naceweb.org/Publications/Spotlight_Online/2009/1111/Job_Outlook_2010__Employers_Cautious_About_Approach_to_Spring_2010_On-Campus_Recruiting.aspx?print=yes
5. http://www.collegeboard.com/parents/pay/scholarships-aid/36990.html

CHAPTER 5

1. http://www.public.iastate.edu/~strategicplan/2010/process/docs/satisfied.shtml.
2. https://www.noellevitz.com/NR/rdonlyres/6F8223F5-1C7D-43E8-886F-F09EE146C67B/0/HowtoAssessSatisfactionandPriorities.pdf
3. http://www.businessweek.com/bschools/content/mar2009/bs2009032_982142.htm
4. http://m.insidehighered.com/news/2009/02/12/tuition

CHAPTER 6

1. http://www.washingtonmonthly.com/features/2007/0709.careyessay.html
2. http://www.collegeboard.com/prod_downloads/press/cost06/trends_college_pricing_06.pdf

3. http://www.thecrimson.com/article/2007/12/12/harvard-lags-in-community-college-recruitment/

4. http://www.virginia.edu/undergradadmission/TransferQA.html

5. http://www.nytimes.com/2007/04/22/education/edlife/22merrow-profile-4.html

6. http://www.universityofcalifornia.edu/admissions/undergrad_adm/paths_to_adm/transfer.html

CHAPTER 7

1. http://www.heri.ucla.edu/cirpoverview.php

2. http://www.nytimes.com/2006/02/20/business/media/20nielsen.html?ex=1298091600&en=1f16787e644d9d08&ei=5090&partner=rssuserland&emc=rss

3. http://www.brockport.edu/career01/upromise.htm

4. http://www.nytimes.com/2009/04/26/business/26every.html

5. http://www.huntingdon.edu/student_services/ccv/students/forms/recreate

6. http://www.cfo.com/article.cfm/5404994?f=related

7. http://oregonbusinessreport.com/2009/08/45-employers-use-facebook-twitter-to-screen-job-candidates/

CHAPTER 10

1. http://www.nytimes.com/2002/11/20/education/20DORM.html?pagewanted=1

INDEX